MAP OF HOPE AND SORROW

Other books by Helen Benedict

Novels
Wolf Season
Sand Queen
The Edge of Eden
The Opposite of Love
The Sailor's Wife
Bad Angel
A World Like This

Non-fiction
The Lonely Soldier: The Private War of Women Serving in Iraq
Virgin or Vamp: How the Press Covers Sex Crimes
Portraits in Print
Safe, Strong, and Streetwise
Recovery: How to Survive Sexual Assault

Play
The Lonely Soldier Monologues

MAP OF HOPE AND SORROW

Stories of Refugees
Trapped in Greece

by

Helen Benedict and
Eyad Awwadawnan

First published in 2022 by
Footnote
www.footnotepress.com

Footnote Press Limited
4th Floor, Victoria House, Bloomsbury Square, London WC1B 4DA
Distributed by Bonnier Books UK
Owned by Bonnier Books
Sveavägen 56, Stockholm, Sweden

First printing
1 3 5 7 9 10 8 6 4 2

Eyad's preface is adapted from his article, 'I Have Become Lost Like
My Homeland', published in *Slate*, August 2, 2018.
Evans' chapter appeared in a different form as 'A Lonesome Journey to
Freedom: The Hidden Struggles of LGBTQ Refugees', in *Arrowsmith
Journal*, vol XVI, 2021.
A version of Mursal's chapter appeared in
The Nation on August 16, 2021.
Epigraph from *Liberty Walks Naked*, poems by Maram al-Masri,
trans. by Theo Dorgan, Southword Editions, Cork, Ireland, 2017.

A CIP catalogue record for this book is available
from the British Library and the Library of Congress.

ISBN (paperback): 978–1–80444–001–8
ISBN (ebook): 978–1–80444–002–5
Cover design by Anna Morrison
Maps by Isabelle Lewis
Typeset by Bonnier Books UK Limited
Printed and bound in Great Britain by
Clays Ltd, Elcograf S.p.A.

MIX
Paper from
responsible sources
FSC
www.fsc.org   FSC® C018072

For Eyad, Hasan and Ali,
who began it all.
And for refugees everywhere and the
people who welcome them
—HB

To Helen, Noor and Ali Jan, and to all the souls
who walk beside me on a journey none
of us ever wanted to take
—EA

I was walking, I was exhausted
I looked behind me
And saw I was dragging
A mountain of sorrow with my right hand,
A mountain of hope with my left.

—Maram al-Masri, *Liberty Walks Naked*, 2017

TABLE OF CONTENTS

LOST, LIKE MY HOMELAND

BY EYAD AWWADAWNAN

Samos, Greece, 2018

I am in my early twenties. I know these are supposed to be the most beautiful days of my life, when I should rise high, make something of myself. Yet I kill my days in sleep. Perhaps I sleep to become nothing, spending all my time in bed in this refugee camp in Samos, Greece, thinking about the journey that brought me here.

March 18, 2011: an unforgettable date. A demonstration against the government in the Syrian province of Daraa. Six demonstrators killed.

At first, people thought this was an isolated incident, that nobody else would die. Days passed and we hoped we could visit our graveyards with flowers instead of new bodies. But the flames of protest only grew and faces in my town became panicked. All over the country, more and more protests broke out, followed by government raids, arrests, executions. When those did not work, President Bashar al-Assad's army and militias adopted a policy of siege, aerial bombardment and artillery. My town of Sabinah, which is just south of Damascus, tumbled into the third century: electricity had once lit its houses, but now its streets disappeared in the dark. Schools closed. Shops emptied of everything except schoolbooks. My family's weekly visits to relatives became memories. And even though I had just been accepted to Damascus University to study law, I could not go to classes. We had been put under house arrest.

My family is made up of eleven members: my father and his wife, my four brothers, three sisters and my grand-mother. After my mother died in 1999, my grandmother took care of us, but by 2011 she was old and sick, and so, at the age of seventeen, I became the one who had to buy bread for the family. It would take me two hours because although the bakery was just a short distance from our home, it was next to an open square guarded by a military sniper. The government had taken control of the town by then and, to prevent rebellion, would shoot anyone out on the streets. I had to walk a long way around, hiding where the sniper couldn't see. I would often see a bullet dance in front of my eyes. Many of my friends fell for bread, one of them lying dead in the street for three days. Because of the sniper, people were afraid to rescue the body.

On February 9, 2012, my uncle Omar was killed by a stray bullet. He was twenty-three, the age I am now, and all he had wanted was a small family and a simple life. Still, although the level of violence increased every day, we had no intention of leaving our home, hoping things would return to the way they used to be. But what happened a short time later to me and my friend Majd made our flight inevitable.

Majd was fourteen. One day, we were running across the street to the bakery with our hands over our heads like helmets when I heard a shot and saw him fall by my side. I ran behind a wall to protect myself from the sniper and looked back. Majd was covered in blood. I carried him to a taxi just as a shell lodged in its back. All sounds disappeared. I only heard Majd groaning.

When I ran home covered in his blood, my grandmother cried out to my father, weeping: 'I will never forgive you if something bad happens to my children! When the siege ends, we must leave. Everything can be rebuilt, but we will not be able to bring our children back if they are killed.'

My father agreed. 'But until the siege is lifted,' he said, 'no one can leave the house.'

I watched their frightened eyes and told them we would be fine – unlike Majd, who will spend the rest of his life in a wheelchair. For the next eight days, rice was our only meal. Then, in the spring of 2012, the way to leave Sabinah opened up because the Syrian army was coming to evacuate the town. We hurried out in our little car with only our dirty clothes, our documents and our memories.

Because my family is so large, we had to split into four groups, each going to a different relative in Syria, as nobody could afford to take us all in. Our hosts were polite to our faces but grumbled behind our backs. We felt ashamed. Every time my father called us, we begged, 'Please take us out of here, we are not welcome.'

After a time, my father rented a house in the small city of Shahba in southern Syria. Our first night there was very beautiful because my family was reunited. My brothers and I took whatever work we could find – shoveling concrete or picking apples – even if it was hard, badly paid or dangerous. We were concerned only about keeping our family safe.

Shahba was quiet, but the streets were full of gangs, drug addicts and thieves who enjoyed finding new prey. One night three of them started beating me. I responded by slapping one of them but I was like a cat trapped between water and fire. People separated us, and I ran to a friend's house covered in blood. 'What happened?' my friend shouted.

'I feel like a stranger in my own country,' I told him. 'I used to feel every village in Syria was my village, all its people were my family. But now I realize my homeland was lost when they fired the first bullet. I have become lost, like my homeland.'

'Things will return to normal,' my friend replied. 'Just have a little patience.'

I told him he was wrong. 'Nothing will be as it was,' I said. 'I think I'll join an armed group to recover my rights, be strong.'

'Recover your rights from whom?' he asked me. 'A little boy or an old man? Then you'll be no better than the men who beat you, a demon possessed with the power of weapons.'

I left feeling angry and went to a cave where I could be alone. I sat there for nearly two hours. Sometimes I told myself to kill the light inside me and become a person without mercy; at other times I asked myself who I would be taking my rights from, people who just want to spend their

4

days in peace? Then what would be the difference between me and this abyss?

At the end of 2015, two of my cousins were killed at the same moment, their bodies torn to pieces by government missiles near their home in Daraa city. When we heard this news, I and every one of my brothers went off on his own to cry without anyone hearing us. When we returned, my father had gone to Daraa to be with his brother whose sons had died.

'I know you would have liked to go with me,' my father said when he came home, 'but you're the age of military service, and on the way to the city of Daraa, there are more than twenty military check points.' He explained that the military would imprison me and my brothers and probably torture and humiliate us, too, because they considered Daraa a city controlled by terrorists.

A few days later, my father made an announcement. 'I have sold our car and we will leave Syria. Every one of you will complete your studies and will achieve your dreams.'

After he spoke, silence fell over us, as if we were at a funeral. My father looked at us sadly and said, 'My children, do not look for honey in a country that kills its bees.'

On February 28, 2016, we left our new city with no luggage but our memories of apples, black city stones and the sounds of animals making our dark nights loud. Tears filled our eyes, perhaps because we realized that this was the end of the country that had given us the elixir of life, the river of papyrus, and apricot orchards in its grottos.

We stayed in Turkey for a year and a half in a small apartment in Antakya. We lived like animals, for our days consisted of work, food, sleep and nothing more. For a while, I repaired trucks, and then I worked in a shoe factory. Employers would often refuse to pay our wages, and if we asked for them we were fired. We were insulted by the people, the police and the army: 'You are traitors. You fled from your country and came here to hide like women behind us.'

At first, I tried hard to explain our war story to them, but in the end, I realized they would never understand. I often sat with my brothers and discussed the dreams we'd had as boys. Now our dreams were ashes blown here and there by the wind between bullets and bodies.

At the beginning of June 2017, my father decided there was no future for us in Turkey. Although we had worked there for a year and a half, we were never paid enough to save anything. We had to borrow the money to go.

The agreement we made with a smuggler was to pay him 500 dollars per person for passage to Greece on a rubber boat with no more than thirty-three passengers, for a crossing to last no longer than an hour. [Smugglers often deal in US dollars.] We were taken to a small hotel in Izmir on the Aegean coast, where the beds were full of bugs and drenched in urine.

The first trip was a failure and we were arrested, an event that I will never be able to expel from my memory. The second trip was with sixty-seven people, adults and children, injured and healthy. We were packed into a closed van, standing like cattle for two hours. It was suffocating, the crying of children and pregnant women, every man cursing.

My father's wife fainted. We beat the roof of the van and shouted. The driver stopped and opened the door. We thought he was going to help us but he only screamed, 'Get out! Stupid people, you could put me in prison.' He threw our luggage on the ground and shouted, 'Go to hell!'

From there we walked for half an hour until we met the Turkish smugglers on the beach. They forced us to carry the boat and inflate it.

Instead of one hour, we spent three hours packed in a boat just seven and a half meters long. Most of us had no life jackets, even though we couldn't swim. The driver was not more than sixteen, steering without a compass to guide us across the Aegean towards an island. With every wave, the boat was forced in a different direction. Vomit filled our luggage. We were crushed together so tightly that an old woman had to sit on my feet. My legs lost all feeling.

Three hours later, we saw a boat approaching us, terrifying everybody. We shouted, 'For God's sake, driver keep us away from that boat!'

The driver panicked and must have flooded the engine because it stopped. 'If we try to escape, I swear to God they will sink our boat,' he said. 'These Turkish border guards don't care about people's lives.' At the time, I didn't understand what he meant, but later I heard stories about the guards stopping the boats by shooting live bullets into the rubber to make them sink.

They came towards us and we saw a banner reading Frontex [the European Border and Coast Guard Agency]. Each passenger raised his child high: we had heard that unless they see children aboard, even the European coast guards might return the boat to Turkey.

The Frontex boat took us to Samos island, where we spent our first night on the floor of the police station in the refugee camp. This was August 19, 2017.

The next day, when we were taken out of the station, we thought they would put us in a container or tent, but the camp official only pointed to an empty patch of ground and said, 'Find a place and make that your house.' I asked an official if it was possible to give us a small tent to protect my nine-month-old sister from summer insects. The answer was shocking: 'I'm sorry, this is not my decision to make. Good luck.' As if to say, 'Who you are to ask for a tent?'

We found an open area in the camp with no tents. The place was very dirty. Then a Syrian man I did not know said: 'My friend, it's better to leave this spot and find somewhere else. There are drunks here who find people to hurt for their own amusement. They might fall over your body while you sleep because they've lost their minds.'

I went looking for another place and finally found one in the woods outside the camp. We spent seventeen days there, my eighty-three-year-old grandmother, my baby sister, all of us. The sky was our roof, the trees our walls, the earth our bed. We would throw some of our food far away from where we slept as bait for insects. The space was covered in bugs and human waste.

After a time, the police drove us from that place to inside the wire and concrete walls of the camp. Although every space in the camp was full, they just repeated, 'Find a place and make it your house.' For three days we looked for a space with no success, until, finally, a friend offered us his tent because we were a family and he was alone. His tent was small, so we used it to shield my baby sister, and tore up a blanket to make another shelter for the rest of the family. Many days, we woke to find rainwater flowing underneath us like a river. And every morning we would have to rise early to stand in a long line for the croissant and small juice box they gave us for breakfast.

I heard a lot of sad stories in the camp. The heat in the nylon tents was so bad that people made covers to keep the sun away from their children, but the police came and cut the covers down, saying they blocked the surveillance cameras. One day, a police officer began to beat a pregnant woman. When a Syrian man came to defend her, they beat him, too, then took him to prison and kept him there until he could not bear it. Finally, he said he wanted to go back to Turkey because there are no rights and no life in Greece.

Now, when we go swimming or walking on the beach, sometimes the police stop us to check our identity cards and order us back to the camp. As obedient as dogs, we go. This is their state, their laws, and we are only refugees who have no right to object. I often see women waiting for hours in front of the clinic in the camp, collapsing when their bodies finally let them down, the nurses saying, 'What can we do for you, with just three nurses and one doctor?'

We often take walks to try and escape the noise in the camp – the fights for toilets, the music and the shouting. Once a man with a razor blade cut his arms in front of a policeman, who did not care that children were watching. The sight of the blood took me back to Syria and to Majd.

On September 4, 2017, two weeks after we had arrived, the asylum office presented my family with a permit to leave the island, with the exception of me and my brothers, Ayham and Ehab. Because we were older than eighteen, we had separate asylum cases. Yet we were happy to know that our family could leave for some place better. We were also certain that the office would give us our own open cards soon so that we could join the rest of our family in Athens.

My older brother, Ayham, received a permit to join my family after three more months. I got one as well, two months after that. But my younger brother's asylum application was denied. Our entire family could stay in Greece, the asylum officials told us, but Ehab alone would be sent back to Turkey. They said they rejected him because Turkey was safe for him. How was that possible when Turkish guards had pushed him back to Syria three times when he had tried to cross the border with two of our young sisters? How was it possible when he had been taken to a police station, hosed with water, insulted and forced to pick up cigarette butts from the floor while being beaten? They never said why Turkey was safe for him but not for all of us.[1]

When my grandmother heard news of his rejection, she could only hide herself away and cry.

Now I must stay on this island because I do not want to leave my younger brother alone while he waits for the appeal court's decision. For ten months now, I have been waiting. I try to sleep, to turn myself again into nothing, but at night I am kept awake by the bedbugs for whom I am prey. I put detergent or chlorine on my body to stop their aggression but it's useless, for they are the natives in my new land. So, I stay awake, examining my life, lighting cigarette followed by cigarette until the sun rises again.

So far, we do not know whether our family will remain together or be torn apart. I no longer care about my future, only about what will happen to my family.

The time is now midnight. After finishing my last cigarette and cup of coffee, I again tell myself to sleep. Ten minutes later, I repeat, 'It is time to sleep.' I stand and walk like a drunk looking for a candle, then throw my tired body on the bed. But the bed is full of bugs and every night they resume their feast.

The time is now one hour after midnight. My last cigarette has given birth to ten more. I look at my cup of coffee in surprise, for I still have not finished it. Did I make another without realizing? The many thoughts in my mind throw me here and there like a boat without an anchor. I have conversations in my head with people who are now only memories, hoping that they will help me sleep.

The time is two hours after midnight and I stop talking to those who are dead. They cannot help me. It is better to light another cigarette and leave the dead lying peacefully in their graves.

INTRODUCTION

Hope and Sorrow

by Helen Benedict

'This is my friend, Hasan. He is a man without hope.'

These were the words that Eyad Awwadawnan used to introduce his fellow Syrian to me when we met in 2018, at just the time Eyad had written the essay above. The three of us were standing inside the foul-smelling, overcrowded refugee camp he describes, surrounded by tents, rubbish and flies, while a police officer eyed us suspiciously from inside his guard booth. Hasan knew little English at the time and I do not speak Arabic, so Eyad translated.

I turned to squint at Hasan through the sun – it was June and Greek-island hot, and I had just failed to find a working toilet or running water, the camp's supply having been cut to two hours a day. He gazed back at me shyly, a slight man of medium height with a gaunt face, dramatic black eyebrows, a crooked nose and a bold streak of white through his black hair. His smile seemed kind but his brow was lined and his mouth pinched, so I took him for more than forty. He was, I later found out, twenty-five.

'Shall we go somewhere private to talk?' I asked, curious to hear what had robbed him of hope.

'Yes, follow us, please,' Eyad replied for him, and led us up the scrubby mountainside above the camp to the spot where he and his family had slept during their first weeks on the island. There, we sat on a fallen log in the shade of an ancient olive tree, encircled by clumps of brittle yellow grass and litter, and gazed out at the sea.

One of the many ironies that comes from installing a hideous refugee camp on a beautiful island like Samos is that, from every angle, the camp looks over a view fit for the gods. The northern Aegean stretches in its glittering turquoises and blues all the way to the sky; the town of Vathi lies like a tumble of sugar cubes at the bottom of the hill below the camp; and the lavender mountains of Turkey rise in the near distance, the very Anatolian range under which Homer had Odysseus glimpse the tortures of Tantalus. It is hard to escape the thought that refugees on Samos suffer a similar fate, taunted wherever they turn by a horizon that promises distant lands they may never see, a beauty they lack the peace of mind to appreciate, and a freedom they fear they will never find.

Eyad, Hasan and the other refugees on Samos and in this book embody an enormous change in modern history. Not only are there some 84 million forcibly displaced people in the world, more than at any time since World War Two[1] (and millions more since President Putin of Russia invaded Ukraine in 2022), but they are fleeing a combination of war, civil unrest, religious conflict, poverty, persecution, local violence and global warming – forces often inextricably intertwined – just at a point when authoritarian governments are rising all over the world and anti-immigrant sentiment is rising with them.

As a result, many refugees are being persecuted, demonized and denied their legal rights, not only by those authoritarian nations, but within Europe, Britain, Australia and the United States, too – the very democracies that are supposed to protect them and that, in some cases, turned them into refugees in the first place. The US's 'War on Terror' alone has displaced more than 37 million people since 2001.[2] Some of the worst of this persecution is being played out in Greece.[3]

Greece has long been a major gateway to Europe for anyone fleeing war or violence in the Middle East and Africa, but, since 2016, it has turned into a trap. Had Eyad and his family arrived at one of the reception centers on the islands of Samos, Lesbos, Chios, Leros or Kos before that date, they would have been registered fairly quickly and given permission to move on to the mainland and then to other, less impoverished countries in Europe, where they might have found a better chance to build new lives. But after more than a million refugees from the wars in Syria, Iraq and Afghanistan arrived in Europe in 2015 and terrorists attacked Paris that same year, anti-immigrant politicians all over the world began blaming and demonizing Muslim refugees (in fact, only one of the ten perpetrators in the Paris attack was a refugee.[4]) The reaction of the European Union (EU) to this was to strike a deal with Turkey to keep such refugees out of the West.

The deal, signed on March 18, 2016, paid Turkey three billion euros and included the bargain that for each refugee Greece sent back to Turkey from the islands – as it was trying to do with Eyad's brother, Ehab – the EU would take one Syrian out; a swap of human beings predicated, as

Amnesty International put it at the time, on the 'untrue, but willfully ignored, premise that Turkey is a safe country for refugees and asylum-seekers'.[5]

The deal also mandated that asylum seekers would no longer be able to move freely about Greece, but would have to stay on the islands where they arrived and undergo a new and much lengthier process to gain asylum, including two interviews, the first to ascertain whether they can be forcibly returned to Turkey, the second to determine whether to grant them official protected status as a refugee.

(Eyad and I use the term 'refugee' to reflect the way the people in this book refer to themselves, but, legally speaking, refugees are only those who have been granted international protection by a government, either through a refugee resettlement program or by winning asylum. Asylum seekers are those who, like everyone we interviewed, fled their homelands to enter another country and request this protection.)

In 2020, the EU-Turkey deal began to fray, partly because of conflicts between Turkey and Greece and partly because the Covid-19 pandemic slowed down people's ability to cross the sea. Yet the EU is still funneling money into Turkey and Greece to keep refugees away, and the effects of the deal's bureaucracy, not to mention corruption and inefficiency, have so clogged Greece's asylum system that the waiting period for these interviews and the subsequent asylum decisions has stretched from months to years, trapping many thousands of people in miserable conditions and agonizing limbo in a country that has neither the resources nor the will to keep them.[6]

Trying to live in a country that does not want you cuts deep into any human soul. We humans are born with a deep-seated need to belong, whether to a nation, family, circle of friends, tribe, language, religion or ideological group. Yet this sense of belonging is exactly what refugees relinquish in order to survive. I would venture that we humans also need to feel that we matter, if only in a small way, yet refugees are increasingly finding themselves in countries where, instead of being welcomed and respected for the skills, fortitude and perseverance they called upon to endure their journeys, they are treated as parasites and criminals, subject to both the ancient racist tropes that still permeate Europe and the more modern fear and distrust of Muslims. Much of the pain expressed by the people in this book is about having risked their lives crossing continents and seas, only to end up belonging nowhere and mattering to nobody.

Some would argue that there is little new about nations trying to keep out refugees and that it is in the nature of a nation state to place its own people over the human rights of outsiders. True as this may be, I would point out that, in the wake of the 2001 attacks on the United States, the senseless invasion of Iraq by the US and its allies, the consequential destabilization of the Middle East and rise of Islamic extremism, and the hyper-attention to a handful of terrorist attacks in Europe, Western nations have been hardening their borders against Middle Eastern and African refugees to an extent never seen since World War Two.

This hardening is not only breaking hearts, it is breaking laws – namely the right to request asylum, enshrined in the 1948 Universal Declaration of Human Rights, and the international laws embedded in the 1951 Refugee Convention.[7] The Convention, held in Geneva by the United Nations in reaction to the shocks of the Holocaust and the ensuing flight and mistreatment of mainly Jewish refugees, was ratified into law by 148 nations, including Greece, Britain, the United States, Canada, Australia and most of Europe.[8] (Some, including the US, signed an updated version later, in 1967.) The idea was never again to allow the spurning of refugees that had sent so many Jews back to their deaths, and to protect the dignity and freedom of human beings everywhere.

With this history in mind, the Convention defined refugees as people who were forced to flee their countries because of 'a well-founded fear of persecution for reasons of race, religion, nationality, political opinion or membership in a particular social group', and who 'cannot return home or [are] afraid to do so'. Such refugees, the Convention declared, have the right to international protection from discrimination and persecution; the right to housing, schooling and the chance to work for a living; the right not to be criminalized for simply seeking asylum; and the right not to be subjected to refoulement – forcible deportation back to the countries they fled.

The UN later expanded the definition of refugees to include people fleeing war, persecution, violence or extreme poverty, but not all governments accepted this amendment, a loophole that allows for many a violation of the rights I list above. Nonetheless, the Convention made Britain, Europe, Canada and the United States respected throughout the world as bastions of human rights, which is why, when people are driven to flee their countries, they head for the safety and dignity they believe they will find in the West. This is the belief that brought Eyad, his family, Hasan and everybody else in this book to Greece.

Shortly after I met Eyad on Samos, he began finding people for me to interview and acting as our translator. A few months later, he and many others were evacuated to the mainland; some sent to live in camps, some to refugee hotels, some to subsidized housing. I followed, visiting Samos and mainland Greece several times over the next two years until, just as I was about to go again in March 2020, the Covid-19 pandemic hit, forcing us to turn to another plan: Eyad would interview Arabic-speakers inside Greece and then translate, while including his own story. I would interview refugees who could speak English or French over video phone until I could return to Greece, as I did in 2021. In this way, we became co-authors.

For the three years between 2018 and the end of 2021, Eyad and I interviewed the people in this book multiple times over many hours and months, sometimes in person, sometimes by phone, recording as we went. Calvin is the only person in the book we never met face to face.

Our approach was informal, sympathetic and transparent. We explained our vision for the book and our wish to allow our subjects to tell their own stories in their own words; we checked facts, went over muddy memories to help clarify them, and promised not to reveal anyone's full name in order to safeguard their asylum status and security. We assured everyone that they were in control of their own stories and were free to put in or leave out what they wished. And even though everybody but Asmahan and some of the women in Chapter Three told their stories in English (Calvin with a sprinkling of French), their second or even third language, we tried to stay as close to their original words as we could, only editing for repetition and clarification.

We interviewed many other people, too, whom, alas, we had no room to include, but everything they told us was equally valuable, helping to build a picture of what it is like to be a refugee in Greece. We refer to several of these people in the book.

As we were working as journalists, not sociologists, we followed conventional ethics and offered no pay to our sources, all of whom accepted this without objection. The argument is that if you offer money up front, you risk making sources feel that they have to talk to you, no matter what, and perhaps even say what they think you want to hear. In short, you might make them feel beholden to you in a way that pollutes the trust between interviewer and interviewee. But we quickly discovered that it feels even worse not to help at all, especially with people you have come to know well, who have lost everything, and for whom even a few dollars can make the difference between eating or not, prison or freedom, shelter or homelessness, safety or danger. So, when help was needed in the form of a phone call, a contact or money, we tried to help as much as we could.

In 2020, I had originally wanted to return to Greece to find out how refugees were being affected by the 2019 election of the blatantly anti-immigrant *Nea Dimokratia* (New Democracy) government. In a disturbing echo of the Trump administration's antagonistic and often deadly policies towards refugees in the United States – policies predicated on both racism and the false idea that making life miserable for refugees will stop them from coming – *Nea Dimokratia* took the line that the majority of 'migrants' in Greece only come to make money and so are not entitled to refugee protections.[9] This reasoning, which willfully ignored the reality that more than 75 percent of asylum seekers in Greece had in fact fled war or violence,[10] allowed the government to make life for asylum seekers and refugees even more punishing than it had been under the EU-Turkey deal. One of its first acts was to decree that it would deport 10,000 asylum seekers before January 2020; and that, after that date, anyone with asylum had one month before being severed from all support.

This meant that, in direct violation of the Geneva Convention, all refugees – even children, pregnant women, the elderly and the sick – would be evicted from their government-supported homes, cut off from cash allowances, denied free medical care except in emergencies, and left to fend for themselves without any of the language, job or integration training offered refugees elsewhere – this in a country that has one of the poorest economies and highest unemployment rates in Europe. In other words, winning international protected status now qualified refugees in Greece for quite the opposite: no protection at all.

How, I wondered, were Eyad, Hasan and every other refugee I knew going to avoid ending up homeless, at the mercy of the criminals and human traffickers who prey on people in exactly such desperate circumstances as these? And so, as Hasan and the other people in this book recounted the tales of their lives up until 2022, our conversations also ranged over the daily crises they were facing in Greece, and how they were struggling to hold on to that most precious of human comforts: hope.

1

HASAN

'You know, my life is funny. I don't want to make people sad or feel sorry for me. I want to make them laugh.'

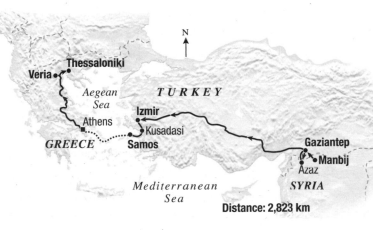

Hasan in Syria

'We have a young man like a rose.'

Helen:

Hasan may not have spoken English when we first met in 2018, but by the time I was interviewing him in 2020, he spoke it as fast as I do. The story here is thus in his own English words, with some editing for clarity. Like all the people in this book, he asked me not to use his last name, both for the sake of his privacy and to protect his asylum status.

Hasan was born in the northern Syrian town of Manbij, eighteen years before the 2011 revolution and the civil war that, as of 2021, had killed some 580,000 civilians and displaced at least 13 million more.[1] Because Manbij lies on the border with Turkey, it quickly became a major battleground for the multiple forces involved in the war. President Bashar al-Assad's forces occupied the town until 2012. The revolutionary Free Syrian Army took over until 2014. ISIS then seized the city and kept it until 2016. And since then Manbij has been in the control of Kurds, with sporadic help from the US but under frequent attack from Assad, Turkey and Russia. Growing up in a political football of a town like this has affected every aspect of Hasan's life.

HASAN IN SYRIA

The history of Syria and its civil war has filled many a book but to understand its basics it helps to go back to World War One, when victorious Britain and France carved up the lands of the previous Ottoman Empire between them, creating Iraq, modern-day Syria, Lebanon, Israel and Jordan. Britain took Iraq, while France took Syria and Lebanon. In essence, European powers were using the same divide-and-conquer methods they had used in Africa to dominate the region, seeding or inflaming ethnic, religious and tribal divisions that only created states destined to fail.

Syrians did not take kindly to French rule and many a revolt erupted through the years until the nation finally won an uneasy independence in 1946. After several more coups and conflicts, fed by the divisions elucidated above, the Arab Socialist Ba'ath Party, which had been gathering members throughout the Middle East, seized power in 1963. Seven years later, the regime was defeated in a coup by the current president's father, Hafez al-Assad.

Assad, who came from the Alawi minority, a Shia sect that had long been persecuted in Syria until the French elevated them, soon sowed his own discontent by proving to be both autocratic and kleptocratic, manipulating patronage to enforce loyalty, suppressing freedom of speech and feeding corruption. When, in February 1982, he ordered a brutal military response to a Muslim Brotherhood uprising in the city of Hama, massacring more than 25,000 people and spreading terror over the land with arbitrary arrests, tortures, imprisonments and executions, he provided a grim model for his son and successor, Bashar, of how to respond to dissent.

As Hasan says, Syrians initially thought well of Bashar. In 2000, at the start of his presidency, he released 600 political prisoners and promised a list of reforms, raising hopes that he would prove less oppressive than his father. Within a year, however, Bashar was as bad if not worse than Hafez, imprisoning, torturing and often killing anyone he deemed a rival or critic.

By the time the so-called Arab Spring swept through the Middle East in early 2011, Syrians were suffering from drought, poverty and a corruption that made it hard for anyone not connected to the regime to advance. All these factors may be why, when a group of boys from the city of Daraa scrawled a juvenile taunt about Bashar on a wall and the regime responded by arresting and torturing them, people were emboldened enough to take to the streets in the peaceful protests Eyad mentions in his Preface. Bashar responded by sending troops to arrest, beat and kill hundreds of protesters and their families, prompting a response that first became a revolution and then the civil war that has lasted ever since.

I will leave the Syrians in this book to tell the rest of this story, but it is important to mention that Europe and the US have played a complicated and inconsistent role in the conflict, in essence leaving Russia, Iran and Turkey to manipulate Syria, while doing little or nothing to help the millions of civilians who have suffered as a result. In 2017, for example, then President Trump subjected Syrians and the citizens from six other predominantly Muslim countries to a travel ban, preventing them from ever entering the United States under his watch.[2] He also suspended all resettlement of Syrian refugees.

Hasan told me bits and pieces of how this history affected his life while we were in Samos with Eyad, but he did not begin his story in earnest until the spring of 2020, when we were both under the coronavirus lockdown. By that time he had been evacuated to a remote hotel forty-four miles west of Thessaloniki in northern Greece, where, almost every day for months, we talked over video phone while his roommates wandered by, occasionally waving into the phone camera as they passed.

During these conversations, Hasan was undergoing a series of crises typically suffered by people who have lost their homes and homelands, including depression and ill-health, all of which spun him into spells of despair, anger and bitterness. He was also withering before my eyes because he found the hotel food inedible, could not afford to buy much of his own, and was forbidden to cook in his room anyway. He seemed to be living on fruit, tea and cigarettes, especially during the Ramadan fast; he could never sleep; and he was often in pain from the old injuries he describes in his story, a pain that he said was like a hot knife in his arm.

'The pain is a shadow that follows me everywhere,' he told me at the time, and he did look exhausted – circles under his eyes, sunken cheeks, a scraggly beard and sallow skin, the lines deeper than ever across his forehead. He had run out of his prescription pain medication, yet the local pharmacist denied him a refill, accusing him of being a drug dealer, which Hasan knew would never have happened had he been Greek. Several times he went to the local hospital, only to be turned away without so much as an examination.

'They do not care about refugees,' he told me with a shrug. 'They believe nothing I say.' Yet whenever I expressed concern, he always replied with his signature phrase, 'No, no, do not worry. It is a small problem.' Then he would drop the subject and return to his memories.

'I am going back to times I have not thought of for years,' he said with a wry smile. 'It helps me get through the days here. There is nothing to do in this hotel, nowhere to go. The nearest town, Veria, is fifteen kilometers away and I have to take two buses to get there, which I cannot afford. There is a small village I can walk to in half an hour, but it has only one market, one pharmacy and no people or cafés, only dogs. And always, all the dogs follow me!' He laughed. 'So, yes, there is nothing to do but remember.'

Being unable to sleep, he took to texting me long messages in the middle of the night, filling in details of the memories he unfolds here.

✳   ✳   ✳

Manbij was like Paris

I am forgetting my mom's smell. I loved her very much, even though she was hard on me. Last month I saw her and my twin in my dreams. They are in heaven, *inshallah*. They looked down at me and smiled.

My twin's name was Hussein. I was born one minute before him on September 17, 1993. We had an elder brother, Mahmoud, and an elder sister, too: Hajar. We were close as a family. All we children slept together on mattresses on the floor. Not because we were poor and couldn't afford beds, we just liked the floor better.

Only my father and sister are alive now. She lives in Saudi Arabia. I have not seen her in eight years.

My mom was twenty-three years younger than my dad. She married him in 1986, when she was seventeen and he was forty. But he worked in Lebanon all the time. He sent her all the money he had every month, but he was gone so much I was scared of him as a child. When he came home, I would say, 'Who is this man?' I didn't get to know him till I went to Beirut with him to work in 2009 when I was fifteen.

We lived in a big house in Manbij and, for me, it was heaven. We had 500 square meters of space, seven bedrooms, the kitchen, living room. Pomegranate trees in the inner courtyard, and pink, yellow and red roses. A small pen for chickens, rabbits. I loved it as a child so much I never wanted to go out.

But between 2005 and 2006, the government decided to open a new street right through our house. They took most of it and left us with eighty square meters. The trees, flowers, chicken coop – all gone. They gave us no money, no other house, nothing. The whole family sat and cried that day.

Still, Manbij was like Paris for me. I knew nothing else but I thought it was beautiful. The smell of the ground after the rain in the winter – I've been in Greece for three years now, but when it rains here, the smell is never the same. Roses grew over the walls. Two rivers wove through the city, dry in the summer, flowing in the winter. Manbij is an ancient city, the market center is more than 500 years old. It was a cocktail of people: Kurds, Armenians, Christians, Turkmen . . . Jews were there too, but they left when Daesh took control.

[Hasan and other Syrians prefer the term Daesh to ISIS or ISIL. Daesh is essentially an acronym formed from the initial letters of the group's previous name in Arabic and sounds similar to an Arabic verb meaning to trample or crush. ISIS supporters object to its use.]

My life in Manbij was not much fun, though. I had to go to school and work so much that I never had time to learn to ride a bicycle or play football or swim or drive a motorcycle. Whoever heard of a person not able to do those things? It's like I'm from Mars.

When I started school, I didn't like it – there were too many other children and the teacher was always shouting at me, hitting me. Later, I learned to like it because I was smart. I say it myself but that's what I think. I would wake up in the morning at 5:00 and eat at 6:00. Mom made us breakfast and tea. We would have *zatoon*, the Syrian bread, and a cheese she made herself from cow's milk, soft and white. We had yogurt, zaatar [a mix of herbs basic to Syrian food, including wild mint, toasted sesame seeds, sumac, salt, thyme, cumin and more] and *labneh*, which is between milk and cheese. My mom used to make the *zaatar* herself. Then she would check to make sure I was clean and tidy and give me one lira. I went to school for six hours a day, six days a week. One week we studied in the morning, the next in the afternoon. At home, I would do my homework, and watch our black-and-white TV. My dad brought it from Lebanon when I was seven. We would watch Turkish cartoons and movies. We were so close to Turkey that the TV had Turkish programs. My mom spoke Turkish instead of Arabic because her village was on the border. Her whole family spoke Turkish – I couldn't understand a word they said.

We didn't have toys to play with. I used to think only girls played with toys. But I remember when my dad brought two footballs for us, one for me, one for my twin. Mine was cream colored and had the name of Pele and other great football players written on it. Hussein's was black and white. I played alone and he played alone. I wanted a bike, too, but I never had one.

My sister Hajar helped take care of us. I called her Mom, I still do, but she is very strong and hard. She and my mom hit me every day. They slapped me in the face, across the back. We were in Syria, not Canada or America, so that was normal. But I was a bad child. I shouted at my mom, I fought with people in the street, my clothes were dirty, I drank tea and left the glass on the floor, I didn't study. I locked the door and ran away. I got my friends to skip school and go play video games or smoke shisha. I taught children to smoke cigarettes. I did all that because I'm a boy. I didn't want anybody telling me what to do. Sometimes I do bad things not because I hate but because I'm angry. And when I'm angry, I'm a stupid person. Because of that, my mom and sister hit me. But I forgive them.

One day, when I was ten or eleven, I went with my mom to the city-center market. I saw children there working, pushing trolleys, carrying shopping bags for people – children ten, twelve years old. I wanted to do that, too! I wanted to earn money because in school I would see the other children with new clothes and shoes and toys, and we didn't have those things. I wanted to buy shoes for my family, not just myself. And to buy sweets for my mom, too. She loved sweets.

So, when I finished my homework, I went to the center without my mom knowing, earned some money and went home to give it to her. I was very proud and excited. But all she did was hit me. And then she called my dad and told him. He said, 'Don't let Hasan do that, I don't want him to work so young.' My mom hit me more, but I told her, 'I'm a man, I want to help.'

Finally, she said I could work during school holidays but otherwise I had to concentrate on my studies. 'You're a child, Hasan, your life should be playing and studying, not working.' But I kept working after that, until I was fourteen.

Umbilical cord

In the eastern regions of Syria, there is a popular belief that if, after a baby is born, you cut the umbilical cord and put it somewhere like a doctor's office, a lawyer's office, a courtroom, a hospital, then your child will join that profession.

I think my mom put the umbilical cord in the hospital. But her plan didn't work because I didn't become a doctor, I became a patient.

It began one day when I was ten and my twin, Hussein, bought a book about how to do martial arts. He needed a human body to train on, so he chose mine, and with the first kick, he hit me in the testicles. I fell to the ground screaming. Mom rushed me to the hospital, where the doctor found a big swelling. He said I was suffering from an inguinal hernia. I thought it meant I was dying, so I cried.

I stayed in the hospital overnight under observation. The doctor said that if I didn't get better, I might need surgery. My mom stayed that night beside me, crying. The next day a doctor told her I was too young to tolerate surgery. He wrote prescriptions for pain relievers and sent us home.

After several years I went to Lebanon with my father and the pain returned, so we went to see a doctor. After some tests, the doctor said I might be sterile, although it could be a medical error, but either way, this beat me down at the time and I refused to speak to Hussein. I held him responsible. In the end I went back to talking to him, but after that I began to reject the idea of marriage and avoid attachment to any girl. I am still doing so now.

The next problem came in the summer of 2008 when I was fourteen. My father sent some money to my mother to build a new home in the village of Karsan, where he was born, twelve kilometers from Manbij. She bought 10,000 bricks for the walls of the house. I helped the construction worker dig and level the foundations, and after we finished, I felt tired and had a headache, so I lay on the floor in a corner, even though it was filled with sharp rocks, and fell asleep for several hours. A few days later, I felt a pain in my right shoulder. I took some medicine but the pain only increased until I was crying. My mom prayed to God to heal me, tears falling from her eyes.

The next day we went to an orthopedic doctor, who took an X-ray of my shoulder and said I had broken bones. He put me in a splint from my shoulder to my wrist. But after fifteen days the pain was worse and my arm was swollen, so I cut the splint off with a knife. The scene was shocking. It was as if a Picasso painting was splashed over my shoulder. Yellow, red, green, blue. I thought it was gangrene. I had something called a purulent abscess and blood poisoning. I went to the Al-Basel National Hospital for surgery and stayed in the operating room three or four hours. When I woke up, my mother was next to me. Blood covered my arm and I was screaming. They did not sew up the wound, they left it open and put a small tube in it to suck out the rest of the pus and tainted blood.

My arm recovered in about a month but I couldn't move my hand. It turned out the surgeon had accidentally cut a tendon or nerve. I had to take physical therapy and medications. This was the beginning of a chronic disability that will accompany me for the rest of my life.

I had other accidents, too. After I left school, I went with my dad to work in Beirut in March 2009. He worked for a Lebanese contractor restoring old buildings, digging foundations and water tunnels, paving the streets, building speed bumps. He kept telling me, 'Don't be like me, keep studying. Be a doctor, a lawyer, something.' But I wanted to help him earn money so my family could live a better life and so I would not have to ask for help from others.

After a short period, I found work in tree trimming. Because I had learned to be a farmer at home, I could do this work. We are all children of the earth and we will all return to it one day.

To trim trees, I had to stand in a basket at the top of a crane and hang in the sky several meters above the ground. One morning, when I was seventeen, I was up there with a large pair of shears and a sharp saw, and I don't know how it happened but I fell off, like a child falling into his mother's arms. At that moment my life passed in front of me at a frightening and terrifying speed, like a movie combining bad and good moments together.

I woke up staring at the white ceiling of a room, asking myself whether I was alive and if this was a nightmare. It was a hospital room and my dad was waiting outside, looking at me from behind glass panels. A doctor asked me: 'Do you feel anything? Can you move your foot?' I couldn't. The next day they took me for an X-ray, which showed I had a lesion in the lumbar spine.

The doctor told my father to buy a truss filled with iron sheets, which was supposed to make my back straight. But it cost 500 dollars and he couldn't afford it. We also had to pay the hospital about 4,000 dollars, which he didn't have either. In the end, my managers paid. After I left hospital, my father decided to send me to Manbij for the best treatment. I said, 'But this is very expensive, Father.'

He told me: 'My son, there are some people in the world who cannot have children, so they pay huge sums to doctors so that they can have one child. We have a young man like a rose. Do you think we will let him die in front of our eyes without doing anything for him?'

Eventually, a neighbor lent my mom an iron belt, which I was forced to wear for six months. I had to sleep on the floor and could only take it off for fifteen minutes a day until I could walk and see the sun again.

I don't care about hijab and age

When I was fifteen, I fell in love. My first time. In school, I would like some girls but not tell. This girl I told. I met her through my Aunt Fida, whose name means silver. She is my mother's sister and I love her a lot. My aunt is a strong woman. She carries a gun, and the men gather around to listen to her with respect when she talks.

My aunt lived in a village called Althyabaa, which means pack of wolves, about twelve kilometers outside the city of Al-Raqqa. I met the girl there because her house was nearby. Her name was Nour and she was about eighteen. She was so beautiful, with white skin and green eyes, blond hair. And she was kind to me, bringing me tea and sweets. We spent all our time together in the two months I was there, smoking and talking. One night we spent the whole night together, just innocently, and when she fell asleep, I stayed up just watching her face in sleep. I was only fifteen but I was so in love. I told my aunt we wanted to get married.

'Fine, but you have to tell your parents,' my aunt said. 'They need to ask her family.'

I said, 'Nour loves me, so it's OK.'

'We are Arab people, Hasan,' my aunt replied. 'It doesn't work this way.'

My parents didn't like the idea at all. 'You are too young, this is not the time to get married,' they told me. 'Your older brother has to marry first.' And they didn't like Nour. They said she smokes and is older than me and she doesn't wear hijab. I said, 'I love her, I don't care about hijab and age!' They said, 'Go get married then. But if you do, forget us. You'll have to go live with her family.' So I had to give up the idea.

I went to Lebanon again to work but I was so angry about Nour I tried to kill myself with pills. I awoke the next day and I was still alive! You cannot take the life from yourself; it is too precious, and it is *haram*, forbidden. Still, I was sad about losing Nour. For two, three months I was sad. But I had a new life in Lebanon. I learned to become a carpenter from my big brother, a job I loved. I became a man there. I had work, a phone, new clothes, I could go back to Syria and give my family money. I learned to think about my family, not myself. I forgot about girls and getting married . . . not now, I decided. Maybe when I have all I want in twelve years. And then I had the other worry I talked about, the one about fertility.

I heard that Nour married someone else after three years, though I am not sure this is true. I met with her before I left Syria. Her sister is pretty, too, so Nour said you can marry her. She was always funny.

War

Between 2010 and 2011, I moved between Syria and Lebanon all the time for work. I had to spend a week in Syria every six months to renew my visa, so I was there when the war started. The dictator Bashar al-Assad sent his army to Manbij between May and July 2011. This was the first time in my life I had seen soldiers in our streets, soldiers with Kalashnikovs. The first time I had ever seen guns in our streets.

Everywhere, Bashar had secret police to spy on us – boys, girls, old men – he didn't care who he hired. And there was a curfew; we weren't allowed out of our homes after ten at night. This is when my family decided to leave the city and go to our farm in Karsan. The Syrian Army was inside Manbij but the rebel Free Army controlled the outside, so we felt safer there. I was in Lebanon when they moved, so it made me feel strange to come back to the village instead of Manbij.

Our village house was big, like our city house – 260 square meters. We had no courtyard with trees but we had trees and flowers outside. We had chickens, five sheep, a cow. We made our own bread. We had about 2,000 olive trees, fifty grape vines, fifty pistachio trees, fifty almond trees. We planted them with a machine. I hated that job. And I didn't like living in the village. I didn't know anybody and the closest house was a kilometer away.

The life was hard. We would harvest the nuts and olives, take the olives to make oil, but none of this could make any real money in Syria. You can have all those trees, two houses and eight hectares [just under twenty acres] of land, but you still can't have a car or anything in the bank. That's why we had to keep going to work in Lebanon. But I never hated my dad for making me work hard like that. He had worked all his life to keep us alive. He built us houses, got us land, planted trees. I want to do that for my children one day, if I ever have them, *inshallah*.

In 2011, when I was eighteen, I was arrested with Hussein and my cousin, Ahmed. We had gone to visit my uncle and his son, who was called Mahmoud, like my brother. We sat with them for a few hours talking about the conditions of the country and the demonstrations against Bashar, and then we left to walk home at about nine o'clock at night.

On the way, we saw a patrol car belonging to the State Security branch in Manbij. We hid in one of the alleys because, at the time, small demonstrations were taking place every evening out of the mosques in Manbij and the police were arresting protesters. The women would throw flowers at the demonstrators and spray them with water and rice from the balcony of the houses to express their opposition to the government. The demonstrations were peaceful. People were only asking for freedom of opinion, that our country and people be together as one, and that the mission of the army be to protect the country and citizens, not persecute them. It was not only Muslims who came out to demonstrate, but people of all nationalities and religions. Initially the security forces suppressed the demonstrations with sticks, electric cables and hoses, but when the protesters started coming out in large numbers in broad daylight, the police began using live bullets.

Anyway, after Ahmed, Hussein and I hid for a while, we kept walking. We felt someone behind us, so we walked faster, scared. A white Peugeot pulled up and the men inside told us to stop. They got out and one said: 'What are you doing out this late? Give me your ID.' We didn't have any papers with us – we didn't need that in our own city. We told him we are from Manbij and that we were going to the bakery to buy bread.

'Don't lie, the bakery isn't open at this time,' he said. Then another said, 'Sir, I was following them and I saw them write anti-state graffiti on the city walls everywhere.' He said we had stabbed him in his hands with a knife and run away. His hand was bleeding but we didn't know who did that to him.

They handcuffed us, shoved us into the back of the car and drove us to the school they had made into a police station for the State Security Branch. After the war began, the Syrian Army closed the schools in Manbij so they could use them for their offices and prisons. In the station, they told us to sit along the wall with our heads down. They beat and insulted us until two o'clock in the morning. For them, this was fun. Hussein had long hair and they grabbed it and threw him around by it. The police were bored, nothing to do, so they insulted and hurt us for entertainment.

Finally, an officer came in and took us to the interrogation room. We were crying. We thought we would never see sunlight again because this often happened to people in the hands of Bashar's police. Everyone knew what they did to people: torture, physical and psychological humiliation, murder, rape, assault.

The officer asked us who we were and what we were doing. I was crying. Then he told us to chant slogans and praise of President Bashar al-Assad, so we obeyed. There was a photo hanging on the wall of the interrogation room of Bashar's father, and we had to salute him as we chanted the slogans. The officer took down the photo and commanded us to kiss it.

After the interrogation ended, they put us in a cell. We sat there the rest of the night. The guard made us mimic animal sounds. We could not sleep.

The next morning, they took us to the chief officer, who made us sign a pledge that we would not leave our houses after ten o'clock in the evening and that we would never tell anyone what we did. I told him again that we didn't do anything but he shouted in my face, saying, 'Shut up and get out of here, stupid!'

We were released at seven in the morning. We went home too afraid to tell our families what happened to us. To this day they don't know.

In December of that year, 2011, I received a letter from the Department of Compulsory Military Service in Manbij stating that I had to report to their center on January 22, 2012 to join the Syrian army for my mandatory one and a half years' service. My brother Mahmoud was already in the service. Now it was my turn.

I ignored the letter. I wanted to be in the revolutionary Free Army, not Bashar's army. I hated Bashar and his father, Hafez, too.

When Hafez died in 2000, I was seven years old. I remember sitting with my dad watching our TV when the news came on saying Hafez was dead. We were eating eggs and my dad began to cry. I cried, too, although I didn't know why. I cried because he cried. Then my dad said: 'I'm crying because I am happy. Now I get my freedom. But don't say that because the walls have ears.' He didn't explain. But then I found out that my dad had been in prison in 1980 because of what was happening in Syria at the time. They beat him up. He had scars. So, my dad taught me, 'You can hate Bashar and his father, but keep it inside your heart, don't say that to people, because they will put us in prison forever.'

When I was a schoolboy, I loved Bashar. He was a doctor, an optometrist, and we thought he was better than his father, we thought he was good. When we woke up and saw the truth, we were shocked.

Near the end of 2011, I had a fight with a friend that made a big change in my life. His dad was in the police, and the next day he went to my uncle's house in anger and told him he was reporting me to the army. My dad didn't want me in the army, so he told me to go to Beirut. I took my ID and passport and gave 100 dollars to a guy who worked in the bus station to hide me in the baggage hold of a bus. He gave half of it to the police as a bribe.

The year I started losing people

Over the next year in Beirut, I lived with my cousin, Abdul Salem, whom I loved. I was a bad person and he put me right. I was always fighting with my family and other people, drinking beer, staying out, smoking, saying bad things about Allah. He led me back to God. We prayed, read the Qur'an together.

One night, he took a shower and sat down with me, looking pale. He was always delicate, fragile. Then he fell over. He never woke up. He died on November 19, 2012. He was only seventeen. He had a heart condition but he didn't know.

Four days later, my friends and I had to take his corpse home on a bus to Manbij so he could be buried. On the border of Lebanon and Syria, the military police checked us. One wanted to arrest me because I was the age for military service, but in Syria, we know how to work with these people: give them money, cigarettes. I gave him fifty dollars and he let us go.

My dad was angry with me for coming home with Abdul Salam's body because it put me in danger of being taken by Assad's army. My big brother was with that army and my twin had joined the Free Army, so they were on opposite sides, and my dad didn't want me to be taken away, too. He shouted in my face, saying: 'Why are you back? It's not safe. Now we'll get into a lot of trouble because of you and your twin. We will die because of you!'

My dad made me hate myself. I couldn't take it anymore, so I left home and went to stay with friends in Manbij.

That was the year I started losing people. My father's grandmother died then, at age 104. I loved her so much. She would tell me stories about my dad when he was young, and we would watch *Tom and Jerry* cartoons together. She was very smart, she never forgot any of our names. She told me that when she got married, her husband put her on a horse and took her from her village to his. I said, 'That's so romantic.' She said: 'Romantic? No, Hasan, it was three days of walking because we had no car.' She always made me laugh.

The black week

When I was twenty, I went with my cousin Mahmoud to Aleppo to join the Free Syrian Army [FSA]. The day was March 28, 2013. My whole family was upset about it, but I wanted our country to have its freedom.

Mahmoud was my father's brother's son, a year younger than me. We didn't know each other until we met at my big sister's wedding when he was fourteen and I was fifteen. I said, 'Who are you, get out of my house!' and we had a fight. But after that we would see each other a lot and study together, so our friendship grew strong. He was so kind, everybody liked him. Soon we were like brothers.

In the beginning with the FSA, I didn't want to fight or kill anybody. I just wanted to help the people under attack in Aleppo. Mahmoud felt the same. We promised each other that if one of us died, the other one would take our body back to our family.

We joined the first regiment, the Tawhid Martyrs Brigade, which was more than 300 people, most of us young students and unpaid volunteers. We were stationed in a small house in the middle of Aleppo, where we cooked food and gave it to the poor. Bashar had the city under siege then, so people were starving. Other cities and people in Turkey sent us bread and food to give out, too. And if someone didn't have a car or money, we would drive them to the border of Turkey or other places so they could escape. We also had volunteer doctors with us from other countries. They worked sometimes for twenty hours with no sleep.

For six or seven months we didn't fight, we just helped. But later on, we did fight because the Syrian Army were dropping bombs on the civilians of Aleppo. Also, people came from Iraq, Afghanistan, Lebanon to fight on Bashar's side, so I would fight them. I didn't want to kill Syrians; they are my brothers. But these other people came to fight us.

My job was to be a lookout – to watch for what the Syrian Army was doing. I spied through a hole in the wall but I also used a laptop and camera to find people. I remember one night in May 2013, at the end of my shift, I was walking away from the wall when suddenly I was flying through the air. I flew maybe five meters and landed hard on the ground. I looked down at myself and I was covered in blood. The Syrian Army had launched an RPG [rocket-propelled grenade] at us. My friends thought I was dead. I think that was the night my hair began to turn white.

Helicopters and planes were in the air twenty-four hours a day – it was so loud. The buildings were in rubble and there were huge craters in the ground made by bombs. If you saw people looking at the sky, you knew to run for cover. Aleppo was such a beautiful ancient city, full of thousands of years of history. It is all destroyed now.

Around the same time I was hurt by the RPG, the pain from my accidents began to grow again. My right arm trembled and swelled, then a fever followed. So, I went to the field hospital in Al-Shaar neighborhood. It was not a real hospital, just a small house with doctors and students and volunteers working there. Aleppo had no doctors at the time and all the hospitals had been bombed, so field hospitals had been opened by civilians in their houses.

The hospital was full of wounded from the barrel bombs that the Assad regime was dropping from helicopters onto civilians. [Barrel bombs are homemade metal containers filled with bits of metal, nails and gasoline.] Blood covered the floor, and women, children and old people were screaming in pain. The space was so narrow and crowded that the doctors were giving people first aid and then asking them to leave so they could help others. Nobody had enough equipment or any anesthetic, so sometimes they did surgery without it.

The doctor I saw – he had been a dentist before the war – looked at my arm, gave me some pain relievers and asked me to come back the next day. When I did, he passed me on to a young volunteer nurse who told me he had not slept for thirty-six hours because he was treating the wounded the whole time, including doing some amputations. He sat me on a sofa and cleaned out the pus that had gathered inside my wound. We discovered we were both from Manbij, so he wouldn't take any payment. He said I should go to hospital in Manbij because I needed surgery.

The next day I left for Manbij and had the surgery. Before I was discharged, the doctor told me I would need another operation to scrape my bones and for that I'd have to go to Turkey. I asked him what would happen if I didn't do it. 'In that case,' he said, 'this problem will remain with you forever and whenever the weather fluctuates, you will have severe pain.' I never had the surgery – my family couldn't afford it – but when I went back to Aleppo, I would go to any clinic nearby to have the wound cleaned.

I stayed in Aleppo for eleven more months, into 2014. It became too dangerous to go back to Manbij because Daesh had taken over by then and they were arresting and imprisoning anyone in the Free Army. During this time, my regiment would fight in the night with the Syrian Army, and in the morning, we would be friends. Sometimes, I swear, we would share cigarettes. I'd give a soldier a cigarette and he would give me a lighter. But sometimes we had to fight to stay alive. We had to stop the army from coming to our place because we had children and women sleeping there. I didn't want to kill anyone. I just wanted them to stay away.

His eyes were talking

While I was in Aleppo with my regiment, a guy who I think was from the BBC came to do an interview with us. He was tall with a thick black beard, and he said his name was Mike. He ate with us, slept with us for three days – he wanted to know how we lived. To me, whatever he wrote, it would be an article about the suffering of a people who wanted freedom.

On May 19, 2014 the group leader told us to prepare for a mission that night. The mission was to measure the distance between us and the regime forces, and to find out the number of their fighters in the building and the types of weapons they had. When the journalist heard this, he insisted on going with us.

We rejected him at first. Non-military persons were forbidden to enter the area because it was a hot zone of fighting. We were only a few meters away from the Syrian Army. There were about 550 fighters there and the fire line was more than ten kilometers long. But in the end, Mike persuaded our group leader to let him to go with us, on condition he would not photograph anything, talk or bring his interpreter. We asked him to take up arms with us, but he said that if he did, it would cause him problems at home.

That night we prayed and read the Qur'an, and at one or two o'clock, we put on special black clothes for the night and waited for the command to go. The reporter wore a helmet, a bulletproof shield and metal plates over his hands and feet. He looked like Iron Man.

We took our Kalashnikovs and crept through trees and alleys to the house where the regime army was stationed, which was maybe 150 meters away through barbed wire, cypress and pine trees, across a paved road and behind a stone wall. It was in Malikiyah village by the Nairab military airport in Aleppo.

The commander told us to cut the barbed wire and put up signs to help us find our way back. We spread out, each of us taking his place. We had opened a hole in the wall the day before, and on the other side a Syrian Army soldier was waiting with an RPG launcher, and another with an automatic machine gun. Our leader told some of the brothers to stay in the woods to provide cover in case something bad happened, while only six people would go on the mission. Mahmoud and I were among those six, along with the journalist.

We managed to cross the road and reach the house where the regime forces were stationed. They were so close we could hear them talking on the other side of the wall. But there was something wrong. Everything was too calm, there was no light, no sound, no movement. When all is quiet, here lies the misfortune.

We listened to them from behind the wall, gathered our intelligence, and then began to creep back. That's when they attacked. They had been listening in on our wireless communications and had prepared a trap. Grenades flew at us from every direction, bullets whizzed over our heads. The gates of hell opened on us.

We ran to hide behind the trees, but we could not exchange fire with the soldiers because that would give away our hiding places, and we only had Kalishes [Kalashnikovs] while they had a cannon. We called for help on our walkie-talkies but it took two hours for the support forces to arrive. Then our brothers began firing machine guns, rifles and mortars to distract the regime forces so we could get out.

We started crawling backwards. The more we were bombed, the more we screamed so we knew we were alive. My friend was shot right through his foot. Another was hit with shrapnel in his shoulder and foot.

Suddenly I remembered Mahmoud. I do not know how I forgot him. I shouted, 'Mahmoud! Mahmoud!' I saw someone lying in the grass, bleeding. I ran over – it was him. He had more than ten bullets in his chest and he was groaning. He was dying at this moment and yet his eyes were talking to me, trying to tell me: 'Hasan, take me with you or kill me, don't leave me here alive. Because we know what they will do to me.' That voice lives inside my head all the time.

I wanted to stay with him but I was scared I'd be killed – everybody just wanted to stay alive at that moment.

So, we dragged him behind a tree and ran for cover. We were screaming and crying into our radios: 'Help us take Mahmoud out. He is still alive. Please send a tank.' No one answered. We couldn't carry him back because it was too far and too dangerous. All we could do was sit behind a wall, praying for him to come to us. I sat there for five or six hours, crying, and hoping he would walk up with a smile and say, 'I'm back, fuckers.'

One of the brothers from the support forces finally managed to reach us – everyone thought we had died. He told us to go back to our base. We wanted to take Mahmoud with us, but daylight began to break and our position became even more vulnerable, so we could not. Our forces on the other side fired heavy gunfire to cover us, and at last we managed to withdraw.

When I got back, I pleaded with our commander, 'Please come with me and get him, please!' I was begging for Mahmoud's soul, shouting and crying. But the commander said, 'Hasan, Mahmoud's dead, we can't, it's too dangerous.'

He was the best cousin I had. I wanted to die with him.

The journalist cried, too. He believed that Mahmoud was killed because of him. Mike was a nice and polite person but sometimes I hate him for Mahmoud's death. I can't help it.

Mahmoud's brother, Abud, was also with the Free Army but in the middle of Aleppo. When he heard his brother had been killed, he came and asked if he could go get Mahmoud's body, but our leaders said no, it was too dangerous.

The next afternoon, the commander told me I should go back to Manbij to tell Mahmoud's father what had happened. I said: 'I don't want to go alone. They will ask me where his body is, what am I going to tell them?' Abud wouldn't go with me because he was quarreling with his father. Their father didn't like his sons being in the Free Army.

So I took some friends with me back to Manbij. We removed our military clothes and dressed normally, then drove in a civilian car with our weapons hidden under the seats so we would not get arrested by Daesh at one of its checkpoints. Daesh were blocking the roads all the way from the countryside of al-Bab to the city of Manbij.

When we arrived, I saw Mahmoud's mom sitting by the door. 'What happened?' she asked me. I told her, 'Don't worry, we just want to say hello to Mahmoud's father.'

We went inside and sat in the room with two of my cousins and my uncle. One of my friends started quoting from the Qur'an and talking about freedom, about Bashar al-Assad and jihad. My uncle cut my friend off and said, 'Which one of my sons is dead, Mahmoud or Abud?'

I gave him Mahmoud's T-shirt and jeans, gun and phone. Then he knew. But all he said was: 'Allah. Drink your tea and you can go.'

Later that day, after we completed reading the Qur'an and saying the special prayers for the dead, my dad came and sat with me. I told him, 'I'm going back to Aleppo to join my regiment.' He said, 'We won't let you.' Then he and my mom, my uncle and aunt locked me in a room, hitting me and shouting, 'You lost your cousin, and you still want to fight?' They took my money, my ID and phone, my shoes to stop me leaving. My mom was crying and pleading with me. She made me feel like a bad guy.

So I gave up on the idea of going back to Aleppo. Daesh had control of Manbij by then and they would have hurt my family if they found out. But in Manbij nobody knew I was with the Free Army, so I could stay there and be relatively safe. Or that's what I thought.

Who has honey in prison?

A few weeks after I had returned to Manbij – this was July 2014 – I was walking down an alleyway when two Daesh men on patrol pulled up in a black Mitsubishi and asked for my ID. I always stayed in alleyways to avoid Daesh, which had patrols all over town, but they found me anyway. They were frightening with their black Afghan clothes and long beards. I told them I didn't have an ID with me, so they searched me and found a pack of cigarettes and my mobile, looked through it and came across some songs and clips of porn videos. Daesh sees smoking and music as *haram* and porn videos as fornication and adultery, so they beat me, threw me in a car and took me to Hisba, a hotel they had made into a prison. All the way, they were kicking and punching me. I was scared they would kill me.

Inside Hisba, there were seven or maybe ten guards – I couldn't see their faces because they were covered. They beat me even more and called me terrible names, telling me I'm *kafir* [unclean] and not a Muslim, accusing me of insulting God and of never praying. They broke my finger, which is still crooked today, and my nose – which is why it is bent now. I was bleeding. When I screamed, they laughed.

The Qur'an says all people are the same, the Muslim, the Christian or the Jew, it doesn't allow this violence. But whenever a new guy came into prison, they had a party like that, laughing and beating people. They enjoyed hurting people.

While they were beating me, they were telling me to confess, and because of pain I confessed to crimes I had nothing to do with, like selling cigarettes and porn.

The Syrians in Daesh were the worst. The people from other countries were a little bit nicer with us. A guy from Iraq or maybe Saudi Arabia said, 'Stop hitting him, he didn't do anything.'

They beat me like that for about an hour, and afterwards I had bruises and cuts all over my body. If I'd had some honey, I could have put it on to make it better, but who has honey in prison? I felt like I was being treated the same way as the people in Guantanamo.

After they stopped beating me, they put me in a room with a lot of other people, Kurds, Syrians, Iraqis. We sat in the cell, looking at the floor, afraid to talk because we didn't know whether anyone sitting with us was a spy from Daesh. We were very scared because some of us had stolen or killed someone and might be executed, and because we didn't know if we would get bombed or if they would kill us or what. In the end, Daesh did kill some of the people there with me. Some they let free: I saw them later on Facebook.

They only beat me that first day. After that, I just sat in the room with the other people and gradually we got to know one another. It was Ramadan, so we prayed together, fasted, read the Qur'an, shared our evening food. I know it is hard to understand but I have some good memories from that prison. Don't get me wrong. Under Islamic rules you don't do what Daesh did. Daesh are bad people. They didn't join to fight Bashar for our freedom – they joined because they needed a job, money, or they wanted to marry a Kurdish woman they had captured from the northern town of Kobani, or to fight the Kurds and the revolutionaries. But at that moment in that place, it wasn't so bad for me because they didn't know I was in the Free Army. This was lucky because they were very cruel to Free Army people and to

Kurds with the PKK [the Kurdistan Workers' Party, an armed guerilla movement fighting for Kurdish independence]. Daesh beat and tortured them. You cannot imagine what they did.

Every Friday, the Daesh guards had a party. They drove a car around Manbij with a megaphone and shouted out to people to pray. Sometimes they gathered maybe 300 people in the central square. They told them through the megaphone that Kurds don't believe in God, that they are infidels, have sex out of marriage, drink alcohol, kill Syrians. Then they put the Kurdish prisoners in the square and cut off their heads. Women, too. All the Kurds in the prison with me were killed this way. Nobody was left.

Every Friday they killed ten to twenty people like that. Everybody had to watch, the women, children, men. That happened for two years all over Syria, sometimes every day, not only in Manbij.

One week after I entered the prison, I saw the investigator, and because of the crimes I had been forced to confess, he sentenced me to twenty-one days in the prison and a whipping. I didn't care. My dad and mom hit me a lot, I was used to it. I was only ashamed because Daesh did it in public. Maybe four or five people stood behind me. They strip you to your underwear and whip you with a piece of plastic in the same place – they hit me eighty times. They pour water on your back, say this is good, then keep whipping you.

I already felt seventy-eight years old when I arrived at that prison. When I left, I felt eighty-two.

Daesh released me after three weeks, but first they said I should ask for their forgiveness. Then they forced me to attend Sharia lessons every evening for fifteen days with a group of other people. They took my ID with my address and told me if I missed any lessons, they would come to my house and arrest me again, or take someone from my family until I turned myself in. I was afraid the whole time that one day I would never come home. My family were afraid for me, too.

The lessons were at the Great Mosque in downtown Manbij near the Manbij Hotel, which later became the headquarters of Daesh. We were taught by Abu Qatada al-Jazrawi, a Saudi terrorist. He taught us Islamic jurisprudence; interpretations of the hadiths of the Prophet of God, Muhammad, may God bless him and grant him peace; and we had to recite and memorize the Holy Qur'an. He talked about jihad, Americans and Russians, Kashmir, and so on. Daesh wanted us to join them and go kill in these countries. They offered to pay you 300 dollars and give you a house if you joined – they would take it from a Free Army guy they'd arrested and give it to you. Or they'd take someone's car or a Kurdish wife or Yazidi women and give them to you. [Yazidi are a mostly Kurdish-speaking and much persecuted minority.]

This is Daesh, this is what they do. But a lot of people agreed to it because there was no work in Manbij, no other opportunity. And because Daesh has a way of making you believe what they say.

When I had finished my Sharia lessons, I knew I had to leave Manbij to save myself. If I stayed, Daesh would send me to Iraq to fight the Shia. They would take people from Iraq and put them to fight in Syria and take people from Syria and put them to fight in Iraq. Why I don't know, but I knew I had to leave. If I had gone back to Aleppo, the FSA would have thought I only survived in Manbij because I had joined Daesh, so they would have put me in prison. My mom said, 'Go to Turkey, work there, you will be safe.'

My heart was not talking

The day I left Manbij, I woke up at dawn, dressed and left my room. My mom, my dad and my brother, Mahmoud, and his wife were all awake and waiting to say farewell with sadness on their faces, as if they knew that, once I went out the door, I would never return.

My mom had prepared some breakfast but I refused it. I asked her: 'Where's my bag? The car will arrive shortly and I want to pack.'

She said: 'Don't worry, my son, I've packed it for you. And I've made some food for your journey. It's in the bag.'

I took out the food and left it on the table. She asked me why. I answered that the bag is too heavy to carry and then I walked to the door. I didn't say goodbye to anyone. It's normal to say goodbye, especially to your mom because she is the closest person to you in the world. But I couldn't.

My mom was crying and everyone was dazed, asking themselves why I was behaving this way. She asked if she could hug me. I said no. I was angry. I didn't want to leave her, didn't want to leave my home, my family. So, I just told her to wish the best for me. I was talking in my anger but my heart was not talking. I wanted to say: 'No, I want to stay with you. I love you. I don't want to leave you, I want to be with you forever.'

But I didn't say that. I don't know why. I'm a bad child.

I turned at the door and asked her one last question: 'Mom, tell me, when am I going to come back home? Because I don't know. When?'

She looked at me and said, 'When I die, my son, this is when you will come home.'

HASAN IN FLIGHT: SYRIA – TURKEY – SAMOS

'MY SUFFERING JOURNEY.'

Helen:

As the Covid spring of 2020 limped by, Hasan's life in the hotel grew ever more onerous. He was wasting away for lack of edible food, the pain in his arm had grown fiercer than ever, he felt dizzy whenever he stood up, and blood was appearing in his stool. He asked the hotel manager to take him to hospital but she refused because of the coronavirus, only relenting after he had argued her to defeat. Yet, when they got there, the doctors kept him waiting almost all day only to give him a cursory examination, say he was fine and turn him away without so much as an aspirin.

'The pain is so bad I bang my head on the wall,' Hasan told me that evening, 'and I am so weak it is hard even to walk. But don't worry, it is a small problem.'

The next day he collapsed, falling unconscious to the floor. The hotel manager rushed him back to hospital, this time with a fellow Syrian who could speak Greek and a social worker to argue on his behalf. They persuaded the doctors to give Hasan a proper medical examination. Diagnosis: severe anemia and an advanced urinary tract infection. They gave him a bed and put him on a drip for two days and nights, as he could no longer eat. They did nothing, however, for the pain in his arm.

'You know what happened on Thursday here in hospital?' he told me a few days later. 'There was an earthquake! I was on the fifth floor, the bed sliding from side to side. People ran outside but I stayed in bed. They asked me why. I said: 'If it's my time to die today, I will die. But it is not my time because I asked my God to give me a long life and I have a lot of things to do.'

The day of his release, May 31, 2020, he met with distressing news: the government had just declared that, now that Greece was opening up after the first wave of the pandemic, it would restart its plan to evict 11,000 refugees from subsidized hotels, camps and houses, beginning the very next morning. Hasan and forty of his fellow refugees in the hotel were on the eviction list. They had exactly one day to get ready to leave.

'One day!' he said to me on the phone. 'I asked the hotel manager why she didn't tell me when she picked me up from hospital. She said, "Hasan, you looked so bad we didn't want to upset you." So now I have to open a bank account in the morning, and then I will take maybe my last shower for a long time. And tonight I will have a last night in my bed. I have a good relationship with my bed, it is a good friend, it's been with me for more than one year. When I sleep, I talk to my blanket about my family, my dreams, about what happened to me today. I tell my bed everything because it's my world.

'They took my family, they took my country, they took my freedom, they took my health, and now they want to take my world. But I will not let them. I will fight.'

HASAN IN FLIGHT

That night, Hasan said goodbye to his friends and went to bed early, rising at five the next morning to take his shower, pack all his clothes in two bags and prepare himself to leave by nine. While he was having breakfast, the hotel manager suddenly told him that she would grant him two more days before he had to go.

'God might close one door in my face but there are ninety-nine more doors and he will always open another,' he messaged me. This gave him forty-eight hours to figure out his next move. 'Maybe I will go tomorrow, Tuesday night,' he told me when we spoke later that day. 'I sold an old phone to a friend, so I have a little money.'

By the time Tuesday dawned, however, he had spun into a panic. 'I don't know what I am going to do,' he told me over video phone. 'I can't find anywhere to stay. I have nothing. I tried to get cash out of my account but there was no cash. And my health is still bad – I need to take medicine all month and I have three appointments at hospital I will have to miss and the pain in my arm still will not let me sleep. The manager of the hotel asked me ten times today when I am going to leave. Everything is closing in on my face.' He rubbed his forehead, which he has the habit of crumpling into a cluster of knots when anxious. 'We refugees are just becoming a burden to ourselves and the world. They broke the hope in us.'

Hasan did have some good news, though. When he had gone to hospital for a checkup that morning, the doctors said he was on the mend. *Inshallah*, everything will be fine,' he said with a shaky smile. 'I will find something. This is not the first time I have had to say goodbye with no idea of what will happen to me.' And he continued his story.

✼   ✼   ✼

I wanted to run to Mars

The morning of July 21, 2014, I left my family and started on my suffering journey out of Syria. There are two ways to reach Turkey: with a smuggler or with a passport, but with a passport you must wait for ten, maybe even twenty-four hours to cross the border and I had nowhere to stay, whereas I had a friend waiting for me on the other side. Plus I was in danger and I wanted to leave fast. So I chose a smuggler, paid him 100 dollars and we made a deal.

A taxi driver helped me find him. Everyone in that city works together – the drivers, smugglers, the Free Army and Turkish border guards. Human trafficking is their livelihood – they all feed off Syrian refugees. But crossing the border illegally means you never know whether you will live or die at the hands of the ferocious beasts called human beings.

Each crossing point differs from the others. Some have barbed wire stretched across an abandoned railway station. Others have a deep trench on both sides of high hills of dirt. At other points there is a wall several meters high with Turkish snipers waiting for you on the other side who will not hesitate to shoot you, whether you are a child, man or woman, in addition to army patrols along the border, although sometimes Turkish border guards work with the smugglers. You must undertake all these risks to cross.

My smuggler took me to an abandoned house near the border. There were maybe fifty other people there, women, men, children, all with lots of bags: the burdens of war. We waited until the middle of the night, then tried to cross, but the border guards fired at us. We had to run back under the bullets.

We waited again until the next afternoon, when the smuggler called one of the Turkish soldiers, who told him we could enter from a specific spot. This time we walked behind the smuggler. He cut through some barbed wire and took us along a path, across some train tracks and a small stream, until we reached a grove of olive trees, pistachios and grapevines, where a Turkish soldier was waiting. He signaled us to follow a road west to avoid the Border Patrol.

In the middle of the road, someone came out of the trees and asked us to go with him without making any sound. He drove us to a house, where we stayed two hours. The house was crowded, men in one place, women in another. The man brought us tea. It was my first time drinking Turkish tea – it was so bad! We couldn't go outside because the police would know he was a smuggler, so he would take two or three people at a time to a small village nearby, leave them in a coffee shop and show how them how to reach the bus station.

When it was my turn, everyone else was already gone. He said he needed more money. I argued. 'How much do you keep wanting me to pay, son of a bitch?' He understood Arabic but I didn't know that. In the end I had to give him the money. He left me at the bus station at eight o'clock and I took the first bus to Gaziantep and my new exile. [Gaziantep is a Turkish town near the border.]

Back in 2013, I had gone to visit Gaziantep with my mom. She had a cousin there and before I left this time, she called and asked him to help me. So when I got off the bus at ten in the evening, I called him and said, I am Hasan. He said, 'Which Hasan?' I told him and he said: 'What's wrong, is everything okay? Is your mother Fatima fine?' I said yes, my mom is fine. Then he said, 'It's the middle of the night, what do you want?' The normal Syrian thing would be to say, 'Where are you? I'm coming to get you.'

At that moment, I felt a great desire to cry, but I did not tell him that I was in Gaziantep with little money and no place to stay – my friend could not give me a place, either. I only hung up and walked until I felt tired. I was also hungry and thirsty, but I was not interested. I just put cardboard on the street and slept there for the next few days. I also slept on doorsteps. Some people would open the door and shout at me. Others said, 'Oh, I'm sorry my friend.' After that, I moved to the park. Lots of people slept in the park, even women. But I was happy enough there. I was OK.

All week I kept moving between sleeping in abandoned buildings and gardens. I also went to the mosque every day because the people there distributed food to the poor and those who had no place to sleep, like me.

One night I was in an abandoned house and it was too cold for sleep, so I made a bed out of an old curtain I found, closed my eyes and pretended I was in bed with a blanket and a light. Then I heard some men come in. They didn't see me at first. They sat and made a fire and drank some beer. Then they saw me. They came over, all five of them, pushed me and talked Turkish and Kurdish at me. I understood nothing. I tried to explain I'm not a bad person, I just want to sleep. They didn't care. They punched and hit me with a beer bottle. Maybe they wanted to rob me, but I had no money, only my bag and some clothes and a small bit of biscuit. One of them saw my bandaged hand from where Daesh had broken my finger in prison, and he bent it until he broke my finger again. I screamed but I refused to cry, I didn't want to be weak. I only wished I was in the Free Syrian Army again with my Kalashnikov so they couldn't do that to me.

After that I ran away. I wanted to run all the way to Mars! I ran for thirty minutes or more, saying, 'My God help me!' I was telling myself if my mom saw what happened to me, she would be sorry she sent me to Turkey.

All that week I was too ashamed to talk to my mom. She and my dad thought I was with my mom's cousin, that I was working and would send them money. But soon I started missing her, so in the end I called her several times. We would talk for one hour, sometimes three. She told me what she'd been doing, we talked about my dad, my brothers. Sometimes she taught me some Turkish.

While I was sleeping in the park, I met a guy from Aleppo who was sleeping there, too. He helped me get a job making furniture, which I knew how to do from when I worked in Lebanon. The job was in the industrial part of the city. The very next day I started working there for a small amount of money, just enough to buy water, food and cigarettes.

My first night at the job, I slept in front of the workshop. I put my shoes under my head, cardboard under my body and covered myself with old cartons. A pack of dogs came up to me, howling and smelling me. I felt no fear. I got used to them standing over me and looking cautiously into my eyes. They knew I was just an innocent animal like them, free of lies. They lay next to me and slept peacefully. Their presence was reassuring. There were at least ten dogs around me!

The next day the owner came and found me sleeping on the sidewalk with all those dogs. 'Why are you sleeping there?' he asked. I could not understand because I did not speak Turkish. At the time we were talking with hand signals.

Then a young Syrian working next door translated and the man understood. He told me I could sleep in his workshop from then on. But nothing in life is free. He increased my working hours and reduced my wages, so I was working fourteen, fifteen hours a day. But he gave me a little money to buy food and brought me cakes, tea, water and sandwiches every day. I didn't care about the low pay. I was alive and safe.

Nothing in Syria

We all know that a raven is a bad omen. The week of November 21, 2014, a black raven wouldn't leave me alone. I used to throw stones at him whenever I saw him. I didn't know he was trying to tell me my mom would die that Friday.

I couldn't understand how she died – she was only forty-five. I called my Aunt Fida, who was the person who washed my mom's body, and asked her. My aunt only said, 'It is not permissible to talk about this now.'

So, I called my father and asked him. He began crying. And then he said: 'That night it was raining. I put out the fire, turned off the light, checked the doors were locked, and we went to sleep. In the middle of the night, I woke up to your mother's voice. She was in pain. I asked her, "Fatima are you okay?" She said, "Yes, but my back hurts between my shoulders." I massaged her until she felt better, and then we went back to sleep.

'Every day your mother wakes up to pray at dawn, but that day she did not. So, I woke before her and went to light the fire and heat some water for our maté tea. Then I did the ablution, prayed the morning prayer and woke your mother for prayer, too. It was four in the morning. While I was reading the Qur'an, I heard a groan. I turned around and she was lying on the floor. I screamed, "Fatima!" I put her head on my lap. We were crying together. She lifted her eyes and looked at me. Then she died.'

All people pray to God to enter Heaven. I pray that I will see my mother just one more time.

Everything I was doing then, I did for my mother. The working, the fighting for our freedom, the coming to Turkey to survive. When she was gone, all my reason for everything was gone.

I wanted to go back to Syria to say goodbye to her body. I remembered her saying that I would go back when she died, and that felt like a promise. But it was risky. My eldest brother was still away with Assad's army. My cousin Abud, Mahmoud's brother, had joined Daesh. And I had been in the Free Army. All that put me in danger. But I wanted to go back anyway, so I told my employer what happened, took my money and caught a bus to Kiels. From there I went by taxi to the Bab al-Salam crossing. [One of the major border crossings in northern Syria.] It was crowded with cars. I couldn't wait, but with money you can buy anything, so I made a deal with a taxi driver, and I was able to bypass the gate on the Turkish border and cross into Syria. I arrived in the city of Azaz on the night of November 22.

As soon as I arrived, I headed to the bus station, but it was closed because all the roads leading to Daesh areas like Manbij were shut down after five in the evening. The border guards asked me how old I was. I showed them my ID. They said I was military age so the army might take me. So I phoned my dad and my cousin Abud and told them, 'I am stuck in Azaz, I need someone to come get me.'

Abud said he wouldn't fetch me unless I went to the Daesh headquarters and signed a paper saying I had gone back to Islam and was not with the Free Army anymore. I was scared. I told him, 'God knows I am Muslim, that's enough for me.' But Abud said: 'If you don't do it, I will kill you. In fact, I will be happy to kill you, because I will have a ticket to heaven because you are not Muslim, you are *kafir*.'

That upset me a lot. I told him: 'You are my cousin. We were in the Free Army together. Your brother died with me in Aleppo. How can you talk to me like that? All I want is to see my mom one last time.'

The next day I received a WhatsApp message from one of my comrades-in-arms saying that some of our brothers in the Free Army had been captured by Daesh. He feared that Daesh would torture them until they gave up all our names, so if I went to Manbij, it would put my life in danger and pose a threat to my family.

My dad called to say the same. 'If you come, Daesh will kill you. Anyway, everything is over. We have buried your mother.'

After that, I felt I had nothing in Syria. Nothing left at all.

The next day, December 1, 2014, I went back to the Bab al-Salam crossing to leave Syria for the last time. More than 3,000 people were waiting in an iron cage to cross. Some had been waiting for a whole week just to get a bus ticket. This was happening because all the borders were under the control of Jabhat al-Nusra, the militant branch of Daesh, which had an agreement with the Turks to open the borders to refugees for only two hours a day.

The border guards gave me a number for my turn to cross. It was more than ten days away. So I decided to enter illegally again, instead of waiting like a chicken in a cage. That gate should not be called the Bab al-Salam [Gate of Peace], it should be called the gate to humiliation and insult. I went back to Azaz to find a smuggler. There were smugglers everywhere. When they see your money, they love you like a dog.

The smuggler led me to a gathering place at midnight, where hundreds of people were waiting to cross. We only had two hours to make it, so we had to move quickly. We walked until we reached a deep trench – I was with a group of women, men and children. The smuggler put a ladder up, then told us to climb it, go down the other side and climb the next ladder, and so on.

A woman with us was carrying about ten bags. She had several children, so I took two of her bags and we ran. Small children running behind me. It was funny but sad. The Turkish army shot at us, but nobody died.

I threw the bags on the other side of the trench and began dropping the children into the hole and helping them climb the ladder and cross to the other side safely. We were all helping each other like that. The children were crying, women screaming.

In the end we managed to cross. I took a bus to Izmir, all the while carrying the pain of losing my mother on my shoulders.

Tell them Hasan is dead

It was in Izmir that I started to lose everything.

I had a place to live there because my twin Hussein sometimes stayed in Izmir with two of our friends from home, Khaled and Qusai. He gave them money to keep a room for him for when he needed a rest from the Free Army. Khaled and Qusai didn't ask me to pay anything, they just took me in.

At their house, I sat doing nothing for two weeks. My mom was dead, I didn't want to move. My health became bad because I was not eating, just smoking. But I didn't care. 'I'm fine,' I told my friends. 'If my dad or anyone else asks how is Hasan, tell them Hasan is dead. Forget Hasan.'

I began looking for jobs. It took a while, but finally I found work as a waiter in a coffee shop. That helped me learn the language. Later, I found another job making sandwiches and cleaning up at night. I liked that but it wasn't many hours and in the winter the coffee shop closed. I worked at a lot of short jobs that way, for one week, a month, selling in the market, cleaning cars, making food. I earned just enough to stay alive. I didn't need more. I just wanted to be alone in my room with my coffee and cigarettes. I didn't want to talk to anybody except Khaled and Qusai. I wanted my mom's death to be a dream and to wake up and find it was not true. Your mom is the first person who is close to you. And I was angry with myself because Hussein and I, we made her suffer. We went away to fight, we did a lot of bad things. She used to say, 'You two make me sad because I love you so much.' I still miss her.

Then my dad married someone else. He was sixty-eight and he married a virgin of twenty-seven. It was only two or three months after my mom died. He should have waited a year! I was so angry that I stopped talking to him for a long time. But there was another reason, too. I was ashamed I wasn't helping him. I didn't have enough money to send him, I had barely enough for myself. Also, he had two houses, a shop . . . at the time I told myself that. Now I just miss him. He was a good husband to my mom and I love him.

Hussein often came to Izmir for short stays while I was there. Because he had a Free Army ID, the police let him go back and forth across the border. He would take his comrades to different hospitals there if they got wounded. He would also come to make money because the Free Army didn't pay him enough. At the beginning of 2016, he came to stay for a month, and he helped me a lot with my Turkish.

Hussein and I have the same face, the same mom and dad, but we fought all the time, as kids and as adults. All day we would fight, then at night we would sleep in the same bed. When he got sick, I got sick, and the other way around. We were true twins, 100 percent the same.

We would play tricks on people when we were boys because we looked exactly alike. The first time I went to school, my teacher said she couldn't tell which of us is which, so she put us in separate classes. We cried, 'No, we want to be together!' So she said OK, you sit here, you sit there. 'No, we want to sit together!' So, she said, OK, then don't wear the uniform but wear different colors. 'But our mom buys us the same clothes.' Which was true. We didn't like it but she always bought us matching outfits.

A few months after Hussein last left Izmir, he and I had another fight and we stopped talking again. I even blocked him on Facebook and WhatsApp. Then, in May, he sent me messages, photos, videos and audio recordings. I deleted and blocked everything without watching or listening to any of it. This still leaves a great wound inside me. He only wanted to talk to me and tell me he was missing me, but I prevented him because I am a person with a black heart.

A few days after he had sent those messages, Hussein was killed in a battle with Daesh. A bullet entered his neck and pierced his head from behind. He was twenty-three.

It happened on the morning of Saturday, May 9, 2016. The news of his death was published on Facebook. Qusai saw it and told me.

My family asked all our relatives, neighbors and friends to tell everyone that Hussein had died when his car got caught in a clash between Daesh and the opposition. They had to say that so Daesh would not know that Hussein had been in the Free Army because that would have put my family in danger. We asked everyone who posted the news of Hussein's death on social media to delete it because that would pose danger to us, too.

I thought about returning to Syria. I wanted to see Hussein and pray for him. I wanted to know where his gravesite was. But the borders were closed, so I couldn't.

My father was also unable to see him. He couldn't fetch Hussein's body home from Azaz because going to the opposition areas like Manbij was forbidden to city residents. At the same time, my brother's friends could not send his body home because Daesh would then know his affiliation with the Free Army. To this day we do not know where he is buried.

After Hussein died, I was lost. He was my twin, my brother, part of me.

I sat alone in my room with the blinds down and the curtains lowered, the lights off. I wanted to stay away from everybody. The summer humidity filled the ceiling, the walls, the floor, until the smell of mold was everywhere. On most days, I stayed awake until dawn and only ate one meal, always the same: milk mixed with olive oil and salt. A piece of bread. A cup of tea.

[Hasan sent me a photograph of Hussein's corpse after he told me this, and it was a shock to see, as if I were staring at a dead Hasan. 'Looking at my dead brother is like looking at myself in death,' Hasan told me later.]

After several months like this, I began having health problems. I had become anemic in 2013 because I wasn't eating meat, but it got worse in Turkey because I was eating so little and smoking two or three packets a day. And it was cold. The cold gave me pain in the old injury in my arm and I was a terrible yellow color. I didn't look human. When I looked at myself in the mirror, I looked like a vampire. I didn't care at first but then I grew so weak I couldn't walk more than a few meters without sitting. I couldn't walk uphill. My body would shiver, I had a severe pain in my knee, my heart beat very fast, I felt dizzy. I could no longer see distances because the poor lighting at home negatively affected my eyes. I had difficulty breathing, pain in my back and shoulder and feet. Every time I went out to buy food, it took an hour, even if the shop was only 500 meters away, because I had to keep sitting down. And I was too weak to work.

I stayed like this until Khaled came to visit me – he was no longer living with me at the time. When I opened the door for him, he took one look at me and said: 'Put on your clothes, we're going to hospital. If you won't go, I'll take you by force.'

He took me to hospital, where the doctor ordered an X-ray, blood and urine tests, and said: 'Why didn't you come to the hospital before? Didn't you know that if you had stayed for another week like this, you would have died?' He told me that my poor nutrition had made it so my bone marrow could no longer produce blood, and that I had to have a blood transfusion right away or die.

They transfused into me the equivalent of a third of the amount of blood in the human body, five blood bags weighing 500 grams each.

When the doctor released me the next evening, I went to stay in my friend Malik's house. His mother nursed me there for several days, feeding me dishes like roast chicken, sweets and fruit. I recovered quickly and managed to stand on my feet and walk again.

Khaled, you are like my guardian angel. And Malik, I will not forget your help. This is a debt in my heart. Thank you.

I'm glad I am still alive. You know, my life is funny. I don't want to make people sad or feel sorry for me. I want to make them laugh.

Love and respect

The next person I lost was my brother Mahmoud. It was September 2017. He was six years older than I am, so we did not share many memories. He had a heart attack caused by choking on food. My father gave him first aid but it didn't work, so a friend rushed him to a hospital. Mahmoud died several days later. He was twenty-nine. He was very kind and when he died, it was hard on everyone in the village because they liked him so much.

Sometimes I'm glad my mom died before she saw the deaths of Hussein and Mahmoud. It would have been too much for her.

When I heard about Mahmoud's death on the phone, I turned off the handset and broke the phone. My friends stared at me. But even though he was my brother and there was love and respect between us, I could not even think of going to Manbij. The borders were still closed and impossible to cross without hiring an expensive smuggler I could not afford. Even if I had the money, the Turkish army and Syrian opposition would have prevented me from reaching Manbij. Also, the PKK would have made me prove that I was not with Daesh.

And then I would have to specify how long I intended to stay in Manbij, give them a residential address and let them confiscate my ID card and passport until I left. And if I decided to stay in Manbij forever, I would have had to pay the price of my protection, approximately 2,000 dollars. My only other option would be to carry arms for the Kurds. This would still be true if I tried to go back today. So I couldn't go back.

I didn't work for months after Mahmoud died. My friends left for other cities and I was alone in the house. That made me want to go back to Syria in spite of all the problems, but a friend, a Kurdish guy called Muhammad Hassan told me, 'That is not a good choice.'

'But I can't stay here, I'm sick and tired and alone,' I told him. 'I tried to starve myself to death. Wherever I look I see my brothers, I see my mother.'

Muhammad Hassan is a smuggler. Izmir is full of smugglers – you can find them anywhere. He explained to me how it all works with the taxi drivers, houses, smugglers, boats, everyone connected with each other. He said: 'I can send you to Greece for 500 dollars. If you can't afford that, you can do something for the smugglers and they won't ask for money.'

'What can I do?'

'You can drive the boat.'

Are you trying to kill us?

The night before I was supposed to leave for Greece – this was January 12, 2018 – Muhammad Hassan took me to a house of his smuggler friends. The house was full of maybe forty-eight people waiting to cross like me: Kurds, Iraqis, Syrians; women, men, children. The smugglers put all the people in one room and told them, 'Turn off the light, don't speak, don't shout, or people outside will guess we are smugglers and call the police.' Then the smugglers told the people that I would steer the boat but not to tell the Greek police if they ask, just say the smuggler left and so we had to drive the boat ourselves.

The smugglers led me into another room and let me sit with them – one Turk and two Syrians. They were smoking hashish but I didn't want any. I was scared. I didn't know how to swim, I couldn't afford a lifejacket, I had never steered a boat. So they gave me vodka to drink and an anti-anxiety pill. I had never had anything stronger than beer or wine before and I was flying! But it stopped me feeling scared.

At midnight, we packed everyone's bags inside a car and drove for an hour and half, arriving at around 1:30 in the morning in Kuşadasi, a town only twenty-seven kilometers across the sea from Samos.

The smugglers walked us to a beach and made us inflate the boat with a pump. It was maybe seven meters long. One of the smugglers drove it for fifty meters to show me how it worked: the outboard motor, the diesel, how to steer, the three speeds. Five minutes instruction and then he said, 'It's ready, let's go.'

We loaded the bags into the boat first, and then the people – all forty-eight of us. I was the last one.

So I am in the sea. When I push the handle right, we go left. When I push the handle left, we go right. The passengers shouted, 'Are you trying to kill us?' I wanted to go back to Turkey and give up.

Then a guy from Iraq said, 'I will steer, but when we cross the border into Greek seas, you take over.' I said OK. We learned that the top speed made the children cry, so we had to go slower. Yet the whole time I felt I was not there. My body was there but my soul was gone. Once we were out in the sea, though, I looked behind me. I couldn't see any land, any light. I knew then where I was and I understood there was no going back now.

It was night, so nobody was allowed to smoke or light up their phone because we could see the Turkish police in the sea with a red light and we didn't want to attract them. We had to steer out of our way for a kilometer to avoid them. Only then could we open a Google map on a phone to find our direction. The wind picked up and because it was January, it was cold. Everything was black: the sea, the sky.

We crossed into Greek waters very slowly – there is an invisible border between Turkey and Greece in the middle of the sea. And soon we saw the Greek coast guard boat coming up behind us. Passengers start waving, crying for help. It was around four o'clock in the morning. We had been in the sea for three hours.

A big boat pulled up and took us aboard, first the children and women, then the men. They asked those of us who had lifejackets to throw them away. My bag was gone. I never saw it again.

We were wet and really cold. They gave blankets to the women and children but not to the men. A guy said we need the toilet. The guards said they didn't care. They made him pee in a bottle in front of all of us and throw the bottle in the sea. The women had to pee on themselves. They were too shy to ask to go to the toilet.

The coast guard took us for two hours to Samos. I was so tired from being scared and the drugs and vodka, I fell asleep on the boat.

When I woke up, I was in Europe.

HASAN IN GREECE

'THE KNIFE DOESN'T CUT THE KNIFE.'

Helen:

Samos, as I have mentioned, is a place of contradictions; beauty and cruelty living side by side. One of the greenest isles in the eastern Aegean, its three mountains rise like emerald pyramids out of the azure sea, attracting tourists and historians alike – birthplace of Pythagoras; home of Hera, Zeus's queen; and, myth has it, where Aesop talked his way out of slavery. Samos even has its own history as a haven for refugees, Hera's eighth-century-BCE temple having been partly built as a sanctuary. Yet, from 2016 to 2021, it held what many have called the most inhumane refugee camp in Europe.

Set on a former military base built to house 648 people, the camp, which was run by the Greek government with help from the United Nations High Commissioner for Refugees (UNHCR), opened in February 2016 as an emergency Reception and Identity Center or 'hot spot'; that is, a temporary holding pen designed to register new arrivals quickly before moving them on to the mainland. But, by the time Eyad and Hasan were there in 2018, the EU-Turkey deal had so clogged the system that there was nothing temporary about the camp at all. Rather, it was bursting with some 3,000 people, most of whom had been living there for at least a year, while more boatloads were arriving every night.

Seared like a gash into the side of Mount Thios, and surrounded by concrete walls and hurricane fences crowned by barbed wire, the camp looked just like a prison, not helped by the enormous lights atop tall poles that glared down at the compound all night long. Inside, dozens of white metal shipping containers were shoved end-to-end and lined up in rows climbing the hill, while stuffed into every inch of space in between were thousands of tents: white UNHCR tents; blue pup tents; green, black, brown and gray camping tents; all draped in laundry and awash in litter, flies, mosquitos and mud. Narrow alleyways threaded between the containers, where barefoot children stood about listlessly or played with broken toys. The stench of sewage filled the air, and rats swarmed the toilets and heaps of rubbish leaning against the fences. It was so crowded that it was no wonder Eyad and his family could find nowhere to sleep when they arrived. Other new arrivals also had to sleep on the ground, some on the bare concrete next to the stinking portable toilets, without so much as a blanket, mat or pillow to protect them from the ground.

Daily life in the camp consisted almost entirely of waiting – not only for asylum interviews and their results, but for hour upon hour in queues: to reach one of the few working toilets, take a shower, find food, or see the camp's single doctor, psychologist or a nurse. Much of the waiting was also to obtain or renew the five different cards a refugee needs to survive in Greece:

1. The *Ausweis*, the all-essential ID card, which you must renew every month. (It is striking that Greece uses the

same German word for an ID card that the Nazis used during World War Two.)

2. The ATM card with which you retrieve the monthly allowance (once from UNHCR but later from the Greek government), which only works if you can keep proving that you live in a camp.

3. AMKA, the health-insurance document without which you will not be admitted to hospital.

4. AFAMI, a tax number you need to work or rent a home.

5. EKA, proof of residence you need to find a legal job.

Every effort to get each of these documents is wrapped so tightly in red tape that asylum seekers are typically forced to wait for months for each one, often over and over again.

When not in one of these queues, the camp dwellers on Samos had to suffer through rain, wind and cold in the winter, desiccating heat in the summer, and the bedbugs Eyad mentions, along with the rats, mice, scabies mites, flies, mosquitos and snakes that constantly invaded tents and containers. All this while being denied the chance to go to school or take a job.

This enforced idleness is one of the most tortuous aspects of being trapped in a refugee camp. Most asylum seekers in Greece are of school or university age, yet by 2020–1, only one in seven children living in mainland camps were in school and those on the islands had no school at all; a sad reflection of the fact that only 5 percent of refugee youth around the world are ever able to continue their educations.[3]

Thwarted ambitions and forced inactivity like this are no help to those suffering the traumas of war and loss, just as waiting for month after month without knowing your fate or having any control over it erodes the very strength a person needs to keep going. As a result, depression, suicide attempts, self-harm and illnesses are rife in camps, especially among the young. As for older refugees, parents and people who had jobs and careers before they fled, the daily idleness is a constant humiliation and reminder that they have lost their place in the world, along with the ability to even provide for their children. The need to resist this paralysis – to feel useful and productive – is so strong that almost everybody I interviewed for this book volunteered for NGOs whenever they could, even though one might think that refugees are the last people who can afford to work for no pay. As Hasan, who became a volunteer himself, kept telling me, 'All we want is the chance to work and look after ourselves.'

To escape the miserable conditions and crowds of the camp, many asylum seekers either roamed the mountain above or drifted down the hill to the port town of Vathi below – a collection of dusty streets, modern shopfronts, old stone houses, cafés and churches – where they could seek shade, dip into the sea, or simply sit somewhere that didn't stink.

This was the world awaiting Hasan when he landed on Samos.

❋   ❋   ❋

Bad dream

As soon as our ferry landed in the port of Vathi at 6:30 in the morning, the first question the police asked us was who had steered our boat. We told him we all did, including me, but already I was scared. Then they took us to the Port Authority building, made us wait in a line, called us inside one by one, and asked us who we were and where we came from. They also made us hold a number up to our chests, took a picture and wrote the number on our hands in black ink.

After that, they put us in white vans with little dark windows and drove us up a hill to the camp. You can't see anything out of those windows except a long road and trees. When we arrived, they opened the door and ordered us out.

At that moment, I felt like I was in a Mexican movie. I'm in handcuffs. A crowd is looking at me and shouting. I don't understand anything. Some are yelling, 'Where are you from? Why did you come? Don't ask for asylum in Greece! Don't give them your passport!' What were they talking about? And they were banging drums, having a party. They always did that when people first arrived, I found out afterwards.

I saw a long line of women and men – later I learned they were waiting for breakfast. That was the first time I ever saw African people, except maybe one guy with Daesh and one in Izmir, but never so many at once. My first time I'd seen Afghan people, too. I thought they were from China.

The police ordered us inside the police station. More police came, put on masks and gloves, checked our bodies and bags, and demanded our papers, passports and so on. I was asking myself, what the fuck, am I in Guantanamo?

The police asked us again who drove the boat. Again, we said we all did, but they arrested two guys from Iraq, one from Jordan and one from Syria. One of the Iraqi guys had a mother and two sisters who started crying. They thought the police would put him in prison and they would never see him again, so one of the sisters told the police that I was the driver. She was trying to save her brother.

The police turned to me. 'Where is your bag?' I told them I lost it in the sea. I hoped this was a bad dream and I'd wake up in five minutes and find myself at home on my sofa. But it was not a dream. They handcuffed me and took me to prison.

That was my first two hours in Europe.

In the prison, they put me in a room and told me to stand and close my eyes. They brought in a translator from Algeria and made me take off all my clothes and turn around and sit and stand while they checked my body. I was so ashamed I looked at the floor. They wrote down what was wrong with my arm, a mark on my ass from when my brother burned me. They let me get dressed again and asked me why I had a streak in my hair.

At the beginning, they were respectful, although they didn't give me water or food. They said I could have a lawyer but there was no lawyer. They asked the same questions a thousand times: 'Are you a smuggler? Who was the driver?' Three hours of that. Two more cops came in the afternoon and asked me the same questions again. I was in handcuffs, sitting on the floor, although sometimes they made me stand.

The last cop came in the evening. He was in a bad mood and started shouting and calling me *malaka* [a vulgar insult in Greek]. He moved the camera so it couldn't see us and shouted at me more. 'Who was the driver?' He slapped my face three times and put a stick on the table to threaten me.

I said, 'Don't slap me, motherfucker, this is democracy, where are my rights? Fuck Europe.' All my anger came out. He slapped me two more times until I saw lights. I kept telling him we all drove the boat, that I only drove it for fifteen minutes. He said, 'I don't believe you.'

Finally, I asked him, 'What do you want from me? All right, tell them I am the driver if you want, I am the smuggler.

Tell them I took money from people.' It wasn't true but I was scared. I told him I attacked America in 2011, not Osama bin Laden. I said, 'I am in Europe, where are my human rights?' The translator cried and hugged me but he said he couldn't help me. The police put him in a car and drove him back to camp.

When I finally said I was the driver, the police said thank you. There were five of them and they made me sign something in Greek. I didn't know what it said. Later, I found out it was a confession.

I stayed in prison from Friday to Tuesday. At one point, the police took me to court. A woman there asked me all the same questions. I said it's all on the paper there. She said, 'Don't worry, we're on your side, we're not the police.' I didn't trust her. Again, they gave me something to sign in Greek and put me back in the prison.

My last day in prison they put another guy in the cell with me, also a Syrian, a huge man. He brought tea and shisha with him, which we shared before they took it away. When we were hungry, we ate out of the trash together. They let him go before me because he had an ID card. 'When you get out, come find me,' he said. 'I'm in the container marked D9.'

Later, I found out that I had been charged with human trafficking. In one year, I would be put on trial.

Ashamed

They released me from prison on a Tuesday afternoon but told me I had to sign in every Monday at the police station. Each time, the police would make me sit for two hours, looking at their phones and ignoring me before they let me sign. They were very rude until I learned a little Greek. 'This is Greece, speak Greek,' they would say. I don't think they liked anyone who wasn't Christian.

When I got out of prison, they sent me to First Reception, an outdoor cage for new arrivals beside the camp police station, gave me a blanket and told me to stay there. I spent three days in that cage, sleeping on a bench. Finally, I went to the office and asked how long I had to stay. They said, 'What are you doing here? Just go find a place to sleep.' I didn't know where to go. I didn't know anyone, I had no tent, I felt shy. So I sat by a wall, put my head on my arms and slept like that.

Then I heard a voice I knew. He was a guy I had met in Izmir three months earlier, Abu Said from Syria. I called out to him. He looked at me. 'Hasan, why are you here?' He had a child named Mohammad, a boy of about twelve who liked me a lot. They invited me to share their tent. The tent was for one person but the three of us slept and ate there together.

The next day, Abu Said took me to a place called Alpha Center. [The headquarters of the NGO, Samos Volunteers.] I saw people inside drinking tea and coffee, reading books and playing chess. It looked so nice, but I thought it was not for free so I couldn't go in, as I had no money. So I walked around the town. I was ashamed of being a refugee, of how the Greek people looked at me. I felt dirty and smelly. I washed in the night but the next morning I had to wear the same clothes again. All I had was my jacket, T-shirt, jeans and a pair of broken shoes, with no money to buy others.

After two days, Abu Said found a place in a container. He said I could go with him, but I said: 'No, you have a child. I'm young, I'll be OK.' I stayed in the tent. The day after that,

I left to find some food and there was a big storm. When I came back, the tent was gone. The storm had stolen it.

Finally, I remembered the guy in prison who said to look for him in container D9. I found it, went inside and asked for him. I couldn't see anyone because the bunks were curtained with gray blankets – there were thirty-four bunk beds in there lined up along the walls. Someone called for him and this huge guy appeared looking like the Incredible Hulk. This was my friend.

All the people in the container were Arabs, most from Syria but also from Egypt, Iraq, Kuwait – those were Bedouins who have no citizenship in Kuwait. They said 'stay with us', and they gave me maté, food, water, cigarettes. Even twenty euros. 'Go take a shower, you smell fucking bad,' they told me, so I did and put a towel around myself, while this guy named Wassim washed my clothes for me and hung them over the heater to dry.

Wassim had lost his wife and their baby, his mom and her sister all on the same day under Bashar's bombs. They lived north of Idlib, but he was working in Lebanon when it happened. He was only three years older than me. We looked after each other in the camp, shared our food and tea, brought each other maté and lunch. I loved him a lot. When he left Samos, he spent six months in a camp, then went to Albania and walked for three months all the way to Germany. Sometimes he took a bus or a train, but mostly he walked. Now he has asylum there, he's learning German. I wish him the best.

My first night in the container I was happy. I had a place to stay, I had friends, I felt safe. But there was no free bed. A guy said you can sleep on the floor or you can share my bed with me, although we are in Europe now so people will think we are gay. I said I don't care what people think. I shared a bed with him for a few nights, then one of the others left and I got his bed.

When I moved into the container, I had no ID, no cash card, just the paper the police had given me at the prison. I didn't understand how anything worked at first. I saw people waiting in long lines but I didn't know what they were waiting for. My friends explained how it all worked – how I had to have two interviews and prove I would not be safe if I was sent back to Turkey. How, when I got my *Ausweis* it might be stamped blue, which would mean I could go anywhere I want inside Greece. Or it might be stamped red, which would mean I couldn't leave Samos.

The police gave me a first interview date of February 14, 2018. They told me I'd get my first cash card at the beginning of March, when I would get ninety euros a month. I thought it was a lot – it was more than I made in Turkey. But I had no money for two months because it was still January, so my friends looked after me. They were so kind. They also told me they knew someone who could help me with the interview. That was how I met Eyad.

Eyad and a student lawyer he knew talked with me for hours, practicing the interviews. They said I had to do it right or I could get rejected and sent back to Turkey.

The night before the interview, I was too nervous to sleep. I did not want to go back to Turkey and lose everything I had done to get to Greece. The next morning, they called my name and I went inside the camp office.

The interviewer was very blond and tall, maybe from Holland. Nice guy. And I had a translator. For seven hours or more, they asked me questions about my family, my health, why I left Syria, why Turkey was not safe for me, why I came to Greece, where I want to go. They gave me two breaks, but we didn't finish till five o'clock, after which they asked me to wait. They gave me the *Ausweis* but told me it was blocked because of the human-trafficking charge. My card was stamped red.

Like family

For the next eight months or so I lived in the container but I also explored the island. Every afternoon, my best friend Trad, who I'd met in Alpha Center, would walk with me to the beach. I couldn't swim and he didn't have swimming clothes, so we would just sit. We would find stray cats and kittens to pet, or watch the sea and talk. One day two men started shouting at refugee teenagers on the beach, telling them: 'Leave, go back to the camp!'

Then the men came to us and said, 'What are you doing here?' I didn't speak English much then but I said we are just sitting here by the sea. 'Where are you from?' We said Syria. 'What are you doing here in Greece?' We said we are refugees. 'I know, I don't care, why did you come here?' We said because of the war and because we don't want to be forced to join any group that kills people. He said, 'You left because you are cowards. Why don't you go to an Arab country or stay in Turkey, why here?' Trad said we don't want to stay here but your government won't let us leave. The man said, 'Europe is for Christians, not Muslims. Because Muslims only like two things, to kill and have sex. I don't want to see you here! Go back to the camp and stay there. Don't come here. This sea, this beach, this country is only for Greek people!'

Later, when we were walking in the street, those same men came back in a white car and threw a bottle of water at us, yelling insults – I don't know what they said. That happened a lot, not only to me, but to other people, too. Locals yelling, 'Go back to your country, this country is for Christians, for Greeks, not you!' Also, sometimes when we were in a café, people would refuse to serve us, or other customers would move to sit as far away from us as possible. The longer I was on the island, the more this was happening.

In August, I began working with Samos Volunteers in Alpha Center. I loved that. My job was in reception, translating when people came to ask about the classes they held. I also took a shift cleaning the classrooms and living room, and shifts in the laundry three days a week washing people's clothes from the camp. I helped with kids' activities, too – drawing, singing ABCs. The people who worked there were not like volunteers coming to help, they were like family.

For a long time, Samos Volunteers was the only NGO in Samos. Then, in late 2018, others opened, and I worked for them also. I started with Refugee 4 Refugees around January 2019. We gave new arrivals shoes, jackets, jeans, T-shirts for children. Shampoo, toothbrushes, soap, blankets, tents. And when Banana House came just before March 2019, I was their first Community Volunteer. [The NGO term for asylum seekers and refugees who volunteer.] I would give out clothes, put people's information into a laptop, translate, help train volunteers. I felt so good doing that.

But otherwise, every day in the camp was the same. Wake up at six o'clock or so in the morning. Go to the food container and wait three hours for juice and croissant. Put the breakfast in a bag and go to Alpha. Drink coffee, eat breakfast. Read a book till noon or so, then go back to wait in line at the restaurant again for two or three more hours. Go back to Alpha and sit and drink tea, or go out and walk or smoke shisha till Alpha closes at six. Wait in line another two hours to get dinner. Then back to the container, sit, go to sleep. It was the same every day for week after week, month after month. And the whole time I was worried about my trial and if I would be put in prison. This is why Eyad said I was a man without hope.

＊　＊　＊

Helen:
Seeking asylum is a right, not a crime. This is made explicit in Article 31 of the Refugee Convention, which states that people entering a country to seek asylum cannot be prosecuted, fined or imprisoned for their illegal entry or stay, even if they breach immigration rules to get there.[4] Hasan drove the boat because he had no other way of pursuing asylum, so he exactly fits the category that should have shielded him. Yet, even though Greece's own Code of Migration also upholds these protections, Greek authorities have accused thousands of asylum seekers like him of human smuggling because they steered their boats. Some have even been sentenced to 50 or 142 years in prison.[5]

His trial was held on October 22, 2018, ten months after he had arrived in Samos, and I returned to attend it. With the help of his friends at Samos Volunteers, he had found a local lawyer to represent him in court, who coached him on what to say. Above all, the lawyer advised, Hasan must on no account ever disclose that the Samos police had beaten him into signing a confession, never mind that it was a confession he could not even read. 'The knife does not cut the knife,' the lawyer said of relations between lawyers and the police on the island.

The Vathi courthouse, where the trial was to take place, is an elegant yellow building reminiscent of a Spanish hacienda, complete with a wrought-iron balcony on the second floor and a palm tree in the front garden. Although the building is at least a century old, inside the courtroom is all sleek, modern wood and large, sunny windows. The audience sits in rows of chairs, each scrape of a leg echoing loudly against the wooden floor and bare white walls, while the judges' bench stretches from one side of the room to the other and is set so high on a platform that it forces one to crane one's neck to look up at it, as if trying to glimpse the Olympian gods. The Greek court system does not use juries but rather a panel of judges; in Hasan's case, a man and two women. The man, the chief judge, tall and white-haired, was the only one in a black robe. The two women, who said virtually nothing, looked weary and, frankly, irritated.

We had to wait four hours for Hasan's trial to start because five other refugees, who had also been charged with human trafficking for having piloted their boats, had their cases scheduled before his, and I was struck by the haphazard nature of the proceedings. The lawyers and interpreters were dressed so casually they looked as though they had just stumbled out of bed. Two of the accused had lawyers, like Hasan, while the other three did not. Only a few were provided with translators. And some of the defendants were handcuffed while others weren't.

Meanwhile, the wait was clearly distressing Hasan. His leg was jiggling, he kept smiling nervously, his brow was crumpled and he looked older than I had ever seen him. Yet whenever

I asked if he was all right, he invariably replied in his much-improved English, 'I'm fine, don't worry – small problem.'

It was not a small problem, however, for, were he to be found guilty, he could face a prison sentence of up to ten years.

A year later, he told me his memories of that day.

�❧ ✦ ✦

A thousand devils

The night before my court date, I could not sleep. I was too scared. I'd cut my hair and borrowed clothes, but all I could think was that the next day I might be alone inside a prison for years.

When we got to court in the morning and had to wait outside, my body was there, but my mind, I don't know where it was. I didn't want to talk. I didn't want to see the inside of the court. I tried to act OK, but I had a thousand devils fighting inside me.

My lawyer told me: 'Hasan, be nice, be polite, don't smile, stand up straight. Be brave.'

Inside, we sat for hours. We had to wait through so many other cases . . . I was the last one. That was hard to take. I wanted badly to smoke. But it helped to have my friends there, as well as Nick van der Steenhoven, a volunteer legal expert from the Netherlands who was helping me and is now my friend. And the lawyer, I like him. He gave me courage, hope.

When it was my turn, I couldn't understand the translator. He was talking classic Arabic, so I didn't know what he was saying. And he couldn't understand my Syrian dialect. I had no idea what the judges or lawyers were saying either. It was all in Greek.

After I was questioned, we were sent away to wait for the verdict. We had lunch, all my friends and me together. It was such a long wait. It was hours and hours.

Finally, my lawyer came and told us something I didn't understand. My English-speaking friends started to cry. I felt so scared when I saw that. I didn't understand why. I thought the police would come and say follow me, you are going to prison. I didn't understand my friends were crying from happiness because I had no prison sentence.

Then Nick told me, 'Hasan, you are lucky, no prison!' I got five years suspended sentence. If I get arrested for anything else, I'll go to prison. But I was free.

The other two guys with lawyers got the same suspended sentence as me. The three without lawyers each got seven years inside. They were taken away in handcuffs.

My lawyer tells me when I've been in Greece for three more years with no trouble with the police, I am cleared. We applied for an appeal to overturn the sentence because, of course, I'm not a trafficker, but nothing's happened. I've been waiting a year and half and still no word. Meanwhile, I am not allowed to leave Greece.

Movie star

By the beginning of 2019, I had been on Samos for a year and three months and I was tired of it. I hated the island, I hated my clothes, my blanket, my friends. I had my open card by then, my blue stamp, and I wanted to leave. Trad pleaded with me not to go. I said: 'I have to go. I have to move on with my life.' All the volunteers agreed. They said if you don't leave, we'll be mad.

The day I left was March 17, 2019.

I had three goodbye parties the night before. My friends from Iraq, Egypt, Africa, Syria, Palestine, they all made parties for me. A woman called Sonia from Cameroon, who would cook for me when I came back to the camp at the end of the day, was there, too. I loved her a lot. She would cook for other people as well. They would give her chicken, spaghetti and pay her to cook for them, but she always gave me food first. All night we danced. We were happy but at the same time we were sad.

The next morning at seven, when everyone was asleep, I got up, packed and left without saying goodbye to anyone. It hurt me too much to say goodbye. Even my close friends from Syria I left asleep.

Trad was waiting for me outside the camp with girls I knew from working as a volunteer. I had to take a bus to the port but they walked. When I got there, it was nine o'clock and the ferry didn't leave till one, so I got permission to go outside with my friends and sit and have coffee. Some of the girls were crying – we had worked together every day for six months.

Then it was time. They checked my ticket and bags and ID, and I boarded the ferry. My friends were waiting on the dock to say goodbye. I bought a coffee and walked out to the deck to see them, but we were already in the middle of the sea!

All around me were Syrians, single men, families. I didn't know them but they all knew me because of my work with Refugee 4 Refugees. They wanted me to help translate their questions, so I did, and they gave me tea and food. I had a family of 300 people! I felt like a movie star.

We arrived in Athens at eleven the next morning. The police called us by our names and ID numbers and put us on a bus to Thessaloniki. We left Athens at two in the afternoon and drove for seven, eight hours, stopping sometimes for juice or food. The driver had a list of where to take people, a hotel or a camp, and everyone was getting off except me and two others, a man from Afghanistan and a married woman from Kuwait. At eight that night, the driver let us off in front of the hotel and drove away. Nobody was there. Now what to do?

Finally, a person from IOM [the International Organization for Migration, the United Nations program that was funding the ninety-three hotels in Greece housing refugees up until June 2020] came and took us into the office. I had to translate for everyone. They explained the rules of the hotel. You can't leave for more than three days. You have to sign in every morning. You get three meals a day.

The married woman with us wanted to find her husband but they wouldn't help her. They just said if you want to leave, leave.

Still, that first hotel was nice. There was a big town ten minutes away and a little market next to the hotel, a lot of coffee shops. After a few weeks, though, they moved me and all the other single men to the hotel where I am now, Hotel Bepola, where everything is far away.

When I was in Samos, I was sleeping in a container. I had no hot water. It was cold some days, hot other days. We had electricity only sometimes, water only sometimes. In this hotel, I have hot water, electricity twenty-four hours, a comfortable bed, a table, a shower, A/C. I can wash my clothes in a machine, not by hand. But I have no classes, no language learning, no volunteering, nowhere to go. For more than a year I've had nothing to do. Just eat and sleep and drink, over and over, like an animal.

I want to work again. I miss working so much. I want to work in the laundry with Samos Volunteers and with Project

Armonia, which cooks food for refugees. I know how to cook – I like that. I want to improve my English and learn Spanish.

I would also like to learn to play guitar some more – I was doing that in Alpha – though I like the violin better. When I sing in Arabic, my friends say, 'Shut up, your voice is terrible.' When I sing with my European friends, they say my voice is good. I don't know who to believe! I don't know when I will get to do that again.

I want to go back to my books. I have only two books with me, one Arabic, one English. I miss the library in Alpha Center.

A kind woman works here at the hotel, a Greek. She comes to clean our rooms but I won't let her clean the toilet. She should not have to do that for me.

I've stopped going out. I've stopped going anywhere except to throw away the trash.

❖　　❖　　❖

Helen:
On Wednesday, June 3, 2020, Hasan said goodbye to Hotel Bepola for the last time and took a bus to Thessaloniki. 'I hate this place so much,' he told me that morning, meaning not the hotel but Greece. 'I don't know what I'm going to do. I'm lost. I have only two options. Go back to Samos, or go to the asylum service and ask them to send me back to Turkey.' And then he confessed that the day before, in a moment of despair, he had used his last euros to buy a ticket to Samos.

This horrified his friends, not only because it was a step backwards but because he had no legal place to stay on the island, which put him in danger of arrest. 'If he gets arrested, it will undo all the work we did to get him a suspended sentence and he'll be put in prison,' his legal expert friend, Nick, explained.

But for Hasan, Samos had taken on a rosy glow, for, as he said, he had found a purpose there, a purpose he had since lost.

By the end of that day, however, he had decided not to go back to Samos after all, but to stay with friends in Thessaloniki until he could find an apartment and a job. 'I am ashamed to depend on them,' he told me unhappily. 'How long will I have to ask people for help?'

In the meantime, the government had thrown so many other refugees onto the streets that week that entire families were camping out in city squares. Hasan spoke about this and his future from his friends' house.

❊   ❊   ❊

Ray of hope

I have a lot of friends sleeping on the roads because of these new rules. I don't worry about single men, we can survive. But when it's families, women, children . . . I saw two families from Iraq sleeping in the square here in Thessaloniki. I asked them what they will do. They said, 'We have money, but when we went to a hotel, they wouldn't give us any rooms.'

You know, when I came to Greece, I had a stereotype in my mind from watching movies and TV that First World countries in Europe, America, Australia, Canada and Britain have democratic constitutions and believe in human rights, justice and equality. That they believe there is no difference between languages, races, skin colors or religions. That there is no racism, no suppression of freedom or opinion. But in Samos I discovered that all of this was just a big lie. All they tell us is: 'Go home! We don't want you here anymore!'

My father called me from Syria yesterday. He said, 'Hasan, we need your help.' At the age of seventy-three, he is trying to support his young wife and my brother Mahmoud's widow and two children in the midst of war, with different forces fighting on every side of Manbij, strangling the life out of it. Before the war, a kilo of sugar would cost twenty-five lira. Now it costs 3,000 or even 5,000. 'You know what we are eating?' my dad said. 'Grape leaves and old bread.'

My dad doesn't know I've been in a camp, he doesn't know what's been happening to me. He asked me to send money . . . he doesn't know I can't find work. He thinks I go to work, come home, eat, shower, watch TV, sleep. He thinks I can come back to Syria. He doesn't know I'm not allowed to leave Greece for three years. I feel so ashamed. I changed my phone number today because I'm afraid someone will call me and tell me my dad is dead. I want to go back and hug him and talk to him before he dies.

Sometimes I say to myself: 'What the fuck, Hasan, why did you leave Syria? People look at you here as if you are a criminal. Police stop you all the time, search your bag.'

But, if I go back to Syria, I will have to join some military group and kill people to stay alive. I don't want to kill anyone, fight anyone. I want to work, take a shower, go to the beach, have a house and a normal family life, time for myself. We all want this, but some can have it and some of us can't. And what do we have in Syria now? We have to fight for one liter of water, one piece of bread. Bombs are falling. Families are freezing to death outside Idlib. It's because of Bashar Assad, yes, but he is the puppet of Iran and Russia. It's the shame of all the world.

But I will not give up because there is still a ray of hope. Somewhere.

2

ASMAHAN

'I have had a lot of pain in my life, but I love my life because it has built me into a strong woman.'

Asmahan in Syria

'I love my life.'

Eyad:

Asmahan and I met in September 2018, when we were both living in a refugee camp in northern Greece. Over our time there together, we ran barefoot to the police station to plead for an ambulance for her newborn son, Aziz; we knocked on doors in the early mornings to ask if we could borrow a cooker when the camp's electricity shut down; we talked for months and we still talk . . .

But first, a memory. My last night in Syria. I remember looking out of my bedroom window, carefully packing all I could bring with me while I tried to escape from the clutches of war and the smell of blood. I started to walk out but stopped to make sure that it was still sleeping there, near my heart. 'It' was my leather wallet containing a piece of paper that held a story of love – a poem for a homeland that had become a feast for hyenas and a cemetery for revolutionaries against tyrants.

Before the sun rose, I boarded a bus and gazed through the window at the darkness outside. Nothing was there but memories so powerful they colored everything, as if I were in broad daylight. I tried to maintain my composure but the questions drummed relentlessly inside my head. Would I be arrested when we crossed the military checkpoints? What would happen to me when I reached territories controlled by the opposition? What if the smuggler took all my money and ran away, or Turkish soldiers shot me at the border? Would my asylum application be accepted or would I be sent back to my death? Would I ever return to my homeland without fear for my life? Would I ever see the people I love again, or would I die alone?

These questions plague all men and women, old or young, forced to escape their homelands. War is a curse that turns everything dark, burying childhoods, devouring dreams.

I and my brother, Ehab, had been living in the Samos refugee camp for a year and two months, waiting to find out if his appeal could save him from being sent back to Turkey, when, on September 20, 2018, we and a group of twenty other refugees were evacuated from the island. Our new home, we were told, was to be Nea Kavala camp, 153 kilometers northeast of Thessaloniki.

While I was in that Samos camp, I had seen so many heartbreaking things. A woman falling to the ground while waiting to see a doctor. A single girl who could find no place to sleep except in the woods. A father who'd had to leave his son alone in Turkey and his family in Syria because of lack of money, yet who still hoped that he could reunite with them in a safe country. So many stories that make sadness infiltrate every inch of you. And all the time, I was forced to be careful. The only way to escape the miserable reality for some of the refugees was either to consume excessive amounts of alcohol or to find someone to curse or beat up, so I avoided getting into conflicts with other refugees or in trouble with the camp workers or the police. I made sure that even my shadow did not touch the shadow of others. Many times, the police stopped us in the town or at the beach to insult us, either with words or physical assault. They would forcefully detain us in front of locals, as if we were raging bulls needing to be punished and disciplined, and they would always finish their fun by shouting in broken English, 'Now go camp,' or, 'Now go sleep.'

One night in the summer of 2018, I was near the main gate of the camp making a call, when a police officer came towards me, saying, 'We know you speak English – come with us to the police station downtown to translate.' I had no choice, so I went. I returned to the camp around five in the morning. Only about an hour later, I was woken by a member of the riot police kicking me and shouting, 'Wake up!' The police took me and two of my roommates to the police station and imprisoned us for two days. Many long hours later, they told us that our crime was having a few kitchen knives in our container and some homemade fitness equipment. This, they said, amounted to possession of deadly weapons.

Soon after, we were put on trial, where we were given a six-month suspended sentence and an 800 euro fine. Helen was in Samos and witnessed the trial herself. She saw how, while I was waiting for my trial in the courtroom, the judge made me stand up in court and translate for a fellow accused Syrian, which put me in the agonizing position of having to represent the law even as I was accused by it.

After that, when I learned that Ehab and I were to be transferred to the mainland, I was not sorry to leave.

To reach Nea Kavala, we sailed on a ferry for more than fifteen hours, and then traveled by bus, arriving at six in the morning, physically exhausted and emotionally drained. Some of us fell asleep on wooden benches, others on the ground. Meanwhile, the camp staff allocated us to our respective shipping containers.

I found this new camp in slightly better condition than the one in Samos, but otherwise nothing was different. We were still prisoners, and we were still forced to feel that we were nothing but creatures made to eat, sleep and submit.

Ehab and I were sent to Container A45. There, we were greeted by a man named Hossam, who was to be our room-mate. Hossam had an inviting face with a soft smile and a quiet voice. He kindly brought us cold drinks and food, and prepared our beds. We fell asleep almost immediately. Five hours later, I woke up to Hossam saying: 'Asmahan, come here. I have a surprise for you. There are two young men from Syria, your country. Come say hello.'

That was the first time I saw Asmahan, a heavy-set woman of forty with a sweet, open face and a husky voice. Her round, slightly plump cheeks are as pale as wheat, although they were darkened back then with pregnancy-induced melasma. Three shallow wrinkles line her forehead, and crows' feet are beginning to appear around her eyes, perhaps because she is constantly smiling. Her eyes are beautiful, neither small nor big, their color the dark brown of roasted Arabic coffee beans, while her inner lids are always lined with black kohl in the traditional style of the Bedouin and so expressive you can see in them a thousand stories. They are crowned by carefully drawn, thin eyebrows that rise and fall with her emotions. She speaks in a mixed Shami (Levantine Arabic) and Deiri (from the Syrian town of Deir al -Zour) accent, and when she laughs, her lips expose small, even teeth. Yet her big hands, wrinkled and rough, as well as her short nails, reveal how hard life has been on her.

The first time we met, she wore an elegant black abaya with embroidery and pearls on the sleeves and around the collar. Over this, she had draped a black woolen shawl decorated with colorful images, its edges embroidered in white, while her hijab was plain black to match. Underneath all this black was a surprise: golden wedged flip-flops.

As the days passed, our friendship grew. Asmahan needed a friend who could listen to the tale of her life without judging her and who would understand the pain of being separated from her homeland and her children. In me, she also saw a son to replace the real son who had rejected her, for I had just turned twenty-four.

At the time I arrived in Nea Kavala, Asmahan was living alone in her sixth month of pregnancy in a camp that lacked even the basic elements of comfort. She would wait for the sun to set and for the neighboring refugees to fall asleep so that she could go in modesty to the communal bathrooms because none of the containers were equipped with toilets or showers.

When the weather was good, we would sit outside the container drinking tea and talking about our memories of our homeland, about her life, her dreams for the future and her fears. Sometimes she rushed inside her container, slamming the door shut behind her because the eyes of certain men were chasing her as if she were prey.

Since that time, we have talked for many hours. I recorded all our conversations and put them into English here.

Asmahan often laughs as she talks, and loves to quote traditional sayings and wisdom from the Qur'an. Her baby, Aziz, now a year and a half as I write, is often on her knee, making faces into the phone while we speak. As she tells me about her life, she cries at times, but more often laughs with a spirit she will not relinquish. Here are her words.

✻　　✻　　✻

There was no justice

I am telling my story because I want everyone to know what our life was in Syria, and I am so grateful that anyone is interested. I did not come here to Greece for money. I came because planes and bombs were killing children. One of my brothers was killed in the war. Another was crossing the street to buy yogurt when he was shot by four bullets. He barely survived. But I would live in Syria again if the war ended.

I have had a lot of pain in my life, but I love my life because it has built me into a strong woman. Because of what I've seen, it's made me feel for others more acutely. I can feel for those who are hungry because I was hungry. I wish to teach this to my children and grandchildren. Life was hard on me but it taught me to be kind and share everything with others.

The funny thing is that my luck has been bad since the day I was born: December 11, 1978. When my mother went into labor with me and asked my father to fetch the local midwife, she was busy helping another woman. By the time he came back, my mother had already given birth to me. He had to cut the umbilical cord himself. Ever since, my father said, I have been unlucky.

My father, may Allah have mercy on him, used to work for the Vehicles Department in Harasta. He was tall with wide shoulders, brown skin, a high forehead. He was more generous than you can imagine and very smart. It is true that he was cruel but he could also treat us kindly and tenderly. More so than my mother. I loved him very much.

During my childhood, we moved several times. Our first house, which had two floors, was in a farming area near the banks of the Tora River between the cities of Douma and Harasta. In the backyard we had a factory for making cement bricks. We were six children while we were there, although later we were more – four boys and four girls. I was born the fourth.

At first my family was somewhat stable. I remember delivering tea to my father in his brick factory when I was six or seven. But then one of his relatives, Abu Ibrahim Shakir, fled Lebanon because of the civil war there and came to us. His arrival forced my father to support his family financially – you know how the Arab tradition of family is. Because of this, my father soon found himself in a sea of debt. He had to sell his factory, the house, most of our possessions. The irony is that he sold the factory to Abu Ibrahim himself. Somehow Abu Ibrahim could find the money to buy my father's property but not to support his own family.

Abu Ibrahim soon became richer than us. He not only bought the factory, he opened a shop and even became the mayor of the neighborhood. But despite this, our relationship with his children remained good. We used to wash wool, make date and grape molasses together, collect firewood. Oh, and watch TV whenever the electricity worked.

My parents often quarreled about our finances. My mother blamed my father for our poverty because my father could not stop himself from spending all our money on visitors and relatives. They also quarreled because they are both stubborn. I remember once my mother wanted to go stay in her brother Taleb's room – we were living in the same house – after having had a fight with my father, so my father beat her violently and pushed her against the wall. The door fell on her head and she started bleeding from her scalp.

I was very afraid when I saw her blood gushing like that and heard her screaming, but my father beat her often.

Their relationship ebbed and flowed. Once he proposed to another woman, and then beat my mother and kicked her out.

[Until 2019, Syrian men were allowed to have more than one wife at a time. Now men can only take a second wife with permission from the first.]

But the village women praised my mother and told her how strong and clever she was. For example, when my father became engaged to that second woman, my mother bribed us and the children of the neighborhood with candy to run after the new woman, calling her 'my father's wife'. We made her believe that my father had dozens of children already, and in the end she annulled the engagement.

After my father lost his factory, he borrowed some money, bought a plot of land and built a three-room house on it, two rooms and a kitchen. We slept in a room no bigger than three by four meters, under a large blanket made of wool that I shared with my siblings and mother. For me, the whole house was just that family bedroom. The other room was for my father's guests, the sheep and wool merchants who would come and stay the night.

The walls of our room were made of cement blocks full of dark holes containing nests of spiders, termites and lizards. There was an old wooden box TV in one corner and a rusty fireplace with a bucket of water on it for my mom to wash us kids. The ceiling was made of tree trunks covered by a layer of nylon and mortar, so low my father's head would touch it when he stood. A single lamp with a dim bulb hung in the middle of the room. During the summer, we had to endure mosquito attacks. We could hear dogs barking, frogs croaking; smell the sewer stench from the river.

Yes, our days were ugly at times but they also had their own beauty. I was always warm. I teased my siblings, tickled them. We wrestled with each other, laughing until my mom ordered us to sleep.

My father borrowed money to rent arable land for growing spinach, and we picked olives. He bought and sold sheep, slaughtering them to sell their meat. Every month he slaughtered a ewe to sell her parts to the neighbors. I used to watch him kill the animal and hang it by its back legs from the branch of a tree, and then skin it and extract its guts and innards. We kids would help by bringing water for him to clean it or mounds of dirt to cover the spilled blood.

We had no toys but we played with things we found in nature, stones and seeds. We liked to run with dandelion seeds to watch them blow away in the wind. My mom would beat us because the seeds would stick to our clothes. And we would keep ladybugs in the room because there were nice stories about them. We would collect animals such as rabbits and sell them for money, play hopscotch with stones. We made small boats with paper from a notebook, even if we got a beating for wasting paper. My mom would write numbers on each page of a notebook, so she could count to see if we'd taken any. That was how poor we were. But it was fine . . . my mother could beat us but the important thing was that we could play.

During the daytime, I washed sheep's wool with my siblings. After that we would fetch firewood for my mom to kindle a fire to make date and grape molasses. My tattered clothes would become smoky and my already dark face would become darker. (*She laughed.*) They called me Blackie, as all my siblings have pale white skin like my mother. She is beautiful, with a face white like snow and blue eyes like the sky. But she was a real tyrant.

One time when I was a child, my father gave her money to buy two matching dresses, one for me and one for my younger sister, Sumaya. Sumaya was blond and beautiful, but I was brown, so my mom decided I didn't need the dress. She took it back to the shop and exchanged it for a curtain. But I had my revenge. I cut the curtain with scissors!

There was no justice from my mother. She was the reason for my unhappiness. Later you will know why.

After a hard morning of work, I would wait impatiently with my brothers for the time to hit one o'clock, hoping that the electricity would be working so we could sit in front of the wooden wonderland box we called TV. We loved to watch a cartoon film called *Heidi*. And *Belle and Sebastian* or *Lady Oscar* [Japanese cartoons popular in Syria]. We would wait for each new episode, anxious to know what happened. By Allah, those were beautiful days compared to now.

Then came a terrible day when I was maybe in first grade. We were playing in one of the orchards, none of my family members were at home, and, because the electricity was unreliable, the TV exploded and a fire spread in our house, the smoke and tongues of flames reaching so high they ate everything in it. My father was shocked, helpless. He clasped his hands, saying, 'There is no strength except in Allah.' My mother slapped herself, wailing and screaming at the sky. Although my father tried to calm her down, you know how we Arab women react in a miserable situation!

The fire killed my father's desire to repair the house, so he sold the land and bought a new plot, on which he built a single room with a kitchenette. The day of the fire, the people of the neighborhood brought some pillows and blankets, and for about a month we slept in the orchard until we finished building the walls and wooden ceiling. When it was ready, the people of Al-Hara flocked again, bringing us additional pillows and some essentials for the new home. I remember well the eight colored woven blankets of cotton they gave us and a large plastic bag filled with clothes. That was a great joy for me because most of my old clothes were shabby. But there was a painful lump in my soul because we could no longer see *Heidi* or *Belle and Sebastian*.

Poverty has an ugly and ruthless face

In the new house, I began fetching bread on top of my other work of washing wool, collecting firewood, carrying grape boxes, herding goats. Because of all that added work, I failed second grade and had to redo the year.

The work with bread was this: I had to wake up at three in the morning with my brothers to ride a bike to the bakery, collect our ration of bread and then resell it. When we were woken up, we would cry and beg to stay warm until the sun rose, but poverty has an ugly and ruthless face. By Allah, I swear my greatest wish was that, instead of being jerked awake by my mother, I might wake up by myself and see that the sun had already shattered the darkness of the night.

Once we were awake, we would leave the house wobbling like drunks, our eyes half-closed. Five of us children would climb onto our bike. Sumaya and I rode on the baggage carrier on the back, Hassan sat on the frame, Ali sat on the seat to pedal, while Yousef perched on the handle bars because he was the smallest.

One morning I was so tired I dropped asleep on the bike and fell off. Ali didn't notice. I ran after him, too afraid to shout in case he got angry and hit me. Because I was wearing a big coat, he thought an old man was chasing him, so he pedaled faster! When he found out it was me, he beat me for falling asleep.

Most of the children in the neighborhood of Al-Deiriyya were racing like us against the speed of sunrise's light to be first to queue for the bread. Whoever got there first had an advantage when it came to reselling it. I would buy my ration of bread, sneak away to change my clothes and put on a hijab to camouflage myself, and then return to the queue to get another ration. I remember giving my veil to Yousef, too, because his features and hair were delicate enough for him to pass as a girl. He really has a beautiful face.

We got bread from three different bakeries. And then, at around six o'clock in the morning, we would go to Souq al-Hal, a big vegetable market in Douma, to repackage it. We left it with our elder brothers, Ali and Hassan, to sell, while the rest of the us walked home on foot, four or five kilometers. We would run near the highway, waving to the passing cars, dreaming that one day we'd be the ones behind the steering wheels. Sometimes we would steal watermelons and soft drinks, if we were lucky and the kiosk owner was snoozing inside.

Once we arrived home we would change into our school clothes quickly. I used to feel like I was from another planet, a planet of no sleep, filled with the smell of bread and goats. Most of our school peers wore clean clothes that smelled fragrant, and they had money to buy potato chips or sweets during recess, even though their bags were already full of bananas, which were expensive. As for us, the teachers scolded and humiliated us because we were sluggish and unmotivated, our notebooks most often empty of homework, our clothes tattered and smelling of goat, and our desire for sleep was bigger than our need for knowledge!

Sometimes, though, I made friends. I felt ecstatic when I became friends with a 'high-class' girl, as if I had suddenly shed the smell of goats on my skin. But mostly I only dreamed of sleep.

I stayed in school until midway through fourth or fifth grade, I am not sure which, but I was twelve at the time. I remember standing on a little platform in the school in 1991 and hearing a missile overhead. There was a war between Iraq and Kuwait. That's the last memory I have of being in school.

※　　※　　※

Eyad:

While Asmahan was telling me stories of her childhood, I was watching her struggle through her pregnancy under the harsh conditions of our camp. Even getting meals was not easy, for she had to walk a long distance to the food line three times a day, and then wait for nearly half an hour each time for a meal so small it was unsuitable for any adult, let alone a pregnant woman. When she was extremely tired, she would ask me or random children roaming what we called the 'streets' of the camp to bring her the food, but sometimes the canteen operators refused to give it to us, insisting that she be present herself, even though she had repeatedly explained that her health was not good enough to allow her to queue multiple times every day.

Once a week, Asmahan would go to the hospital for prenatal check-ups, and often there was no interpreter to help her communicate with the doctors. It took her half an hour just to walk to the bus stop because her pregnancy had so slowed her pace. Her monthly allowance was ninety euros, minus the 2.50 euros the government took in taxes – not nearly enough to buy the healthy food or the vitamins she needed to keep her and her unborn child healthy.

Single and pregnant women are supposed to have special protection under the refugee rules, yet Asmahan seemed invisible to the human rights organizations at the camp. I often went with her to visit the office responsible for vulnerable people to hurry them into finding her proper accommodation. But, time after time, they only answered, 'The request has been submitted to the Ministry and we are waiting, just like you.'

Asmahan and I would talk sarcastically on the way back: 'She says she is just "like" us? No way! She is not pregnant and urgently waiting for the night so she can use the bathroom. She is not sleeping alone in a container with her eyes half-open for fear someone might storm in and steal or rape. She does not wake up in a panic when a drunk kicks the thin container walls and screams at the top of his lungs, taking everyone back to the sounds of incoming missiles.'

Once, when someone invited himself over to drink tea with Asmahan, she asked me not to leave her alone with him because she feared his intentions. It is a nightmare to be a woman in a place like that camp.

I learned about the details of her past as time crept along and I enjoyed trying to outdo her in cooking. We would compete over who made a certain dish best. I remember her laughing hard when my friends and I began shouting at each other; I think it was about whose turn it was to wash the heaps of dirty dishes. I finally gave in and carried them outside to wash. But then a friend called me over, so I put them down and went to him. When I came back, Asmahan had washed them all. I felt genuinely ashamed.

The days went by slowly in that camp, so our only entertainment was to dig up memories and tell stories – both the beautiful and the ugly, including the tale of her marriage.

❊   ❊   ❊

I lay like a ring on a man's finger

When I was thirteen, a relative of my mother called Khalil asked for my older sister Asmaa's hand in marriage. He was a soldier in the third division of the army, twenty-six or twenty-seven, so old to me that I called him Uncle. He was dark-skinned, with small eyes – not ugly but not beautiful either, without much character or charisma.

One of our cousins also wanted to marry Asmaa – an orphan who was studying English literature in Damascus. Asmaa chose him. Khalil tried to compete by selling his house for the dowry and proposing to her again, but the orphan was faster. After the engagement, Khalil came to us and blamed my father for having made him put up his house for sale based on the false promise that Asmaa would be his bride.

The conversation took place at night while we were all sitting in the room where we slept. My father had sold our second family room because he was going through another financial hardship, so the whole family was living in one room. I was on the bed with my sleeping siblings when my mother asked Khalil, 'Where is this house?'

Khalil said it was in the Al-Tahouh area. That was where my mother's sister lived. So my mother said to my father: 'What do you think, Hussein? We could have a house there, close to my sister and the city.' My father was silent. Then she said to Khalil: 'No need to sell, we will marry you to one of ours. Asmaa is gone but you have other options.' She pointed at me. 'What do you think of this one, even though she is young?'

Khalil said: 'It is not a problem. What matters to me that my wife would be from this family.' Perhaps he hoped that Asmaa would change her mind and marry him after all. But our family had a reputation for being good, respectable people, so he wanted that, too.

My mother nodded at me to follow her outside, saying she needed to wash the teacups. Then she told me what I had to say, and I so feared her extreme cruelty that I obeyed. We re-entered and my father asked me, 'What do you think, Blackie, do you agree to this?'

I said what my mother told me to say: 'I will not find anyone better than my cousin . . . But I do not know anything.'

My father slapped his hand on his neck, a sign of surprise, and said, 'Whoever answers in this way is not a child or a little girl; you know everything.' He didn't realize I had been rehearsed by my mother.

They used to call me another nickname as well as Blackie, which is Hathfal Hashtar, after a lady we knew who was very short – black, old, skinny. I was perhaps not even a meter tall then because I had not finished growing – my puberty had not begun. My hair was still in a ponytail and I smelled of goats. But let me come back to the story of my engagement.

My father said: 'Khalil, we agree to this marriage. You give us the house and we give you the girl, but she's still young, so will you wait a bit?'

Khalil said he would wait. In this way, my parents sold me to get a house.

Because we had no space for Khalil to move in with us, he rented a room in another house. I saw him bringing a closet one day, and then a desk, clothes, blankets and a mattress. I had no understanding of what was going on. He even bought me a gold necklace that weighed five grams, and two rings.

On February 14, 1992, the weather was very cold. A well-known man had died around this time and all the people from my neighborhood had gone to the city of Deir al-Zour for his funeral. My family took advantage of this and told Khalil to come and marry me right away while everyone was gone. Because I was a child, they didn't want people to stir up trouble against my family.

[In Syria at this time, a girl was not supposed to marry until she was fifteen, although the rules could be bent with her father's consent. Nowadays, it is against the law for a girl to marry before age eighteen.]

At midnight, everyone was asleep except my sister, Sumaya, who woke me up, saying that my mother needed help with a stack of mattresses that had toppled over in Khalil's house. Then my mother came in carrying a small heater. She put it down and began washing my hair, combing it, spraying perfume on me. I was confused. She made me put on Hathfal Hashtar's jalabeya, which was so long for me my mother had to pin it up, and gave me plastic shoes that kept slipping off, I was so small.

We were walking to Khalil's house when Sumaya said: 'They will marry you, unlucky girl. Believe it or not, this is your wedding day.'

I hit her. But she said it again. So I asked my mother what was going on. Her answer was, 'Nothing.' After that, my mother looked at my sister Sumaya with angry eyes and said, 'Shut your mouth, red-face.' *Ya hamra* [red-face], was her nickname because she was blond and pink-skinned. Then my mother said to me, 'Hurry, Blackie, your father is about to arrive.'

We were nearly in front of Khalil's building when Sumaya shouted again, 'They will marry you! I swear to God.' I hit her so hard on her shoulder she cried. 'Is that the truth?' I asked my mother. And she said: 'Yes. Now shut up and go into the house.'

The building was close to my uncle Taleb's house, and I knew my mother was afraid of her brother, so I ran towards his door shouting at her: 'By Allah, I will tell your brother what you are doing to me, that you are kidnapping me. I swear I will tell him that you threw me away for a house!'

In a panic my mother yelled, '*Ya kelba* [you dog], come here right now! Your father has arrived.'

I saw the figures of my father and Khalil approaching, which raised a fear in my heart, so I ran to my mother obediently. When I later told my uncle Taleb about this, he said, 'I swear that if you had come to me that night, I would have killed your father at that very moment.'

My father was dressed up in a brown jalabeya, Khalil in a black one. My father told me to enter the room, and my mother put bedding on the floor and the old electric heater. Then my father ordered her and Sumaya to leave the house. 'As for you, Blackie, you stay right where you are.'

Right after they left, my father walked up to me, held a bone-handled knife to my throat and said, 'Blackie, if you cause any trouble, big or small, I will slaughter you with this knife as I slaughter my ewes and extract their guts, and you know how I do this.'

I could not forget the image of him slicing the necks of our sheep, skinning them and extracting their guts. I began trembling.

He pointed to Khalil. 'Anything this man wants, you do it, anything he asks for, you immediately say yes. Do not speak up or whisper or even breathe, or else I will kill you with this knife, you understand?'

My father was afraid I would run away and tell people what had been done to me, which would result in a shameful scandal for him. He also knew that, because I was a child, marital relations could result in my bleeding to death. So he said to Khalil: 'She knows nothing and is completely ignorant. Be careful.'

Khalil was watching but he didn't do anything. My father told him to lock the door and windows so I wouldn't escape. Then he left, locking the door behind him. Khalil saw that I was shaking, so he said, 'I will turn on the heater.'

'I am not afraid of turning on the heater by myself,' I told him.

'Step aside, I'll do it,' he said.

'So now you've suddenly become a man?'

'Why are you talking to me this way?' Khalil asked.

'Why did you agree to get married like this?' I answered, 'I thought you agreed. I heard it from you.'

'Even if I said yes, why did you agree?' I said. 'Did I do a nefarious act that brought shame upon my family and this is my punishment? What is wrong with me that you have to bring me here so secretly? I object to this marriage!'

'Why did you not say this in front of your father? Khalil replied. 'Because if you had, I would have told him to take you back.'

I answered: 'Are you the man here or am I? You saw my father put the knife against my throat – how do you expect me to speak? You're the one who has to speak.'

'Me? I'm a young man. Someone told me to take this girl and go with her, she is yours, did you think I would say no? Of course I would say yes!'

That is what happened between us that night. The weather was cold as death, so I climbed under the blanket and wrapped my body in it. Soon he was touching me, caressing me from the outside to the inside. I dared not refuse because of the memory of my father's knife against my throat, so I lay silently like a ring on a man's finger. But Khalil did not have sex with me that night, so I would not be hurt.

That was my wedding night. At five in the morning, he took me back to my family's house and went to work, so my stay at his place was only about four hours.

By Allah, though, it wasn't Khalil who destroyed my life. The one who destroyed it was my mother. But they were all partners in this, my parents, Khalil; each wanted what was in their own interest. Still, it was my mother I blamed. I no longer loved her, I hated her. That was my reaction to what she had done to me.

[Asmahan fell silent here, then began to cry.]

I am ashamed of what I am about to say, but imagine that you have been carrying a backpack full of bricks . . . In the end, either you will fall or have to sit immobile, or the bag will tear or explode.

After Khalil dropped me off, my parents asked me what happened in the night. I felt shy, so I said nothing happened. Then my mother asked if there was blood. I told her 'no'. Suspicion began to arise in her mind, so she insisted on examining me. I will die without ever forgetting that moment when I had to expose myself to show my mother my hymen. As soon as she finished examining me, my father entered and she told him, 'Everything is fine.' He asked me again what happened last night. I felt afraid, so I told them that Khalil had licked me down there like a cat, and they started laughing.

My mother's father cut off contact with my parents for two years after what they did to me. He was extremely religious and didn't agree with the marriage at all. He said that I was still just a child, so it was *haram* [forbidden]. But otherwise, no one tried to help me. My brother, Ali, was on my side, but he was under seventeen when this happened, so he didn't have the power to do anything about it.

Now I feel my parents killed my childhood, stripped me of my adolescence. I have the right to love someone like any other girl, and to feel someone loving me. I look at my sisters. This one is courted by that man, and that one quarrels with another suitor who wants to win her . . .

I want to experience love like that. I want a love that will make me feel like a person of value.

✻   ✻   ✻

Eyad:
On November 8, 2018, Asmahan went into labor and needed to go to hospital. So, at six that morning, I carried an old bag of clothes for her and her unborn child while we walked to the bus

stop, which was about thirty minutes away. We were trembling with the cold. I waited with her until her bus came, when I wished her safety and health, and returned to the camp.

Al Aziz Yousef was born by Cesarean section the next day. Asmahan told me that her treatment by the hospital staff had been excellent, but communication with them had been almost impossible because there was no interpreter and no friend visited her. I had to be elsewhere and so could not visit either.

After five days, Asmahan discharged herself against the doctors' wishes because she was so frustrated by the lack of communication. 'At least at the camp I know people who can understand me,' she insisted. But when she returned to Nea Kavala, her face was jaundiced, she could barely speak, and the baby was so little that he almost disappeared between my hands.

In the days that followed, I helped her as much as I could. I found a neighbor willing to lend her a gas canister to heat water for the baby formula, and I regularly changed Aziz's diapers – with all my younger siblings, I knew what to do. Aziz was a striking baby, with black eyes and thick, black hair. But at night, I would often see Asmahan pulling herself painfully across the ground and breathing irregularly on her way to the public toilets. Her laughing eyes had lost their luster. She looked as if part of her had died.

Having had a tough start in life, Aziz suffered from breathing problems. On his third night in the camp, as Asmahan was feeding him, he suddenly went limp. Asmahan shouted in terror: 'Eyad, look at him, he's not moving! My child has died!' She started crying, saying to him, 'I fought for you, I crossed the seas to keep you alive, and now you've left me!' In a panic, I grabbed Aziz from her and ran out of the container, where the air was fresher. Asmahan tried to catch me but she could not – it was as if she were paralyzed, only managing to squeeze out, 'Eyad, is my child dead?'

I went back inside and told her I could feel a weak pulse and that everything would be fine. Then I gave her Aziz and ran barefoot to the army base inside the camp, but all the officers were asleep because it was two in the morning. It took five minutes of frantic knocking on their doors before they finally responded. They told me that an ambulance would arrive within half an hour outside the main gate of the camp.

I dreaded telling Asmahan this because when your child is dying, half an hour seems an eternity. On my way back, I saw her carrying Aziz to the police container by the gate, dragging her bare feet as if chains were around her ankles, her tears flowing. She was wailing that her child had died, her child was gone, while a young Algerian man named Reda tried to calm her down.

We begged the police again to help us, until one of the officers finally seemed worried enough to offer to drive her and Aziz to hospital. As only one person was allowed to accompany them, Reda went with her because he speaks Greek. Later, he told me that he had broken down crying while he watched Asmahan begging her child through wails and sobs not to leave her alone, to take just a single breath, for Allah's sake, just one breath.

Aziz was sent to Thessaloniki Hospital, where I visited and saw him in an incubator, lost among wires and tubes. But he grew stronger.

Asmahan and Aziz came back to the camp after a week and upon their return the news she had so long awaited finally arrived: 'You can leave the camp. We have found you a house.'

Now to return to the story of her days as a child bride.

✻   ✻   ✻

The most unjust people

The first three weeks of our marriage, Khalil didn't have sex with me. But when he did, I was so scared of him. I hated him so much, I even hated the ground under his feet. I felt disgusted every time he came to bed with me.

The night after Khalil consummated our marriage, my cousin, Ahmed Al-Fahad, came to visit us because he loved me and considered me his little sister. I had washed myself and changed my clothes but Khalil was still wearing his white jalabeya, so when Ahmed knocked on the door and Khalil opened it, Ahmed saw my blood on Khalil's clothes. Ahmed hit his head with his hands and left for my family's home without speaking a word.

I know that he went to speak to my father, asking him, 'You are not afraid of Allah, that your daughter might die of bleeding?' Then Ahmed came back and shouted at Khalil: 'Get out of my sight! You and Abu Asmahan [Asmahan's father] are not human, get out of my face!' He really wanted to hit him hard. He said to me, crying, 'You are the best girl but you have been thrown among the most unjust people.'

This was the last time I saw Ahmed because he died a few days later when he tried to pull two drowning children out of a reservoir. He jumped in and never came out. There was an electrical cord in the water tank, so he was electrocuted. He was the only brother among eight sisters. His wife gave birth to a baby girl after his death.

Many people spoke to my father against my marriage but he would just say, 'It's none of your business.' The story by that time was already finished and my brothers could not stand against him.

Every night with Khalil after that was an ugly night until I had my first child, Ibrahim, when I was fifteen. It was July 2, 1994, the day Syria defeated Saudi Arabia in a football match. I was in labor in Douma Hospital, screaming – you can't imagine the pain of childbirth – but the nurses only hit me, saying, 'Shut up, enough shouting!' and left to watch the football game. I swear to Allah, the doctor said, 'Let her give birth alone, like a wild sheep.' They all left me alone so they could watch the game.

My mother and Khalil were waiting in the hallway because they were forbidden from entering until I had birthed the baby. Ibrahim was born around three in the afternoon and the medical staff asked us for sweets as gifts, for having helped me give birth to a healthy child!

All this time, whenever my father wanted money, Khalil would loan him some. This was already happening before our marriage but continued after it as well. Look, Khalil was a good person, but I hated him for what he did to me. I hated him for two years straight and lived with utter bitterness towards him and my own family. I hated having to wash anything that belonged to him or even to prepare his food. I would close my eyes and pretend to be asleep most of the night until he left in the morning. It is impossible for anyone to understand it except those who have lived it like me.

Many other things made me hate Khalil, too, like the fact that he used to hit me, complain to my mother about me, and tell my sister that I visited some of our neighbors. His brothers kept their eyes on me, too, making sure I didn't leave the home, beating me. My family hit me with water hoses and ordered me not to go outside Khalil's house or visit anyone. They even forbade me from visiting Uncle Abu Ibrahim to see my cousins. My family stalked every step I took because they were afraid I would bring shame upon them.

Khalil beat me from the beginning. He beat me if he found that our utensils were dirty or when I refused to sleep with him. It happened a lot that he had sex with me against my will and this fueled my hatred for him. These regular beatings lasted for two or three years, until I grew a bit older, became more aware and imposed my personality on him.

[Asmahan's words made me think of the proverb: 'When you are hungry, you may eat food that disgusts you, when you are thirsty you may drink even dirty water, but it is impossible for someone you hate to enter the world of your heart.']

Divorce me or I'll kill you

Khalil was working selling cigarettes and one day he came home after work and saw that cigarette cartons filled our room, along with a notebook of accounts. He told me to clean up and throw away the empty cartons and notebook, then he went out to get falafel. When he came back, he found the room clean but he hit and insulted me because I had thrown out the account book without copying the notes about our rent on another paper. I got so angry that I pulled out a knife, pushed him on the ground and put the knife to his neck. He screamed, 'You crazy donkey, get away from me!'

'In the name of Allah the Almighty,' I told him, 'either divorce me or I'm going to kill you.' I was fuming.

'You're crazy! Get out, go to your family,' he shouted.

I replied, 'Not without a divorce, because otherwise my family will beat me and force me to return here.'

This all happened in the yard of the house, so the neighbors saw everything and came running, yelling at me not to kill him. Khalil felt ashamed that people saw him with a knife to his neck, so as soon as the neighbors arrived, he divorced me to save the water of his face [a saying about protecting your pride]. I threw the knife down in front of him and said, 'Give me Ibrahim.' Khalil refused, so I said, 'All right.' And I left.

[Under Islam, a married man has the right to initiate a type of divorce called *al-talaq al-ba'en baynunah al-sughra* by saying out loud, 'You are now divorced,' or words to that effect. This leads to a separation of up to three months. Within that time, the couple can reconcile without legal formalities if they both wish, but if neither tries in three months, then the couple is fully divorced and free to remarry.]

After I left, Khalil took Ibrahim – who was a year and three months old – to his brother's wife. I wanted to have him with me but my father refused, saying: 'He dies or he lives, I don't care. The child stays with his father.'

Khalil's brother's wife lived next to my family's house, so I would see her sitting outside, ignoring my baby. I often went up to the roof to watch him from a distance, but I had to do it secretly because my mother would prevent me from going. The day I saw my little Ibrahim crawling on the ground and raising one hand and then the other, crying, because of the intense heat of the cobblestones, my heart burned for him. So I went back to Khalil and swore to Allah that I would never leave the house again for Ibrahim's sake, even if Khalil and I quarreled. I never again wanted to see my son in a messy, unhappy state, never again wanted to see him kidnapped from me and given to another woman.

From then on, I put up with everything and anything from Khalil for the sake of my children.

My own house

At the time, Khalil and I were living with my uncle, who asked us every day to leave because we were late paying the rent. So I gave my brother money Khalil had earned selling cigarettes and he built a two-room house for us, just a living room and a kitchen, not even a toilet.

My second child, Ismail, was seventeen days old the day I moved in, but our conditions were bad and our debts accumulating. Creditors were demanding their money. We had no electricity, our doors were just curtains, our floor was dirt, our house nothing more than walls and a ceiling. I was so anxious that I could no longer breastfeed.

Khalil's family had a cow and chickens in Deir al-Zour so, for Ismail's sake, I traveled there to feed him milk, yogurt and eggs. I started working there picking fruit and cucumbers. I worked mornings and evenings for two months, until I basically paid off all our debts. Then I returned.

After I got back to Douma, I found that our living conditions were still the same, so I decided to do something about it. I contacted two military truck drivers I knew who would bring smuggled goods from Lebanon. I would borrow some and sell them in Douma; things like glassware and children's clothing. When I had earned back the value of the goods, I would pay it back to the truck drivers and keep the profits.

As for Khalil, after the birth of our first two children, his treatment of me changed for the better. You know that after puberty a girl changes her features, the shape of her body? This is what happened to me after I gave birth to Ibrahim. I became prettier. I was no longer the short, skinny, black one. My skin was lighter like my sisters', my figure filled out. After that, Khalil would do anything I wanted. But I did all I could to avoid him when he was at home, either by sleeping or by staying out of the house. When I was afraid of him, he was able to control me, but I got rid of that fear and instead became indifferent.

To be fair, I know that he was tormented by this because he loved me. But I did not love him. Despite all the time that had passed, I could not accept him.

[In the years following, Asmahan gave birth to six more children in rapid succession: Nadine in 1997, Hadeel in 1999, Yamama in 2000, another daughter also called Yamama in 2003, Muhammad in 2004 and Shehab in 2009.]

The final straw

My relationship with my family was as bad as it had always been. I had hatred for my mother, and they still surveilled and controlled me all the time, as if I were a prisoner. I wanted to get away from them but I did not know how.

Then something happened that was the straw that broke the camel's back: the death of Yamama, my eight-month-old girl.

During the summer nights, because of the heat, I used to keep her sleeping on the roof. One night, my daughter, Nadine, or maybe it was Hadeel, was running around on the roof with a friend when suddenly a disturbing sound came out of Yamama. I ran to her and found that one of them had stepped on her belly. I was so angry, I hit my daughter and kicked her friend out.

I remember touching Yamama's clothes after she fell back asleep and finding them damp, but there were no lights on the roof of the house, so I just changed her clothes and sent the damp ones down for washing. I thought the damp was spilled tea.

The next morning Yamama was not at all well. I knocked on my neighbors' doors asking to borrow 200 Syrian pounds so that I could take her to Al-Nour Hospital, but no one would give me the money because they knew we would not be able to pay it back.

Under normal circumstances, we could have gone to Harasta Military Hospital due to the nature of Khalil's work, but Yamama was not yet registered in the family book so was not eligible to go there. I grew desperate, so I forced Khalil to forge her name in the book. I made it to the hospital and, after waiting for three hours, I asked one of the nurses about her condition. He responded coldly, 'Your daughter is in the refrigerator.'

I screamed, 'What? How?' and he just responded, 'Yes, she's in the fridge.' I hurried hysterically to the morgue and found a doctor explaining to medical students the possible causes of her death: 'Dry throat, swollen head, holes in her body.' Holes because they hadn't been able to find her veins.

It turned out that my child had meningitis – the doctors said something about a vaccine that women are supposed to take during their pregnancy, but I did not know about it. Also, she had internal bleeding. Days later, my neighbor came to visit me, she was a nurse, and as she watched me hugging my Yamama's clothes, she noticed stains on one of the white shirts and said it was blood. I thought back to that night when I found her clothes damp. It was not tea, as I had thought.

Back at the hospital, tears filled my face. I was in a state of hysteria. Khalil was with me but when I asked them to give me my child, the hospital administration refused because we had forged her name. Khalil remained silent, afraid of punishment because of his work as a soldier. I shouted: 'Yes, we wrote the name ourselves, but falsification of a document is better than letting your child die! She's dead now anyway, *yalla yalla*, give me my daughter, don't you have a heart?'

After three hours they brought her to me in a shroud.

I carried her out, crying. We took a small bus home, just us and the driver. I looked at her face and hugged her. The driver muttered, 'God bless her,' and called her a bird of paradise. He was kind and refused to let us pay the fare.

I knew then that I had to get away from Douma.

If I'd had a husband I loved, would my life have been better? If I'd had a better family, would my life would have been easier?

All these events motivated me to go to see Khalil's boss and tell him that I was married to a soldier but living in a house with no bathroom or kitchen. Within forty-five days, we were given a prefabricated house in the military complex in Al-Qutayfah. Because the house was not fully equipped, I let out our house in Douma and asked for three months' rent in advance. With that money, I decorated the new house, little by little, painting and putting up wallpaper. I did all this myself.

I didn't want them to suffer as I had

After I moved away from my family, I became more free. My new location was full of people from the educated class – officers, engineers, military women – and the majority of our neighbors were from the Alawite sect, so had privileged access to public state positions. [President al-Assad is an Alawite.]

I saw the huge difference between the poorer neighborhoods and ours, between our lives and theirs. I saw how different they were with their children. When I was living in Douma, I would lock my children inside after feeding them and leave them alone all day while I went to work. I realized that this was not the way to be a good mother. So I decided not to have any more children and instead take better care of the ones I had. I wanted them to see themselves as equal to other children; as educated, not ignorant or illiterate like me. I wanted their future to be better than my past.

I opened a clothes shop in my house, so Khalil's salary could go towards the household. All my profit was for my children. I thought perhaps I will never be like the people around me because I haven't finished my studies, but I will be better through my children and their accomplishments. Even my mother and other family members grew proud of me. My father said that I was like a fifth son because I had fixed up our house and taken care of our children.

Ibrahim and Ismail were old enough by then to work in a restaurant. Nadine and Hadeel were bullied so badly at school for their accents, their looks, the color of their skin and their clothing, that they decided to leave. Nadine trained as a hairdresser.

By then, Khalil was no more than formally a husband to me and the father of my children. He had rights and respect but, as I told you, I had no love for him. Love was caring for my children.

From the year 2000 until I left, this period in Al-Qutayfah was the best phase in my life, for both myself and my children. I had managed to remove them from the misery I had lived in and give them a new life.

His money was stained with blood

Life stayed fairly quiet for my family until the first flames of the Syrian revolution were sparked. The Syrian security forces kept arbitrarily detaining Ibrahim and Ismail on their way to school, accusing them of planning demonstrations against the regime. Ibrahim was studying electronics, while Ismail was specializing in technical maintenance of medical equipment. But their schools were far enough away to raise the security forces' suspicions.

I became so afraid for their safety that, in 2013, I decided to move back to Deir al-Zour. I told Khalil that we could no longer accept his money, it being stained with the blood of innocent people from our homeland. After all, he served with the army. I told him I would take my children away, whether he was coming or not.

Khalil dared not go with us, so I and the children went back alone. We ended up in the city of Al-Muhassan in eastern Syria. But soon afterwards, the government buildings in Al-Rahiba that housed Khalil and other army officers were burned to the ground. Six days later, Khalil defected and joined us.

Ten months after his defection, Daesh began its offensive on the city of Deir al-Zour, and rumors spread amongst the residents that Daesh would kill and crucify anyone working or who had worked with the regime, including deserters like Khalil. When Daesh began bombing properties belonging to anyone who had connections to the Syrian Army, fear flooded Khalil's heart. He surrendered to the army and they put him in prison for defecting.

Daesh was slowly extending its control over all areas of the city by then. Despite this, I secretly submitted more than one request to the regime forces to release Khalil and my persistence paid off. He was freed on condition that he continued to serve the army loyally and did not leave the small area still controlled by the regime, which at this point was completely surrounded by Daesh.

Only nineteen kilometers separated Al-Muhassan from the neighborhood of Harabesh, where Khalil was stuck, but any meeting between us was impossible. Daesh formed an impenetrable fortress around us. Even the meager rations of food given to the civilians in Khalil's neighborhood had to be dropped in packages by helicopter.

The biggest surprise, however, was that, about six months later, in 2014, Khalil married another woman. [As is permitted by Islamic law.] This traumatized me even more deeply than the darkest years of the war.

Until the pain itself sleeps

Now I was a mother who had to face life under the shadow of Daesh and the inferno of war alone. My family lived nowhere near me. The days were becoming more and more bitter. In May 2014 Daesh tried to seize my house on the pretext that it belonged to a tyrant, namely Khalil, working with the tyrant regime. All I could do was to present them with the deed to my house proving that I was its rightful owner. This was not enough for them. They gave me a choice: either divorce my 'tyrant' husband and keep the house, or surrender it to Daesh, who would make of it a headquarters. I chose to keep the house.

I divorced Khalil *in absentia* and had to make many difficult decisions to find enough money for Ibrahim and Ismail to flee to Turkey. Daesh had prevented them from completing their studies, but their greatest fear was that Daesh would forcibly recruit them to fight for their cause.

At first, I had just enough for one of my sons to go, so Ismail went. After he found work in Turkey, he was able to send money to bring over Ibrahim and their younger brother, Muhammad. After a while, I married off Hadeel and sent her and her new husband to Turkey, as well.

By then it was 2017 and I was living a miserable life under Daesh, alone with my daughter, Yamama, who was twelve, and seven-year-old Shehab, who suffers from numerous growth problems and congenital malformations. There is no freedom for a woman under Daesh. She cannot leave her home without a husband or a close male relative, such as a brother or father, so she cannot work.

The only way I could free myself from these chains and survive was to enter into a Sharia marriage of convenience with a young man named Moh, who was already married and the father of a child, but who agreed to accept me. We married in the summer of 2017 in complete secrecy. The only ones who knew were some seven close friends; my younger brother, Yousef; and Yamama.

Life in Turkey is not easy and even the money my children sent me was not enough to sustain us. You can ignore your own pangs of hunger, you can cry from pain in the darkness until the pain itself sleeps, without making even a whisper to alert your children of your suffering. But, tell me, would you be able to see your child starving, crying in pain, without access to a doctor, without money to buy medicine, without the power to do anything to ease their suffering? I had to do this – marry Moh – without thinking about the long-term consequences.

For several months, Moh, my sham husband, and I drove from one place to another on a motorbike to buy used items, repair and re-sell them. We sold a lot of generators because of constant power outages. After work every day, each of us would go to our own homes, except the rare times when Moh had some unfinished tasks and worked overtime.

The days went normally until my daughter Hadeel's brothers-in-law contacted a Daesh security branch called al-Hisba to report the presence of people in my house late in the evening. The brothers-in-law were angry with me because they believed I had sent their brother to Turkey, which to them is a land of infidels. They refused to believe I did it to protect him from forced recruitment into Daesh and to spare Hadeel the pain of becoming a widow.

Al-Hisba raided the house and arrested Moh and his two brothers, as well as a mechanic who worked with us. I was forced to show al-Hisba the Sharia marriage contract, otherwise Moh and I would have faced flogging and death. The contract saved our lives in that moment, but it also began a series of clashes between me and my children, as well as within Moh's family.

Moh divorced me after that trouble, so I found a man to smuggle me and my two youngest children out of the Daesh-controlled zone. It was not easy. We traveled on a motorbike during the night. On the Kasra road, we were shot at by Daesh militants. A bullet lodged in the driver's leg and we all fell to the ground.

The driver, a young man of nineteen or twenty, moaned to us to go hide, so we huddled into a small ditch while he went in another direction. He was afraid he would be caught and face two charges, the first for smuggling people out of 'Caliphate' land, the second for carrying a non-related woman on his motorcycle.

After we had been hiding for a while, some Daesh members appeared and began detaining a number of other people who were caught trying to leave Daesh territory. Then a Daeshi caught sight of a woman with a crying baby hiding next to us, spotted us all and dragged us back to the group of escapees. Unfortunately, he caught our driver, too, and brought him back with a gun to his head. He was bleeding, hopping on his uninjured leg. They threw him onto the ground near us. He was moaning in pain, begging me, 'For God's sake, give me water,' so I wet his face and lips. A Daeshi turned the motorcycle's light on us and yelled at me, 'Get away from him, whore, stay away from him.' I think he was Moroccan. I screamed, 'Don't you fear Allah?' But he just yelled again, 'You are all whores, you want to go to the land of infidels, get out of my face!'

I screamed back: 'Why are you calling me a whore, isn't that defamation? Yes, I want to leave and it's because of you people!'

He replied, 'Shut up, your voice is *awrah*.' [A word describing the profane or unwelcome voice of a woman.]

'So my voice is *awrah*, but does not keeping silent about the truth make me a mute devil? Syria has been destroyed because of people like you!'

After I said that, the man got angry and shot the driver in the feet and body again, in front of my children and everyone else. 'Don't you fear Allah?' I screamed. 'You are shooting an unarmed man in front of children!' By Allah, Eyad, he fired the fifth bullet and it flew just past my ear. I could feel its air. Yamama started vomiting. People begged me, 'For the sake of Allah, stop talking or they will keep shooting him.' So I closed my mouth.

I felt so guilty about what happened to that young driver. But he did miraculously survive. Perhaps one of the local Daesh members went to tell his family where he was because Daesh left him behind, covered in blood, and drove us back to Al-Mohassan. There were two cars, one for the men and one for the women and children.

Back in Al-Mohassan, I swore to Daesh that I would not attempt to leave again, but we only spent four days there before we managed to escape with the help of a new smuggler. This time we made it to Ain Issa camp in northeast Syria, but the conditions there were so dire that I decided to continue on to Idlib and from there try to cross the border on foot to Turkey.

Asmahan in flight:
Syria – Turkey – Lesbos

'I had to put my trust in anyone who could help.'

Eyad:
The stories of those fleeing for their lives across the border are all similar, including my own. Yet the memory remains painful for me, just as it does for Asmahan.

On April 19, 2016, I climbed the wall that Turkey had built along the border to keep out refugees like me. I was alone. Once I landed on Turkish ground, I began running, afraid of a predator I couldn't even see and of a bullet that might come from anywhere. My bag was heavier than I imagined, my thoughts fighting one another.

'Toss it away so you can run faster . . .'

'No, I can't! All that remains of my life, documents, poems and pieces of memories are in it.'

In the end, I held on to it as if it were my only child.

I had reached the highway between the cities of Reyhanli and Antakya when the Turkish smuggler we had hired arrived

on a motorcycle, shouting in broken Arabic, 'Get on quickly.'
As soon as we began moving, he said, 'How much money do
you have?'

'I have fifty Turkish lira for you,' I told him. 'That's the amount
I agreed with the Syrian smuggler to give you.' [This was worth
sixteen dollars in 2016.]

'I won't accept it. I'll hand you over to the border guards if
you don't tell me how much you have.' The idea of being arrested
by the border guards was so terrifying that I told him the truth:
that I had 150 lira.

'Give it to me.' He took everything I had, leaving me with
nothing but some Turkish change amounting to about thirteen
lira. As soon as we arrived, he snatched even that out of my hand
to buy food I did not even want, looking at me with an ugly face.
Man is a very dirty creature when greed possesses him. And
greed can find a way even to milk an ant.

I thought, if all this and more happened to me as a young
man in my prime, how much harder it must be for a woman alone
like Asmahan in a world where so many see women as nothing
but prey.

Asmahan continued her story.

✻   ✻   ✻

I threatened to scream

The walk to Turkey took us through mountains and dense
forests, where for two days, my children and I slept under the
trees without food or water. On the third day, I almost lost
Yamama twice when she fell into clefts in the rock. Finally,
I told the smuggler that we were too tired to continue. He
promised to come back to fetch us soon, but he never did.

I spent that night alone with my children, with only fruit from the trees to eat. Then, in the early morning, I heard the sounds of another group trying to cross. I shouted and turned on the flashlight on my phone so they would notice us. The smuggler refused at first, but I threatened to scream until we were discovered by the Turkish border guards, so he gave in and took us with him.

After hours of walking, we crossed the border and I called a number the smuggler had given me. A Turk who spoke broken Arabic answered. I asked him to help us get to Istanbul. After we waited many hours, he came and took all of us to a small room, locked the door and left.

For hours we screamed for someone to let us out. My children even urinated on the ground. I even forgot to call my son, Ibrahim, because of the panic that overtook me.

After we had waited and shouted for several hours, the Turk returned and said through a small window, 'You have to pay 1,000 dollars or I will keep you here and hand you over to the police.'

I told him I only had 400. After long negotiations, he finally believed me and brought us to a couple with a car, who drove us to a bus stop. On the bus to Istanbul, I called Ibrahim and told him what happened, adding that the children and I were hungry but had no money.

A young man on the bus had been listening, so when we stopped for a driving break, he bought sandwiches and tea for us. His name was Muhammad and he came from the Syrian city of Hama. He was so kind. Before he got off, he gave me his phone number.

After arriving in Istanbul, my life became like a boat swinging on angry waves. Khalil kept demeaning and criticizing me on the phone to my children, especially to Ibrahim and Ismail. 'You see what your mother did?' he would say. 'She married a younger man and brought shame upon us, and as if all this was not enough, she is now working in Istanbul. Shame on her.'

All this was a time bomb that finally exploded in the faces of my family and utterly disintegrated it.

At the beginning of January 2018, the weather was cold and everything was covered in snow. The quarrels kept going until, one day, Ismail kicked me out of the house. I was defeated on the inside, but despite this I was laughing in his face. I did not want him to see my weakness and Shehab was witnessing everything and crying. Seeing him cry like that is a memory that haunts me to this day. He was only nine.

When I told Ismail I wanted to take Shehab with me, he took Shehab's hand and said, 'No, Shehab stays with us.'

'Well, then give me the 800 Turkish lira that I gave you a few days ago,' I said. But Ismail refused that, too.

Shehab grabbed me. 'Do not go, do not leave me, take me with you.' I was under pressure and desperate. I didn't know what would happen even to myself, let alone what would happen to him if I took him with me. So I told Shehab to go with Ismail. Then I went to Ibrahim's room and took 500 lira from the money I had given him. And I left. [This was worth around 100 dollars in 2018.]

It was a cruel situation, crueler than any I had been exposed to. Many bad things have happened to me over the course of my life, but expulsion by my own children was like a stab at my dignity. Try to put yourself in my shoes – someone you gave birth to, raised and loved, ends up doing this to you. I had so many conflicting feelings: being insulted, humiliated and stripped of my dignity, but also love and fear. On the one hand, I did not want to leave them, afraid that something bad might happen to them. On the other hand, I felt betrayed by them, wanted to take revenge and leave them. All these feelings melted together until I could no longer distinguish between them.

After Ismail threw me out, I boarded a bus to the Syrian border, only to be kicked off in Adana because I lacked a travel permit. I spent three nights at the bus station before remembering that Muhammad, the boy I met on the bus, was in Adana, so I called him. I ended up staying at his house for five nights, until Moh, who had since fled to Turkey, contacted me and invited me to live in a house near him, promising to take care of me while the storm between me and my children calmed down.

'Remember, Asmahan,' he said, 'that regardless of the fact that our marriage was merely one of convenience, we are still friends and must help each other.'

Under the circumstances, I had to put my trust in anyone who would lend a helping hand without knowing whether that hand would help or use me, for by then I felt that I was a nobody, a pariah living in a state of nothingness.

His face became like a wolf's

Two days after Moh's call, I decided to join him in the Turkish city of Mardin. I could not do it on my own because I lacked a travel permit, so Muhammad helped me. He was like a glimmer of light leading me out of a black tunnel, even though he was just a young refugee working like a machine to send money to his family in Hama. To his own detriment, he gave me 300 Turkish lira [sixty dollars]. Can you believe that there are people in this world like Muhammad, with such manners and generosity?

When I reached a town near Mardin, a woman Moh knew helped me find a small apartment, which I paid for with the money Muhammad gave me.

The weather was cold, snow filling the streets. The apartment had no heating, not even so much as a blanket or mattress. It was a naked, empty place, but a paradise for me. I made a bed from my abaya and coat, and went to sleep.

Three hours later, I woke up terrified by a loud banging on the door. Had Moh come to check on me? But no, it was a group of three men and a woman concerned with the affairs of Syrians in their city. At first I thought they were a security committee and felt afraid. I had grown completely phobic about any security services, whether they served a legitimate state or a religious, tyrannical one like Daesh.

With open mouths and eyes full of tears, they absorbed the bare room, my open suitcase, my abaya on the floor. I told them I am Syrian, I don't know anyone here and I don't have enough money to last for more than a few days. An hour later, two of them came back with a heater and some essentials for the house.

I spent the next few days looking for work during the day and seeking to get news of my children at night, drowning in a sea of my own tears until I slept.

One day, I was looking for work when a young Syrian stopped me and tried to give me a meal. Although for several nights I had gone to sleep hungry, I thanked him politely but refused, and continued on to my house. Would you believe, he followed me to the flat, knocked on the door and put the meal at my doorstep before running off? He did this every day. I was receiving the care of children who were not mine; while those who had inhabited my body for nine months had hearts so cruel that they abandoned me in a foreign country. And when they learned that I lived near Moh, the flood only overflowed and drowned everything green.

Part of me wanted to return to Syria then but I could not. Perhaps I stayed because my heart believed that the ice of cruelty between us would melt. Does a fish dare to abandon its sea, even if its waves crash strongly? Surely my sons would give in eventually.

While my relationship with my family was like a shattered vase, Moh took advantage of my distress. Using his youthful, innocent face, he made me believe that he wanted to marry me again, for real this time, raising my hope that my family would finally accept and bless our marriage.

Moh and I married, and with the passing of time, despite taking precautions and despite my old age, I fell pregnant. Moh's beautiful face suddenly became like a wolf's then, grimacing and baring his fangs. Repeatedly, he tried to persuade me to abort my child, as did his first wife and his family.

How could he want me to kill my child? Was this not his child, too? I wouldn't do such a forbidden thing, ever. When I refused, Moh began to beat me severely, trying to kill the fetus inside me.

In Syria, under the shadow of Daesh, I had repeatedly risked my life to keep my children safe from the hand of death, but now I had to struggle to keep my child alive in my womb. The forbidden nature of abortion, and my certainty that Moh would abandon me even if I went through with it, as well as knowing that I had become an eternal enemy to my existing children, gave me the strength to hold onto my unborn child. That child might be the only family I would have left.

This is when I decided to flee Moh's hell and his constant threats of death. Europe, I thought, would be a safe haven for me and my unborn child.

Golden ticket

Around May 8, 2018, I boarded a bus without telling anyone and went to Izmir, where I made a deal with a smuggler to get me to Greece. Because I had no money, I paid him with all the golden jewelry I owned.

Fearful thoughts invaded my mind like locusts. What if the smuggler scammed me and deprived me of my golden ticket to safety? What if the boat sank and my child was killed, when my only reason for sailing was to save him? My one comfort was knowing that, if he died, I would die with him.

A week later, the smuggler drove me and about fifty people in a small van to a gathering point in the woods. This was during Ramadan, so we had no food or water, except a little for the children, because the smuggler had assured us that our journey would last no more than an hour. But this is not what happened. We had to hide among the trees, still as the dead, from four in the morning until late the next evening. Between the fasting and the high temperatures, our clothes were sticking to our bodies with sweat. And all the while, the Turkish border guard was lying in wait.

Finally, the smuggler called, '*Yalla, yalla, yalla!*' in a whispered scream and ordered us to put our boat in the water and get in. The boat left at nine, its driver nothing but a frightened young man with no compass to direct him except the dim lights from Mytilene Island [Lesbos]. The sea was calm initially but after four hours the waves grew stronger. The boat was swinging heavily, the engine kept stalling, the water leaking in to mix with the vomit on the floor, and the wooden transom holding the engine broke. The passengers panicked, adults screaming, children crying. It was as if the sea had roared awake with a hideous face to devour us in the night.

My gaze darted between the silhouettes of the many people aboard. Feeling that I had to do something about the helplessness that had seized everyone, I turned on my phone. A man screamed at me, saying we would be caught by the border guards. I shouted back: 'So let them catch us. Better that than to end up dead on the ocean floor!' I sent a message to the smuggler who, in turn, sent our location to Frontex.

The engine then stopped completely, turning the boat into a mere floating plank of wood heaving with every wave. Every one of us froze. After a second of total silence, fear overtook us, causing some to throw up, others to weep and yet others to emit screams that would frighten the dead. Then we saw a bright light and a loud engine approached us, so we began shouting. The ship sounded its horn several times – a rescue boat.

We were taken aboard and sailed until five in the morning. The ship stopped to pick up passengers from two other dinghies whose passengers, like us, had been begging the sea to sleep.

After eight hours at sea, the boat arrived at a port, and I, along with more than 130 other refugees, was kept in the harbor until nine o'clock the next morning. We had landed on the island of Lesbos.

ASMAHAN IN GREECE

'WHO CARES ABOUT CHILDREN?'

Eyad:

Lesbos holds the largest and most notorious refugee camp in Europe: Moria. Like the camp on Samos, Moria was supposed to be a temporary reception center, but had since turned into what everyone there called an open prison from hell. Built to hold some 3,500 people, the camp was sheltering about 7,000 by the time Asmahan arrived in May 2018, many spilled out into the streets and fields, with no shelter regardless of the weather. These dire conditions were only worsened by fights within the camp and by members of the then-popular far-right party, Golden Dawn, who were attacking refugees there with bats, rocks and sticks, while shouting slogans like, 'Burn them alive!'[1]

While Asmahan was telling me this part of her story, she was living in a one-bedroom apartment in the Sondos suburb of Thessaloniki, where she had moved after leaving Nea Kavala in late November 2018. She stayed in that apartment for two years.

The first time I visited her there was in May 2020, after the long Covid lockdown of that year. Her building was run for refugees by the NGO, Solidarity Now,[2] so its lobby was pasted with posters for the United Nations and other organizations concerned with refugee affairs. The building was five floors high but we had to take the stairs because, she told me, the lift was out of order almost all the time. On every floor, the corridors were crowded with people. I could see blankets covering the doors, baby carriages and shoes, shopping carts, women laden with clothes waddling towards the washing machine.

The gaps in the stair railing were so big, just looking at them made me nervous. Even an adult would be able to fall through those gaps, so I asked Asmahan what she did when Aziz wanted to leave the room. She smiled and said, 'I tie him with a rope.'

On the fifth floor, at the end of the hallway, a door opened to a narrow corridor covered with carpet, with a small bathroom on the left. At the end was her room, no bigger than twelve square meters. On one side was a small kitchenette, barely larger than a child's play-kitchen, with a little sink, an old hot plate for a stove, and her dishes and cleaning supplies crammed into its few shelves. Along one wall was the single bed she shared with Aziz, over which she had tacked up some colored fairy lights spelling out her name. I remember her childlike smile when we talked about her little art installation. Across the room was a simple foam mattress for guests, topped with pillows, and on the western wall was the room's only window, draped with dreary curtains but without any child protective gates. She had placed a table and an air conditioner under the window, but was constantly worried that Aziz would find a way to open it and fall out.

Aziz was a year and seven months old by then, a bundle of energy, with a beautiful face and the same thick black hair he had been born with, only long. He ran around, climbed the table, jumped onto the bed and often tried to get out of the room, but the door was locked and he would scream whenever Asmahan tried to stop him pulling on the door handle. At one point, he wrapped a small blanket around himself and began hitting his head against the wall repeatedly, while biting the edge of the blanket with his teeth. I tried to stop him, but Asmahan told me with a tired face that this was his way of soothing himself to sleep. Still, I could not help but think of them as being prisoners in this tiny place, especially while the pandemic lockdown from March to May had forced them to stay inside. If they ever went out, Asmahan spent the entire time terrified that she would be stopped by the police and fined when she could hardly afford household basics and food. She also worried about the effect of the lockdown on Aziz, who could no longer go to preschool or see other children. 'He has very little socialization, very few toys to keep him stimulated,' she told me. 'I can't buy him what he needs, let alone what he desires.'

The whole time Asmahan lived in that refugee building in Sondos, she was struggling to make ends meet. The 270 euros a month she was getting from UNHCR was not enough. 'I have to call everyone I know just to secure what little we need. As for Aziz's clothing, no organizations will help us. I went to a place that supposedly deals out second-hand clothing but all they can give me is a diaper pack once a month. The only person who frequently helps us is a man called Saber, who brings us milk and food. Once he gave me 100 euros.'

She did not care about her own food, she added, saying she could eat 'anything.' Once, during a video call with Helen, she pointed her phone camera at a plate with a smear of yogurt on it and, with much embarrassment, told her, 'This is my dinner,' ending her sentence with a laugh. Her main concern was not to starve her child.

The next time I visited Asmahan, we met in a local park. It was sunny, so we sat under a tree, where we ate chips and drank juice, while Aziz ran around nonstop, laughing loudly, happiness clear on his face. He was like a bird who had escaped its cage.

Suddenly Asmahan looked at a nearby store and said, 'I am ashamed in front of the owner of that store because I have borrowed several cartons of milk for Aziz and haven't paid for them yet. Before the lockdown, friends would visit me, bringing milk and food. It wasn't much but it was a pebble propping up a jar. Now, *wallahy* [I swear], I do not throw away even stale or moldy bread.'

During this time, like all of us, Asmahan was undergoing the lengthy procedures required to apply for asylum. 'I am very upset with the asylum procedures,' she told me. 'It is a form of abuse. It is indignity itself. Yes, they let you live in their country, but beyond that, there is no concern about whether you live or die. Even a tortoise could bring you your documents faster than the government here can wrap up your procedures.'

She then returned to the story of when she first landed in Greece.

※ ※ ※

Why are you locking me up?

After the boat arrived, we were taken by bus to the camp and put in a large tent with about sixty bunkbeds inside. It was so crowded that you couldn't find an empty bed. But seeing the camp was such a shock to me that I told myself Syria would be better: the children crying, the food being thrown out because it was bad, the people who lacked the money even to feed and clothe their children.

144

As soon as I arrived, I was interrogated by a Greek and an Iraqi translator, tall and bald, green-eyed, grim-faced, full-bodied. I swear to Allah, the fear that possessed me as I crossed the sea was nothing compared to the fear caused by that man.

The interrogator asked me about my name, age, marital status and nationality, and if I had any papers proving my identity. My phone had pictures of me with my brothers, in which I was wearing a black abaya and a burqa, although the burqa was not covering my face. When the interrogator left the room, the translator suddenly asked, 'What is this black abaya and burqa, and these bearded men? You divorced your military husband so you could go work for Daesh? Here we are atheists, all of Europe is atheist, curse your Muhammad!'

I asked him, 'Why would you say something like that?' and I tried to explain why I had to marry Moh and told him that I had come to Greece to save my unborn child. I then asked the translator whether my baby should be registered in his father's name. He responded: 'Who cares about children? Here in Europe, we spend every night with a different woman. As for children, the bathrooms are full of them. [By this, he implied that men were masturbating there.] Register the child in your name and have lots more children with different men.'

By Allah, I was terrified of being framed, that I might rot in prison till I died. And I felt disgust that he would speak to me like this.

After the interview, the camp workers gave me a blanket and a mattress. At first I slept on the floor in the big tent, near the food-distribution place, but I was not comfortable, so I found somewhere between the outside bathrooms, where I hung up a blanket for privacy. One day the weather was bad, so I went inside the tent to find an empty bed. I found one and lay on it to sleep, only to be woken up by someone saying, 'Get up, this woman is tired and it's her bed.' So I found another and as soon as I sat on it, a young man told in a harsh tone, 'This is mine, go!'

I was eight weeks pregnant by then and hungry, so I went to fetch a meal. And I don't know what happened to me, but suddenly I threw down the meal, took off my shoes and threw them, sat next to the barbed wire and began crying. I didn't say a word. All I did was cry until people gathered and asked: 'What's wrong? What happened?' All I could answer while weeping was: 'Take me back to Syria! Get me out of this prison! Let me be imprisoned in Syria, why are you locking me up here?' I was screaming and yanking at the barbed wire.

Did we escape from prison, murder and terrorism only to die either in the sea or of humiliation near the piled-up garbage? I would say that death in our country would be more honorable.

You forget your own tragedy

In the Moria camp, the majority of the Greek workers were very bad to us, except the EuroRelief[3] volunteers, who come from all over the world. They wear orange to help the refugees and they treated us as humans, even though they didn't have enough capacity to help us all.

As for the camp workers, they say they give priority to pregnant women and children, but none of this is true. They do not even help the cases that are thousands of times more tragic than mine – people who have cancer, heart disease, a severed hand or leg, permanent disabilities, paralysis, brain diseases. There were people dying because of drugs, people cutting themselves in front of everyone, scenes that make you hate life in every sense of the word. Every day you find a suicide or an attempted suicide, either by cutting wrists or taking medicines. This happened in front of me in abundance. The situation is so tragic, you forget your own tragedy and think instead of other people.

There were fights in the camp all the time. I remember a big quarrel between the Kurds and the Arabs, leading a young man named Mukhlis to come running into the reception tent to hide out. I had to protect him. After this, Mukhlis and I, as well as another young Kurdish man named Mustafa, became friends.

Finally, after spending a month and a half in the tent, I was transferred to a small container for pregnant women, which held seven other women of different nationalities. We had four bunkbeds to sleep on but there was no hygiene at all, so we lived with scabies infestations, lice and a constant putrid smell. One of the women was always throwing up because of the food. I felt sad for her but whenever I saw her vomiting, I felt like throwing up, too. And, because I was pregnant, I craved a lot of things – ice cream, grilled meat – but I didn't have the money to buy them. Psychologically, I was very low. I couldn't stand the situation anymore. I had to do something.

So, I paid ninety euros for five sticks and blankets that were sewn together to make a shelter, and moved in. During the daytime, the shelter felt like an oven, but it was still better than being in that container. My friends and I used to meet inside and we made some sweet memories, laughed, fixed food and even invited EuroRelief members to eat with us. It felt like a family.

I lived on Lesbos for four and a half months, until, on August 28, 2018, I was taken with two single women to Fakhoury camp in Thessaloniki. I stayed there for a week. It was a decent camp, pretty clean, but there was no electricity and of course it was burning hot in the daytime. To get food or get to the bathrooms, I had to walk a long distance, which was hard because I was six months pregnant by then. So, another woman and I submitted a request to be moved to a better place. We were approved for transfer to the Nea Kavala camp but at our own expense. I borrowed twenty euros from a friend and we left.

You know, Eyad, we came here because the West is merciful and sympathetic to humans, but that time on Lesbos dispelled any image of mercy, pity and kindness I had. There, we were just like the homeless cats around us, crowding around an empty tin of sardines, fighting each other just to get fish oil or leftovers. You will see people of different nationalities quarreling over one tomato, a massacre for a bottle of milk. Meaning that what is happening in Syria is happening in Greece as well.

✻   ✻   ✻

Eyad:
Asmahan was finally granted asylum at the end of July 2020. However, instead of improving her life, this only made it worse because, under the new government rules, all her financial aid would be cut off and she would have to leave her apartment within a month.

ASMAHAN IN GREECE

Asmahan was experiencing the new reality in Greece that Helen describes in her introduction: that being recognized as a refugee is no light at the end of a tunnel, but rather sends you into a downward spiral that seems never to end. When one of my good friends won asylum, he was shocked to discover that the date of his 'fingerprint appointment' – when your fingerprints are digitally recorded and tied to your case number, a necessary prerequisite for getting your residence permit and passport – was more than a year into the future, and that, even after this was done, he would have to wait several more months to receive the documents. This meant that in front of him lay at least a whole year of stress and struggle over how to pay rent and buy food for himself and his family, while they bounced from cramped container to container, mildewy room to room, cockroach-infested flat to flat.

A man in this situation told me once, 'Do you think I would send my child to school on a rainy day in his worn-out flip flops, just to let him look with hungry eyes and empty hands at the Greek children with their snacks?' Another man cried to me, saying: '*Wallahy*, my children only eat bread and drink watered-down tea, and I put medicine in the tea to make them sleepy. When you've got no money and no hope, the only way you can think of to protect your children is to let them dream.'

The only help left for Asmahan was the HELIOS program, a subsidiary of the UN's IOM program for refugees,[4] which would give her 300 euros a month towards rent for a period of six months only. Yet, to register with HELIOS, she first had to find an apartment, conclude the contract with the landlord and pay the deposit, insurance and other costs; an impossible burden for most refugees with no jobs or sources of income. It is such a tortuous procedure, not helped by racist or crooked landlords and language barriers, that many a refugee gives up on HELIOS altogether. Asmahan only managed it by borrowing from friends.

'The irony is that the HELIOS money is only just enough to pay the rent, not food or clothes or anything else Aziz needs,' she told me at the time. She also needed to pay the electricity bill so she could turn on the heat for Aziz in the winter. The only way she could meet these expenses was to rent out a room illegally to undocumented refugees.

At the same time, she was also struggling through the endless red tape required to obtain a passport, which cost so much that she had to call around again for loans. 'I am drowning in a sea of debt,' she told me.

I, too, was undergoing these headaches to get my own and my brothers' passports. Our main concern as refugees in Greece is to secure these documents so we can leave the country and escape its inhumane camps, only fit for sewer rats; its police brutality; and the unrelenting feeling of unbearable insecurity. Yet the wait is so long that many of us go to a middleman in an attempt to speed it up, although this is prohibitively expensive and might not even work. This is what happened to Asmahan, who was charged 600 euros by a middleman and a corrupt Greek lawyer just to receive her documents a tad faster. She tried borrowing money. 'But everyone either said they couldn't help me or wanted me to pay with you-know-what.'

Despair makes us all easy targets for such predators, whether in the form of smugglers, landlords or middlemen who promise to help procure papers or find jobs or apartments.

I, too, have experience with fraudsters. In the summer of 2020, I contacted a man who said he could schedule a fingerprint appointment for my brother, Ehab, in September. Although I paid the man 400 euros, nothing happened. Ehab had to wait until July

2021. And even then it took three more months for the authorities to release his documents.

Despite all this misery inflicted on refugees, I do want to say that in Greece, like everywhere else, there is always goodness to be found among the bad. I have seen an old woman give up her seat on a bus to a little refugee girl, touching her hair and cheeks with trembling hands, as if to tell her, in the common language of humanity, 'Do not worry, my child, you are safe and everything will be fine.'

For Asmahan, there was also a ray of sun through all this: the rift with her eldest sons finally began to mend, and, once she received her passport in January 2021, she could not wait to visit them in Turkey. Sadly, when she paid a man to help her obtain a visa, he turned out to be yet another con artist and defrauded her of 2,000 euros, so she was unable to go. She had to save for another four more months before she could afford to leave Greece.

Finally, on April 14, 2021, she took a flight to Austria and then a train to Germany. She called me from the train to describe her feelings.

✳   ✳   ✳

No refugee crisis

I am happy to leave Greece. For four years, Greece has given me nothing but fear, tension and tragedy. Four years of just waiting to get the papers that would allow me to travel to see my children.

In Germany, I will have to go through the asylum procedures again. I hope they accept me so I can reunite with my youngest boys. Shehab is twelve now, and Muhammad is turning eighteen soon. Muhammad tried entering Greece illegally, but as soon as he crossed the Evros river, he was arrested by the Greek police, who insulted him, stripped and beat him, and confiscated his phone. He spent the night sleeping in only his underwear in a cold room, and then they sent him back to Turkey. He swore to Allah that he won't do it again, so the only way I can be with him is through the family reunification procedure.

As for Shehab, he is a special case for me. I will never forget when I left the house that night in Turkey and he was shedding tears, a disabled child growing up without a father or mother who sees himself as different from the rest of the children; a child his own brother registered at school as an orphan; a child who has now left school to help his brothers survive the poor living conditions in Turkey. He is working for no more than 250 Turkish lira per week [a mere eighteen dollars]. During one of our recent calls, he said: 'It seems that the procedures for our reunification will never happen. I better focus on working hard to become a man.'

I felt despair when I heard that. I felt that he has lost hope of reaching me.

We always hear about the refugee crisis in Greece but if I had received a travel document from the very beginning, I would not have stayed for even one day after what I saw there. If everyone received their passports straight away, there would be no overcrowding. There would be no refugee crisis in Greece.

3

WOMEN ON SAMOS

BY HELEN BENEDICT

In March 2019, five months after I first met Eyad and Hasan, I returned to Samos for the third time with the express purpose of talking to women, curious to know how they endured the rough life of the camp and what sort of conditions they faced. One of the first women I spoke to, whom I shall call Leila, was an elegant Afghan of thirty-four, dressed in a black abaya with lacy sleeves and an embroidered bodice. A business owner who had once taught devout women marketable skills in Iran, she had been forced to flee with her husband and children because of the discrimination and violence they faced there as Afghans. By the time I met her, she was one of thousands of refugees struggling to get by in the camp.

Like the other women in this chapter, Leila chose to use a pseudonym because she was afraid that speaking the truth about life in the camp under even her real first name might jeopardize her chances of winning asylum.

'When we arrived here in December, I thought at least there would be rules and security,' she told me through a sister Afghan refugee who could speak English. 'But there are no rules. People have fights in the camp and you see them bleeding but no one does anything. Men drink and party all night, so it's too loud to sleep. It's so frightening that my family has to go to the toilet together, holding hands.'

In the months since my last visit, the camp's population had ballooned from 3,000 to 4,000,[1] forcing camp authorities to build what they called an 'extended area' that looked like a collection of upside-down, U-shaped pipes. The containers, too, were painfully overcrowded. Leila told me that she and her husband had to squeeze onto the narrow bottom mattress of their bunkbed, while their teenaged daughter and eleven-year-old son squashed together on the mattress above. Eighteen inches away, another family was crammed into another bunk, and down the row stretched twenty more, their only privacy the gray blankets with which they curtained their beds.

And people kept coming.[2] On March 19 alone, two rubber boats were hauled to Samos, one containing sixty-two people from Africa, the other fifty-five from Syria and Iraq. I found the boats lying on the seafront dock: long flaps of deflated black and gray rubber, patched with duct tape and filled with sodden sweaters, children's shoes, inner tubes, soaked lifejackets and the plastic garbage bags that had served as suitcases.

Although the number of refugees on Samos was not as great as on Lesbos, the official camp was so much smaller that the overcrowding was actually worse. This forced thousands of people to build themselves a sprawling village of shelters and tents in the surrounding olive groves, which everyone called the Jungle. Here, children, women and men lived without security, electricity, running water or toilets – conditions especially dangerous for teenage girls and women, who were outnumbered by men by five to one.[3]

Women who arrive on a Greek island alone are supposed to be granted heightened vulnerability status and rapid transfers to safer places on the mainland, but this rarely happened. Most had no protection at all, not even special zones or housing. All they had was their own refusal to go out after dark and the little padlock some fastened to the zippers of their tents.

Still I Rise, an NGO which ran a small but much-needed school for refugee children on the island, sued the camp manager that year for abusing the rights of refugees by keeping them in these inhumane conditions – in particular the hundreds of unaccompanied children there at the time, many of whom were living by themselves without even the most basic security mandated by international law. (The camp manager responded by suing Still I Rise in turn for defamation.)[4] In late 2019, the UN declared the Samos camp a human rights catastrophe.[5]

The crowds made daily life even harder than it had been during Eyad and Hasan's time. Leila told me that, to use the toilet or shower, she and her family had to wait for at least an hour among their forty or so neighbors in the container, by which time the water, always cold, had often run out. To eat, they rose at three in the morning to queue for six hours, just to receive the miniature juice box, croissant and single piece of fruit that made their breakfast. To wash their clothes, they had to make their way to one of the eight taps of cold water shared by the thousands of people living around them, and line up yet again.

For women living in tents, these tasks were even more arduous. Because every one of the camp toilets was broken, clogged and foul, the floors caved in and the walls black with filth, women needed to use the toilets and showers inside the containers. Yet most of those containers were occupied only by men, some of whom wouldn't allow children or women inside at all, while others charged them money to enter. This forced many women either to resort to the woods or to use buckets inside their tents. Such lack of sanitation is unhealthy for anyone, but especially for menstruating or lactating women.

'The rates of infection among women are very high because of how unsanitary the camp is,' I was told by Dr Sophie Gedeon, who ran a small medical NGO called Med'Equali outside the camp.[6] (Med'Equali was a lifesaver, for the camp still had only one doctor, two nurses and no dentist.)

Another woman I met, a twenty-three-year-old Somali mother who chose the name Zainab, echoed much of what Leila said. We sipped tea together around an outdoor table at an NGO called Banana House, while a young Palestinian man with one eye translated between Arabic and English. Sitting with us was Zainab's friend, Mala, also Somali and, at twenty-six, a mother. Both fled Somalia to escape the Islamist militant group, al-Shabab, an al-Qaeda affiliate that has been terrorizing Somalis for years.[7] The women met on Samos and had been inseparable ever since.

Zainab, tall and slender, was wearing a flowing yellow abaya and matching hijab draped gracefully over her head. Mala, small and round-faced, was in a similar outfit, only in striking scarlet. The conversation between them went like this.

Mala: 'My parents are dead, so I was left to care for my younger siblings, a girl and a boy. I worked in a restaurant but it was attacked all the time by al-Shabab. I was trying to make a good life for my brother and sister, and then my baby, but I couldn't. It was too dangerous. I don't care about my life but I do care about theirs.' She pulled up a photograph on her phone of her son when he was a tiny infant, and then another as he was now, an alert, robust baby – everything she had missed.

'I have been here for five months and I must still wait two years for my asylum interview. My boy was only four months old when I left him with my mother-in-law. Now he's nine months. I came here to change my life for the better, to save money and bring my brother and sister and son here. I came peacefully. I don't want to hurt anyone, I just want to escape war and have a normal life. But now I feel crushed and I cry a lot when I am alone. It's so painful not to know when or how this life here at the camp will end.'

Zainab nodded in agreement: 'It is so dangerous for children in Somalia. There are landmines everywhere taking off people's legs. Attacks, explosions . . . civil war and endless other small wars. Al-Shabab and ISIS fighting each other.' Tears swam in her eyes. 'When you are there, you can't save the children from this. There is no way. If you try, al-Shabab will kill you. They force us all out into the street to watch while they cut the throats of people. Even the children. If you won't watch, they attack you.'

Zainab then explained that she had fled to avoid being forcibly married to an al-Shabab militant. 'My husband went to Libya to escape them two years ago. Now I don't know if he is alive or dead, if I am a widow or not. So they came to take me. My father was so afraid for me that he died of a heart attack right there in front of us.' She paused, unable to speak for a moment. 'I also came here hoping to find safety, to work and send for my child. And it is safe here from bombs and war. But I can't make any life here while I'm stuck in this camp.'

Mala: 'And the Greeks, they do not want to help us. A friend of ours collapsed on the street in pain and asked the people around him to please call an ambulance. The locals wouldn't do it. "Where is your mercy?" he asked. All they said was, "The mercy is in your country. No ambulances for Black people."'

Zainab: 'And when we go to shops to buy something, people say it's not for sale. Then we see them sell it to a Greek.'

Mala: 'Here, I am sleeping in one of those pipes in the extended area. I cannot go to the bathroom at night because I'm afraid of the drunks. The men have the right to drink. They need to forget, as we all do. I understand this. But every night there's a fight and the police do nothing. I feel scared all the time. For single women like us, our tents become a prison at night.'

The threat of sexual violence in the camp is traumatic for anyone, but even more so for those who endured the torture of rape before they arrived. Several teachers at Samos Volunteers told me that they had never met a woman at the camp who had not been raped in the past, while two staffers at Med'Equali told a visiting doctor in June 2019 that they were seeing some thirty reported cases of rape in the camp every week. The number of women who had been raped in the past was so high, the doctors said, that they could only take on cases that had occurred within the past six months.[8]

Women who come from countries at war, where rape is used as a weapon or a method of genocide, are, of course, particularly likely to have suffered such attacks. But for those making their journeys alone, the risk is also high. Smugglers, soldiers, police officers – all often rape. Yet, for most of 2019, the camp still had only one psychologist, whose main job was to assess and report the traumas of asylum seekers as evidence for their interviews, which meant that she was too overwhelmed to see anybody more than once.

To make matters worse, that same year, the Greek government took Post-Traumatic Stress Disorder (PTSD), a common reaction to rape, off the list of vulnerabilities that qualify a person to be quickly transferred from the islands to the mainland. This effectively closed off escape to safer conditions and treatment for all who had been raped or otherwise tortured.[9]

As for reporting a rape or assault to the police or camp officials, refugees and NGO volunteers alike told me that this, too, was almost always futile. Most women are too distrustful of officials and afraid of social stigma and reprisal from their assailants to report an assault. Many also believe that, if they do, they will get into trouble with asylum officials and be stuck in the camp forever. And even those few who do report find that their cases usually go nowhere. As a result, women and men who have been assaulted are left without help, while their assailants meet with no consequences.

Four women I met on this visit told me about the rapes they had endured, two in their home countries of Congo and Syria respectively, one in Turkey and the fourth in the camp itself, but most found it too painful to speak about. All the women I met, however, were explicit about how afraid they were, especially at night.

I was unable to meet women inside the camp on this visit, the manager having banned journalists, perhaps because she was unhappy with the bad publicity she was getting from an international array of appalled reporters. But I still managed to visit people in the Jungle. An English-speaking refugee I shall call Beth took me there, leading me up the scrubby hillside beside the camp and hiding me from the police officer guarding the back entrance from inside a booth. I followed her along a dirt path as narrow as a goat trail, around rocks and ancient olive trees, and through the haphazard sprawl of tents and box-like shelters crammed up against the outside of the camp's chain-link fence and scattered all over the hill. Flies buzzed around our faces, and sacks of garbage and loose litter lay about in muddy heaps. Discarded plastic water bottles were particularly abundant – an environmental nightmare but, given the lack of running water in the woods and the fact that even the water in Vathi is often not potable, there seemed to be no choice but to clog up the island with plastic.

Many of the shelters were impressive, tall enough to stand in, with curtained windows, lamps, decorations, even strings of fairy lights. Enterprising businesses had also sprung up everywhere: seamstresses, barbers and hairdressers, carpenters, cooks, electricians, builders. It is often thought that refugees, especially women, are all poor and unedu-cated, but this is far from the truth. Among the women I met were an architectural engineer and a certified midwife, both Palestinian; Leila, the Afghan business owner; a professional photographer from Syria; a university lecturer; and a Syrian who had counseled widows in, ironically, a Syrian refugee camp, which, she told me, had been much more humane than the one in Samos.

In the Jungle, Beth showed me her own house first: a wooden cube the length and height of a bed, tightly wrapped in blue tarp, like a present. It had no windows but it did have a wooden front door and a padlock. Inside, I was struck by how clean and orderly it looked, like a ship's cabin. The floor, ceiling and walls were all lined with taut gray UNHCR blankets, putting me in mind of a padded cell, while a mattress stretched from wall to wall across the back. Beside it, she had installed a little table for books and her battery lamp.

The builders of these box houses were a group of enterprising young men, mostly from the Congo or Nigeria, who charged 200–50 euros per house, and a little more to tap into the electricity from a nearby streetlamp and bring it into a shelter via a network of tangled wires. But the inside was Beth's doing. In one corner she had installed her bathroom: a bucket, toilet paper and basin. Her makeshift kitchen lay along the left side, and on the blanketed walls she had hung a cloth panel of pockets for her toothbrush and toiletries. 'I hang up as much as I can because of the rats,' she explained.

Rats are a plague in the camp and have been for years. Beth said they are so enormous and plentiful that even the island's populous feral cats are afraid to chase them. 'My little wooden house is built over stones, layers of cardboard, wooden pallets, a plastic-covered floor and then a carpet, but the rats dig through it all. I keep an umbrella to hit them with. One night I dreamed someone was massaging my legs. A rat was nibbling my toes!'

Beth then took me to one of the largest shelters in the Jungle to meet seven young Eritreans, five women and two men, most of them no older than twenty. Inside their giant wooden box, they had built a huge bed on a high platform that took up half the room, where they sat together. One, a petite girl of nineteen with a small, delicate face and huge eyes, spoke very good English. She asked me to call her Smeunit.

Smeunit told me that she had been a small child when her father was killed in the ongoing war between Eritrea and Ethiopia. 'My mother kept getting arrested and beaten, and even I kept getting interrogated as a little kid. Most of our fathers were killed in Ethiopia. That's why we had to leave. I bought a fake passport when I was seventeen and went to North Sudan. Then I flew to Turkey.'

Her friends took different routes, traveling through Libya, Beirut, Somalia, Sudan. Walking, hiding in trucks, boarding planes and boats. 'In Turkey, I was always running from the police, being subjected to sexual harassment, and I was working all the time for almost no pay,' Smeunit said, adding that she was often called derogatory names for Black people. 'The Turks are very racist against Blacks,' she told me, an observation echoed by every African I interviewed for this book.

Smeunit and her friends, who had been on Samos for two months, all had dates for their first asylum interviews two and a half years in the future, during which time they would not be allowed to leave the island. One of the holdups, they explained, was lack of translators from Amharic to Greek.

After admitting that she and her friends almost never left their box, not even to see the sea or take a walk, Smeunit added: 'It feels so dangerous here for women. We are so outnumbered and the men take everything first – the meat, the space, the food. And we keep hearing about rape and assault. So we walk together everywhere and pee out in the woods.' She shrugged. 'But I have given up expecting anything. Look, we are rich, look at our house!' Laughing, she pointed around the cube, its blanketed walls hung with colorful posters; a lion in one, landscapes in the others. A narrow wooden shelf stretched across the front wall, lined with miniature Christian Orthodox icons.

Before we took our leave, Beth urged the women to at least try to walk out into the island's beauty while they were there, for their mental and physical health, if nothing else. They shook their heads. 'We don't care about the beauty,' Smeunit said. 'We just want to move on with our lives.'

Beth told me that many women in the camp stay inside all day, every day, too afraid, ill or depressed to venture outside.

When I returned to Samos two years later, in May 2021, I found conditions for women in the camp as dire as ever: still the fear of going to the toilet at night, still the rapes and assaults, still no protection or legal recourse for those who are attacked. The only improvement was the presence of Médecins Sans Frontières (MSF/Doctors Without Borders) and one or two new NGOs offering counseling and safe spaces for women. Several other NGOs had been forced to leave by the government's new stringent rules excluding them (see Calvin's story in Chapter 6), or had shut down because of Covid.

'I see a lot of women here who are traumatized and have nightmares,' said Nora Dinah Keim, a German psychologist working at a small center for women and children called We Are One.[10] 'They also become obsessed with thinking about what might happen to them next, whether they will get asylum or an open card. Their thoughts go round and round.' One of the saddest fallouts from this waiting and worrying, she said, is that it drains away all the resolve and hope people used to flee their countries and reach Greece.

'It takes a lot of strength to survive the journey – strength and determination and resilience,' Nora said. 'In counseling, I try to support this strength they have in them. The women here are very strong.'

4

EVANS

'A lot of people here, when they see me, they shout *haram*. It means forbidden in Arabic.'

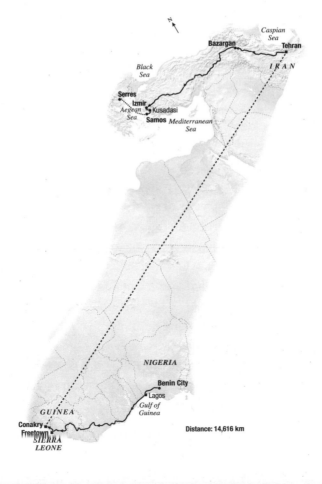

Evans in Nigeria

'I don't like to remember.'

Helen:
Evans first fell in love when he was fifteen.

'His name was Nosa. We lived in the same room at boarding school. He was average height, a little plump, playful. There was something special between us we could both feel. We became so close. Nosa was my first relationship, my first love. I was addicted to him.

'We were together for two years, until we got caught at the end-of-school party. We were in the broom closet in a classroom. A teacher found us and beat us with a stick. Then he called the rest of the staff. They came with the parents. My mother was there. They hit us with pieces of wood and beat us with their feet. The manager of the school said that, because I was seventeen, they wouldn't send me to jail, but I was expelled to save the reputation of the school and not to affect the other children. Nosa was expelled also. I never heard about him again.

'Because my mother was present that day, she felt ashamed. For her, I had done an unforgivable forbidden act. After the beatings at school, when we got home, she had two men tie me up. I don't know who they were. One man was holding my legs and the other was holding my hands and I was on the floor. They were older than me and bigger, so I couldn't resist. There, she hit me and left a mark on my stomach with a razor blade. She took a stick and broke it on me, and she kicked me. Now I have scars on my stomach. My mom did that. She put a knife in the fire and burned my stomach. I was screaming. She kept doing it. After that, she said I should get out, I'm not her son anymore. She doesn't want to see me, have anything to do with me, she is no longer my mother. I almost died.'

Evans is a tall young man with a strikingly beautiful face; a deep, melodious voice; and the lanky but muscular build of the dancer he once was. He likes to dress in jeans and crisply clean white or turquoise T-shirts, is deeply earnest and unfailingly polite, very religious, and also a fanatic devotee of exercise. Working out, music and Christianity are clearly what keep him sane.

He grew up in a Christian Pentecostal family in the city of Benin, Nigeria, his father a doctor who held a position at Benin City's university teaching hospital, his mother the proprietor of a small restaurant. Born on July 28, 1998, Evans was only twenty-one when he fled – young for someone who has to build a new life from nothing but his own resilience. Now he is a refugee, and when he and I first began to talk in November 2020, he was, like so many others in this book, trapped in the camp on Samos.

Homosexuality is illegal in Nigeria. Or, as Nigerian lawyer and activist, Richard Akuson, put it, 'In Nigeria, gay men are portrayed as cancers eating deeply into the fabric of society – tumors that must be obliterated.'[1] The law that dictates this, the Same-Sex (Prohibition) Bill, signed on January 7, 2014 by Nigeria's former president, Goodluck Jonathan, essentially criminalizes all LGBTQI+ persons and those who support them, while giving license to the population to persecute, attack, beat and torture anyone they see as queer. Indeed, a deep religious and cultural hostility to LGBTQI+ people persists among both the country's religious leaders and the general population. The

Islamic Sharia law that is practiced in twelve of the northern Nigerian states imposes a death penalty for homosexuality by stoning, while many Christian priests and ministers preach against it, too. In 2017, a survey by a Nigerian human rights organization showed that 90 percent of Nigerians still support the laws.[2] As Evans put it, 'People think we pollute the earth.'

Nigeria is far from alone in its homophobic attitudes and laws, laws that, for the most part, originated with British colonizers back in 1861 – namely, Section 61 of the Offences Against the Person Act outlawing 'Sodomy and Bestiality,' defined as the 'abominable Crime of Buggery, committed either with Mankind or with any Animal.'[3] At least seventy-one countries around the world criminalize consensual same-sex sexual activity; forty-three specifically outlaw such activity between women, which in many cases encourages the practice of 'corrective' rape; eleven impose the death penalty for homosexual activity; and fifteen criminalize trans people.[4] Most of these countries are in Africa, the Middle East and the Caribbean, but Indonesia, Pakistan and Guyana are also on the list.

The Samos camp holds people from many of these nations. The cruel irony is that, even as they escaped death or imprisonment by fleeing home, in Greece they now face homophobia from their fellow refugees who come from the same countries they fled, as well as racism from many Greeks.

When Evans and I spoke over the phone during the Covid winter of 2020, he was usually in the dark of night because of the seven-hour time difference between Greece and New York, so sometimes I could barely see him, only that he was huddled in his tent, lit by the light of his cell phone, or standing by the towering chain-link fence that surrounded the camp, under one of the giant spotlights glaring down on him like the eye of a cyclops. Often, as we talked, he cast nervous looks around. 'A lot of people here, when they see me, they shout *haram*. It means sinful and forbidden in Arabic.'

He also had to keep an eye out for the police, he added, plucking at the scrap of cloth dangling under his chin. 'If they catch you without a mask, they fine you 300 euros.' Evans and other single refugees in the camp were no longer given ninety euros a month, as Hasan and Eyad had been, but only seventy-five.

I began by asking him what he most wanted people to know about himself and his situation. Speaking in a formal British English, although he is more at home in his own language, Edo, he offered this reply:

'I am twenty-two and a very simple person. I hate to see someone being oppressed. I hate this with so much passion. It is only yesterday that I saw a policeman hit a woman who was carrying a baby. Oh God . . . it makes me go crazy, it makes me want to cry. I like a place where there is justice. Where every human is equal, whether you are white, Black, I don't care. One day, I want to be a human rights lawyer so I can help refugees like us.'

He went on to speak about his past and his life in the camp, sometimes hesitating and avoiding my eyes when the subject was painful; other times plunging into bursts of earnest passion. When I asked him why he wanted to speak about all this in the first place, he replied simply, 'I needed to talk.'

'I came to Samos in October of 2019,' he told me early on in our conversations. 'My country, my mom, they made me want to commit suicide or harm myself. I don't want more persecution and bullying. I just want to live my life. But I've never seen anything like this camp in Samos. I've never lived like this before, where they treat us humans as if we are animals.

'I don't make friends here because they've hurt me in the past. Also, because of my sexual orientation, I don't feel safe.

But my asylum interview is not until next year, September. Until then I'm not allowed to leave.

'I asked my psychologist today, "What is the definition of life?" She said, "Life is like a circle, it has good, it has bad." I said: "No. Life is useful when you have freedom of speech, freedom of movement, freedom of association. When these things are lacking, life becomes worthless." The life we are living here is like that. Worthless.'

Dan Chapman, who runs an undercover LGBTQI+ support group for refugees out of Samos Volunteers – undercover because to be overt would put its members in danger from their compatriots – says he hears despairing comments like this all the time. 'The camp offers no protection for people who are facing attacks and discrimination for being queer,' he told me. 'This comes as a shock to most people because they think that as soon as they arrive in Europe, they'll have their rights protected, at least more than they were before. And then they find out that they are not protected at all.'

Dan, who is twenty-three, British and queer himself, has been working with Samos Volunteers for more than three years now, but this has not dulled his frustration. 'Today I had to tell an eighteen-year-old boy that the best protection I could offer him from the middle-aged man threatening daily to rape him is an attack alarm,' he wrote on Facebook in September 2020. 'And last week I had to explain to a woman that even though she'd been raped multiple times for being LGBT by the same man, the passivity of the hospital and the police mean she still has to live in the camp with him. She is petrified that tonight it will happen again . . . I don't know how anyone survives the camp at all.'

One of the women in Dan's support group, who asked to be called Liliane, told me with much distress that, after being ejected from her family in Cameroon and forcibly separated from her two children for being a lesbian, she was raped by two men in the camp for the same reason. 'My two girlfriends who are in a relationship were physically and sexually assaulted here because they are lesbians,' she added in French. 'That panicked all of us. I was very afraid because the assailants told my friends, "We know you all and we will kill you." I still live in fear.'

Another young man I met through Dan's group, a twenty-two-year-old Sierra Leonean named York, who had also fled homophobic persecution in his home country, told me that he had managed to hide his sexual identity from his compatriots in the camp and was even one of his community's leaders, until they found out, ostracized and threatened him. This put him in such fear for his life that he fled the island illegally, relinquishing all governmental support. He ended up jobless, undocumented and homeless in Athens; a refugee from other refugees.

As a boy, Evans was lucky enough to live far from such dangers, at least for a time. Here is his story.

✽   ✽   ✽

She said I had a good heart

My parents were strict but we had a loving home, a good family, a nice apartment on a city street. Every morning, the first thing I did was go to my father's room and say, 'Good morning, Father,' and then go to my mother's room and greet her the same way. Then I would tidy my room, make the bed. My parents didn't let me go out and play with friends, so I would put on my earphones and dance, or play with my little brother.

Now I am not talking to my mother or brother because of the way they treated me.

Even as a child I could not bear to see people suffer. If people came in hungry to my mother's restaurant but couldn't pay, I would plead with her to feed them anyway.

She liked that about me. She said I had a good heart. But she didn't like me to be in the restaurant because I kept giving away the food to people who couldn't afford to eat!' [Evans cracked a rare smile when he said this, laughing at himself.]

When I was thirteen years old, in 2011, that is when I began to have feelings for men. I felt OK with my sexuality because I didn't cause it, I just grew up that way. I was fine with it. But I saw some videos on the internet of people who had caught gay people red-handed, abused them, flogged them, treated them disparagingly. This created fear in me. I thought that if my mother or someone else found out, the same might happen to me. That's why I didn't tell my mother about my feelings. I never told my classmates, either.

My parents sent me to boarding school around this time and that's where I met Nosa. They wanted me to attend a mixed school with girls but I insisted on going to a boys-only school. I did not want to be with girls, to deal with the pressure people would put on me to court and marry.

My father had just died in a car accident a few months before Nosa and I were caught, but my father would have treated me just the same as my mother did. Sometimes, things like that, I just don't want to remember . . .

[Evans fell silent here and looked away, his young face creased into a knot of pain.]

After my mom told me she's no longer my mother, I had to get out of her house for good. I was bleeding, I was in pain, I had bruises and cuts all over my body, but I was afraid to go to hospital because I didn't want anyone to know what had happened. So I went to the ring road area in Benin, pushed a mat together with cardboard, and slept on the street. I stayed like that for about four days until I found a job at a gas station. The owner paid me a month in advance, so I could rent a place. Later I found someone to teach me how to make furniture, so I started doing that, too. But I don't like to remember my mother now.

Dino Dancers

While I was working at the gas station, pumping petrol, I found out about a dance group named Dino Dancers from a guy named Usaro. He approached me to give me a brochure, and something inside me made me understand this was a group for gays. In the brochure, the dancers were all men. I always had a passion for dancing, even as a little boy. So, I joined the group.

We got well known, going to carnivals and parties to perform. Everybody in the group was gay but we used the dance group as a cover. We picked up some lesbians so we would not look suspicious because if you are never seen with women in my country, it is very, very risky. We danced to any song. Congo, Cameroon. Just mention any dance, I know the steps. I was assiduous. I practice even here. I have a mirror and little speakers in my tent and I practice in front of the mirror and try to learn new moves. We got paid good money for our dancing and if the crowd liked what we were doing, they would throw money at us, too. My dream was to be on *Nigerian Idol*!

Dancing used to make me so happy. I miss it. But most of all I miss singing and playing the drum in church. I did that every Sunday. I love doing that more than anything. Church was very important to me at home. I loved my pastor. It is very important to me here, too. I go to the church that refugees built in the camp, and I go to an American church down in the town.

[Evans showed me this church when I saw him in Samos, which was no more than a storefront. It was closed because of Covid.]

They have a lot of Iranians and Afghans in the American church and some missionaries. When I joined, some of the Afghans were shaking hands with everybody. But they kept skipping me because I am the only Black in the congregation. Then a man tried to hug me, welcome me, but his wife screamed at him not to touch me. I don't care. If people want to be evil, they will find a way to be evil anywhere. It is not my problem. I know who I am and what I need. I know my God. They will not keep me from church.

But we had no LGBTQ support groups at home, nothing like that. In Nigeria, people think we gays are useless people in society. Look at this.

[Here, Evans texted me several photos of the Dino Dancers, himself among them, a dashing group of young men dressed in white sports shirts and artfully torn jeans, making the goofy faces and victory signs everyone makes in selfies. He also sent me a video of several young men who, having been accused of being gay, were forced to strip by a crowd, whipped, and then made to dance naked, while the women and men circling them shouted and jeered.]

Those guys in the video, they were my friends. Once you are caught like that, it's only by the grace of God you will even get to the police station. The people will kill you before that. I didn't call my friends there to find out the outcome. I know they were arrested. They will go to court, then jail, but before that they will be tortured and the police will beat them.

Charles

It was in Dino Dancers that I met Charles. We were both eighteen years of age, he a few months older. We were in a deep relationship from 2017 to 2019, until we got caught.

It is very hard but sometimes it releases me to talk about it.

Charles was very handsome. He had a nice body, muscular, he went to the gym, he was dark-complexioned and tall. I loved him very much.

I would see him Mondays and Saturdays because those were the days we rehearsed. After rehearsals, we'd go to my house, sit together, just like someone would with their boyfriend or girlfriend. We talked about a lot of things. Normal talk, like about something we might have seen on the street.

He's very funny, he's got a lot of energy, he smiles a lot, he was playful. Sometimes when I called him to see where he was, he wouldn't pick up the phone. Sometimes he would make me jealous. But he was such a nice man.

On September 18, 2019, we went to a funeral – it was for the mother of one of the other dancers. A funeral is usually a two-day party in my country. We drank until we were drunk. When we got back to my house around seven or eight at night, we put on music so the neighbors wouldn't hear us. The house was kind of like a hotel, with opposite rooms down a hallway and one bathroom everyone shared. This is common in my country.

We started making love. We locked the door but we didn't know the neighbors were listening. They broke down the door and found us. I can't explain how they found out, but they saw us all the time going into the room together and we acted like you do when you have a girl.

Over ten people came in, saying, 'We suspected you' in local English. They hit us with sticks, kicked us. For over half an hour, they beat us up, shouted, caught more neighbors' attention.

Some of the people, they had beards, some were fat. I didn't see well, the room was dark. I could only see there were a lot of them. There were women there, too, shouting, 'To jail with you!' The only face I saw was of the man hitting me. He had a thick beard.

They beat us not only with sticks but cutlasses. I have scars on my buttocks and head and leg from the cutlass. I had my pants down to my knees when we were found and someone tried to cut me off with the knife, so I put my hand in front to protect myself. I have a scar on my hand from that now. Then this same man hit me in the face. You can still see marks on my face from that, too.

[Indeed, Evans has a wide and shiny scar that curves from his left ear to his jaw, but it only shows in certain light.]

One of the men was holding me by the pants and the others were hitting me. I realized they were about to kill us, so with all my might I hit the guy who was holding me, pulled up my pants, jumped out the window and ran. I was chased, other people in the area joining in. I didn't look behind me to see how many there were but there must have been ten and they were yelling.

I ran and I jumped into a place like a hole . . . in Nigeria we have a lot of moats. People don't normally go into those places, they are full of bushes and trees. I stayed there for two days, hiding.

When I climbed out of the ditch in the night, I went to find a woman who owed me money. I had made her a chair she never paid for. There were bruises all over my body, blood and injuries on my face. She tried to find out what happened to me. I would not tell her. I just asked her to pay me the money she owed me, which was about 3,000 in Naira, Nigerian money [around eight dollars at the time].

I found shoes on the street, put them on, and boarded a bus to Lagos. There, I went to a friend of my father called

Robert. He and my father had worked together, they were close. Robert already knew what had happened. He was the one who told me . . . [long silence] . . . he told me that the mob beat my lover Charles to death.

Robert was so, so angry with me because of his friendship with my father. But he wouldn't allow me into his house. He said it was not safe for me or him because the Nigerian police were after me for being gay. They had put out a warrant for my arrest. I was a wanted criminal. [Evans showed me the warrant, which, absurdly, also charged Charles. Issued by the Magistrate's Court of Edo State in Nigeria on behalf of the Commissioner of Police and posted all over the state, the charge read in typically convoluted legal language (I have deleted the surnames for Evans' protection):

'That you – Charles *** (deceased) and Evans *** – now at large on 18th day of September, 2019 . . . conspired among yourselves to commit Same Sex Amorous Relationship to wit by being homosexuals, an act of homosexuality and thereby committed an offense punishable under Section 1 subsection 2(a)(b) . . . of the Same Sex Marriage Prohibition Act of 2013 as applicable in Edo State.']

Robert gave me some money and sent me away. With the money, I bought clothes and took a bus from Lagos to Sierra Leone. It took a whole day and all night. I was just looking for a place that was far away from home. I didn't know where I was going, I just wanted to be safe from people who would do to me what they did to Charles. And I was crying, crying because Charles was dead.

Evans in flight: Nigeria – Sierra Leone – Guinea – Iran – Turkey – Samos

'I was someone who was sold.'

Helen:

The next time I talked to Evans, in early 2021, he was cooking in what he called his tent, which was really a homemade wooden box covered with tarpaulin and tightly lined with gray UNHCR blankets, just like the ones Beth had shown me in 2019. He had bought the box from another refugee for twenty euros. The population in the camp had plummeted in recent months, partly because Covid had prevented refugees from leaving Turkey and partly because the new government had speeded up deportations and evacuations, so it had become a buyer's market.

Evans used his phone to show me what he was cooking on his single propane cylinder burner. 'Maybe, when you come, I will cook this for you,' he said, stirring chicken into a saucepan. 'Fou-fou, which is made with cassava. Eat it with igussi soup:

you peel a melon, take the white fruit inside, grind it, cook it. It's sweet. I don't use too many spices. I have my ghee, pepper, salt.'

Evans was careful not only to eat healthily and eschew smoking and drinking, but to exercise every day, either by lifting weights and boxing in the gym refugees had built in the Jungle, or by jogging several kilometers around the hills of Samos. During my visit in May, he took me for a walk along the route he ran every week high above the town of Vathi, which climbs so steeply up the mountain that the flights of stairs between streets are almost as vertical as ladders. When we reached the top, we stood and looked out at the glittering blues of the Aegean stretching all the way to the horizon. 'One day, I will be on a boat sailing out there,' he said wistfully. 'I watch the boats every day and I wish.'

Later that day, he grew more animated than I had ever seen him, telling me about the various Nigerian dances he knows, showing me videos of them and explaining how they evolved from traditional dances. 'I love music. Fast African music. Some American music, Tupac, Justin Bieber. My best American artist is Akon. I like dancing to this. Drake. Rihanna. Beyoncé. I dance to any music, African, anything.

'Some people in the camp, they saw me rehearsing. Arab guys, Sierra Leoneans, some from Sudan and Cameroon, they were all begging me to teach them how to dance. I said no, I don't have the time. The truth is, dancing in front of people makes me feel bad now. It brings back bad memories.'

Evans looked away, as he often did when those memories hurt, jiggling his legs, his whole body clearly yearning to flee. That he had lost his career as a dancer on top of everything else was a heartbreak he did not wish to discuss.

Instead, he continued the story of his escape.

❖   ❖   ❖

I didn't know what he was planning

I was so scared of being caught that I didn't even know where I was when the bus dropped me in Sierra Leone. This was, I think, September 21, 2019. I was in a very busy place, a market, scared and crying. Then I saw a man who said his name was Abdul. I begged him to help me, so he invited me to come to his house. But when he got there, he said he wanted to take me to his mosque. I said, 'But I am a Christian.' He said he could not allow me to stay in his house if I am a Christian, that I would have to change my religion if I wanted to stay. I said I could not change my religion for anything, but please, just help me. He would not.

So I went into the streets, saw an unfinished building and slept there. A man noticed me and asked why I was sleeping there. I didn't tell him my sexual orientation or anything about myself, just that I didn't have any family, any relatives, anywhere to go, and that I needed help.

He told me his name was Mohammad and that he was from Guinea. He sounded like he was just being kind. He bought food for me. I was scared and he was willing to help me, so I just grabbed on to that. I didn't know what he was planning.

Mohammad took me on a bus over the border to Guinea. In Guinea they speak French and it's also a Muslim country, so I was scared. I felt I was moving from the frying pan to the fire.

When we arrived, Mohammad brought me to this big marketplace and told me to wait for him by the road. The police came to ask me what I was doing but I could not explain because I do not speak French. They seized me and took me to the police station. My phone battery was dead, so I had no way to reach Mohammad. I tried to explain my situation but they just threw me inside the cell. I was there for three days. On the third day, they released me because they couldn't find anything about me.

I found a way to charge my phone and finally I was able to reach Mohammad and explain what had happened. He told me, 'Don't worry, I'll take you someplace safe.' I was thinking maybe he felt pity for me. I never knew he had negative plans, that he wanted to capture my heart so he could do what he wanted with me.

[Evans paused here, looking upset, so I asked if it was too hard for him, digging up all these painful memories. He smiled. 'I'm enjoying the conversation. It is painful but sometimes when I talk about it, it relieves me a little.' This reminded me of something another refugee had said to me about recounting his story: 'The choice is between the pain of telling and the pain of not telling.']

Mohammad took me to a house and gave me instructions not to go out, just to stay indoors. The house was gated, fenced. He was there but I never saw anybody like family or anything, so we were alone. But I was happy. I thought he was a godsend. He'd promised that he was going to help me leave the country for a safer place. He was giving me food, being kind. I didn't feel like a prisoner. I was just seeing freedom, that I was OK, I was alive. And he never asked me for sexual favors, he wasn't touching me. I didn't disclose my sexual orientation to him, you understand, because I was scared.

I was there for nine days. Then he said he had documents to help me leave. He gave me an envelope and instructions not to open it until I got to the place I was going. I was so happy.

He took me to the main airport in Guinea and told me he was sending me to a better place, to Turkey.

But when I got off the plane, I was not in Turkey. I was in Iran.

God, provide for me!

In Iran, as soon as the police at the airport took the envelope and saw that it contained a fake passport, they arrested me. I didn't know what was in it! Mohammad had just given me instructions and the envelope.

Before I left Guinea, Mohammad gave me a number to call when I arrived, to reach someone to get me. So I called the number but I couldn't reach anybody. The police also called. Nobody answered. I tried to explain to the police what was happening but they couldn't understand English. I gave them Mohammad's number but when Mohammad picked up the phone and heard a voice that wasn't mine, he ended the call. After that, the police couldn't reach him. So with no information about me, they put me in prison for five weeks.

The prison in Iran . . . I was badly treated there. The guards shouted at me, hit my back with their hands, insulted me, dragged me around. I was separated from other people, I was just alone, nobody came close to me. Sometimes I eat, sometimes I don't eat. So horrible. As I'm talking to you right now about that I just feel like crying remembering it.

When they let me go, the police took me from the airport prison and dumped me on the street. They didn't know what else to do with me. I don't know where I was. I don't know anything about Iran.

When they dumped me, I found a place to charge my phone, called Mohammad's friend and finally reached him. He said he would come to get me.

When this man came, he was looking all around, very nervous. He didn't speak English but he beckoned me to follow him fast. He pushed me into a car and told me to bend down in the back while he was driving. Then he drove at full speed to a very far place. He stopped the car and locked me inside the boot [trunk].

I was in there a long, long time. I was crying a lot. I didn't know what was going on. He was driving at high speed with me inside the boot all night. It was so frightening.

When he let me out in the morning, the land around us was very wide, very big. Mountains all around. It was a big farm with a single house. He took me to a tent and I saw some white people there . . . they were from Afghanistan. He left me there.

That's when one of the Afghans told me that I had been trafficked. He told me I was sold.

Yes, I was someone who was sold . . .

The Afghans had been sold, too. I was the only Black among them and they were very kind to me, those guys. They tried to calm me down because I was so scared, I was crying. They said, 'Don't worry, we are going to escape.' They had a plan.

We worked on the farm all day, digging cucumbers, water-melons and vegetables out of the earth. It was like a desert area, you can't grow much in that place. The farmers made us work long, long hours and sleep in a tent. All we had to eat was bread and water from the water trough. Nowhere to wash, so we just washed our hands and legs and arms. No toilet.

We were hungry and thirsty all the time. One of the guys, he took a cucumber from the crop and ate from it. The men on the farm took the food from his mouth and beat him seriously. There were bruises all over his body just because he tried to eat a cucumber.

I don't know who we were working for. There were a lot of people there but they kept away from us. They didn't want us to see their faces. But it was hard to escape from that place. We were surrounded by a high wall and we were only allowed out to work.

After we worked for five days, the Afghans said the time had come for our escape. They had found a way over the wall. That night, we climbed over and dug a hole and hid our bags inside it. Later, at around 2am, when everybody was asleep, we sneaked out one by one, all five of us. And we ran.

We ran throughout two whole nights and days. We had nothing to eat and only the water from streams to drink. I got sick from that water. And I was so exhausted and hungry, I was crawling through the desert, praying to God. 'God, you provided for the Israelites in the desert. Now I am in the desert. Provide for me!' Thirty seconds later, I found a biscuit on the ground. Just lying there. So I ate it.

Finally one morning, we met a man in a truck. We begged him to help us and he agreed. After driving for some distance, he dropped us off in a village. We continued walking. Then we met a group of people, some Black, some white. When I saw Blacks, I felt a bit of relief, you understand? They spoke French but one understood English a little, so I asked him, where are we, what's happening?

He said we are going to Turkey. So we followed them. We walked for hours. My leg has been hurting me a lot lately and I think that's because I injured it during that long walk. And then I helped to carry a sick lady yesterday and that made it worse.

I couldn't see anything but clouds

The Turkish border was very difficult for us to pass over. It was all high fences and police guarding it. The police began shooting at us, so everybody scattered and I lost sight of my friends. I could not find anybody. I thought maybe they had already crossed and I was alone. I knew I had to go, I was crying tears, but for a long time, I could not move. Finally, I started crawling through the grass. It was very dark but the border police almost caught me. They shined their torch where I was lying. I lay there flat, without moving, for more than thirty minutes, my heart pounding, waiting for them to remove their attention. When they finally did, I continued crawling, crawling, until I passed them. The fence was very high. I climbed over it and jumped.

On the other side, I didn't know where to go. I was just running. I saw some people who had already crossed – they were all white. There were very many of them, so I followed them until we got to a village. I don't know them, they don't know me, so they went their way. That's when the police came and arrested me again!

The police drove me all night and all the next day till the evening, and then they put me in Abangi prison. That was the first time I had food since I had run away with the Afghans. I never saw them again. I don't know what happened to them.

I was in the prison for about two weeks, then I was released. When they released me, I discovered that I was in Izmir.

I found a park to sleep in and stayed there about two days. That's where I met a guy from Ghana. His name was Nana. He told me he could help me get to a place where I could get asylum, not like in Turkey.

I wasn't expecting anything because I thought he was just a fraudster, like the other gangsters in the area. But to avoid a struggle, I gave him 100 dollars I had left over from the money my father's friend, Robert, gave me. I didn't have any confidence in Nana but when he came later that evening and said to follow him, I just followed him, not knowing what else to do.

Nana put me in a truck. Other people were there. Black, white, all sorts. We were taken to a mechanic's shop full of old cars. We waited there a day.

They came to take us in the evening and drove us in a bus for a very long time. I imagined myself in the sea and I got scared. We arrived at night and waited in some long grass from about ten to four in the morning. We were told to be very quiet.

Then a boat came and took us. It was one of those balloon boats. I thought I would die! [Evans laughed at himself for a long time when he said this.] I know a little how to swim but there were too many people on the boat. The sound of the sea . . . oh God, I almost met it, seriously. I started off sitting on the edge but then I moved towards the middle because I didn't want any shark coming to get me. I'd watched movies about sharks eating people. Oh God!

[He was laughing more than ever now. There are few sharks in the Aegean, and none that pose a risk to humans, but many people believe otherwise.]

I was crying, so scared. It was October 21, very cold and windy. At some points, the waves were so big and I couldn't see anything in front of me but clouds. I look behind me, I see clouds. I look to the left, I see clouds. I look to the right, I see clouds.

When the sun rose, we could see rocks. The Coast Guard boat came. Everyone is rejoicing, shouting, 'Thank you, God!' but I'm, 'What's happening?' The rescue team pulled us close and transferred us into their boat. They gave us nothing to eat or drink, no blankets. They took us here to Vathi at eight in the morning.

Evans in Greece

'Fear is the beginning of failure for me.'

Helen:

Evans was right to be so frightened of crossing the sea on such a flimsy, overcrowded dinghy, for so many thousands of refugees drown this way, some because their boat deflates or snaps in two, some because it sinks or capsizes, that Pope Francis has called the Mediterranean the 'largest cemetery in Europe.'[5] The Palestinian engineer I met on Samos in 2019 told me that she, her husband and five-year-old son had left from Izmir at four in the morning and sailed for eighteen hours before their boat broke to pieces, throwing all forty-nine of its passengers into the sea.

'I spent six hours in the water with nothing but a rubber tire to hold me up, clutching my son the whole time,' she said through Google Translate on her phone. 'We weren't rescued until a helicopter finally spotted us and let down a ladder.' She typed in a few words, then held up her phone for me to see. It read, JOURNEY OF DEATH.

When Evans finally arrived in Samos, he, like everyone else in this book, was shocked by the filth, crowds and chaos that greeted him — not at all what he had expected from Europe.

'Never had I seen a place so dirty.' Inside the camp, there was not one millimeter of room to sleep, so, like Eyad and so many others, once he had been registered, he had to find a patch of ground in the fields. Eventually, he found a box and lived in it for months. Twice he lost his home in fires, along with most of his belongings and clothes; fires spread quickly in camps because the gas cylinders everyone uses for cooking explode so easily. And on October 30, 2020, the camp was shaken by a 6.7-magnitude earthquake, the worst Samos had experienced in decades. 'That was so scary!' Evans said with a chuckle. 'I was sitting on the floor of my tent and the ground began moving back and forth. I ran out. Everyone was screaming, running helter-skelter.'

Nonetheless, during those first days on Samos, he mainly felt relief. 'I was OK because I had just been through hell and now at least nobody was trying to kill me. I had some peace. But then I started having nightmares about people chasing me, and those made me go to see the psychologist at MSF. She gave me some medication. It helped but I don't take it anymore. But life is just a mess here. I was coming from the city the other day – I'd gone to buy some food – when some police shouted at me to go back to the camp. The next day I saw one of those police and he shouted, 'I'll mess you up.' He used his head to hit me on my nose and he hit my back with his cosh. The police know there is nothing we can do about it, so they treat us anyhow they want.' A cosh is a bludgeon.

There was a time when many Samians were kind to the desperate people landing on their shores, welcoming them with food and clothes, but over the years this welcome has all but disappeared. Indeed, as I walked around town with Evans in the summer of 2021, I could see how much more hostile both the police and civilians had grown to the new arrivals than they had been even on my previous visits – especially towards Africans. With Evans, I witnessed so many incidents of unabashed racism that I felt as though I'd stepped into the Jim Crow American South. Sometimes it was the look on a person's face or an outright refusal to serve him, but more often it was people shouting at him as if he were a dog, or talking to me, a white woman, about him as if he were an idiot child. As Evans said, 'I have swapped homophobia in Nigeria for racism in Europe.' This racism was so widely recognized by refugees and NGO volunteers alike that they routinely avoided certain restaurants, cafés and shops where the bigotry was most brazen. It was not so easy, however, to avoid the police.

Back in January 2021, the winter before my visit, Evans texted me to report that he had received surprising news: his asylum interview had suddenly been moved up from the following September to that very week, January 27. We spoke again two days after it. Evans told me that his volunteer lawyer had not been allowed to accompany him, so he'd had to go it alone. 'Fear is the beginning of failure for me, so I tried to contain every atom of fear inside me. But they noticed it and told me to calm down. Once I began speaking, I felt calmer. Then they asked me so many questions that even the interpreter was tired. It was frustrating and exhausting going through the interpreter.'

In the translated interview Evans showed me later, his country is written as the Republic of Congo, not Nigeria, which does make one wonder how skilled – or indifferent – that interpreter was.

'I didn't eat all day, I was too nervous,' Evans went on. 'And the interview lasted six hours! But it went well. They didn't ask me what I went through on my journey, only in Nigeria.

What happened, why I left. They asked about my partner, what did he look like, when did it happen, how did it happen? What happened to me in school and how did I know I was having feelings for the same sex? It wasn't that difficult. I could answer their questions.'

Often in these interviews, LGBTQI+ asylum seekers are asked to prove their sexual identity by answering graphically invasive questions about sexual acts with their partners. 'This kind of humiliation is routine,' Dan told me, which is certainly how such questions feel to the interviewees. But the larger picture is that asylum officials are often intent on ferreting out lies, looking for reasons not to grant people protection, but to reject them.

'Meanwhile, right now, life in the camp is very, very difficult,' Evans went on. 'Everybody fighting, anxious. But there's a proverb, what cannot kill you makes you stronger. So when I wake up, the first thing I do, I walk to the gym. I love our gym here. Or I go running to the beach so I can swim. Then I come back to my tent, wash my dishes, clean up. After that, I don't go out. People fight all the time here and I don't want a fight. So I keep to myself.

'When I first came to the camp and the nightmares started, I cried for two months, just crying, tears and tears. Now I know that all the time I spend crying, it is not really helping. Sometimes I have mood swings and sometimes I don't want to talk to anybody, I just want to be alone and cry, but not compared to last year. There's a little improvement with the help of my psychologist, Katerina, who I see every week, but only with the help of God will I get through this.

'But I cannot stop thinking about what will happen with my decision, my future. It is what we all think about here, all the time.'

Even though it might seem obvious that someone like Evans should easily qualify for asylum as having 'a well-founded fear of being persecuted for . . . membership of a particular social group,' not all governments agree. Some do not consider homosexuality a protected category at all, while others regard the claim with an arbitrary and even capricious range of opinions.[6] Take Greece. 'The more someone has been traumatized, raped or tortured, the more likely it is that their asylum will be rejected here,' Dan told me. 'I see this all the time, to the point where I can predict it. It sounds like the opposite of what should happen, but it's because traumatized people often can't tell their stories consistently. This has been documented for decades, yet the asylum officials don't get it. So they decide the asylum seeker is lying.' Asylum is often denied because the interviewer or immigration judge simply refuses to believe that a woman was raped, for example, or that an applicant is queer.

This is exactly what happened to the Sierra Leonean, York, I mention earlier. York was beaten to unconsciousness when he was caught with his partner at home, the police sentenced his partner to life imprisonment with hard labor – a sentence he is serving to this day – and York barely escaped with his life. Yet his application for asylum was rejected. Twice. 'The asylum people did not believe me,' he said. His case was further harmed by the fact that all his papers proving his story, including the warrant for his arrest, were burned in one of the Samos fires, and the asylum service refused to give him time to replace them.

While Evans awaited his own asylum decision, everyone was talking about the new, closed detention center that was being built in a remote location in the Samian mountains, where some 3,000 refugees would be locked up and kept out of sight. Named Camp Zervou, it was officially called a Closed Controlled Access

Centre and it instilled fear in all who heard of it. Construction was almost finished, at a cost of 38 million euros;[7] local protests had been numerous yet ignored; and transfers to the camp seemed imminent, especially, the rumor ran, for those whose asylum applications had been rejected and for people from Africa.

I went to see Zervou while I was on Samos and there is no way to describe it except to say that it looks like a shiny new concentration camp. Set in a valley between mountains, far out of reach of any village, shop, hospital or NGO office, it is a vast patch of bare earth holding row upon row of white metal shipping containers, squeezed tightly together and surrounded by two layers of six-meter-tall hurricane fences, topped with barbed wire. Nary a tree, shrub or flower is in sight. It is exposed, hot and hideous.

'They are talking about putting families there, children, people whose asylum applications have been rejected,' Dan told me. 'I think it's really going to happen.'

It did. In September 2021, Zervou was opened to great fanfare, EU and Greek officials attending the opening as if it were a gala. Soon the transfers began.

The European Union is the major funder of this camp, giving Greece 155 billion euros to build it and four other such remote, closed camps on the Aegean islands, including one on Lesbos, with the idea of 'better fortifying the EU's borders' – in other words, as a way of locking refugees out of Western Europe.[8] Some money also came from the Internal Security Fund, which funds the management of the EU's external borders, along with further help from the Recovery Fund for pandemic aid.[9]

During a visit to the island of Lesbos to announce the gift of this sum on March 29, 2021, the European Commissioner for Home Affairs, Ylva Johansson, was met with a large crowd of protesters. One sign read: 'No to European Guantánamos. Shame on you, Europe.'[10]

MSF, the International Rescue Committee (IRC) and Amnesty International, along with many other well-known international human rights groups, all vehemently object to Zervou and other similar camps, calling them inhumane and punitive.[11] One of the most egregious aspects of the camps, they point out, is the use of an elaborate new surveillance system named Centaur. From a base in Athens, a closed-circuit system of video monitors tracks the movements of detainees inside. Everyone in the camp must wear an electronic bracelet. Drones hover constantly overhead. Perimeter alarms are festooned with cameras. Gates are controlled with metal detectors and x-ray machines. Nobody is allowed out between 8:00pm and 8:00am. And an automated system for public announcements blasts out of loudspeakers throughout the day. This Orwellian surveillance system cost more than 33 million euros to build.[12]

Greek migration ministers and certain EU politicians claim that these prison camps protect refugees from the dangers they fled to escape – dangers from 'the East,' as one put it[13] – while also providing asylum seekers with more physical comforts than they had in the camps. But, as critics have pointed out, not only is it an absurd twist of logic to claim that imprisoning the victims of persecution and war protects them, but how are fingerprints, electric bracelets, AI and barbed-wire gates going to safeguard people's rights or keep them safe from one another? The new camp offers no special protection or safe spaces for LGBTQI+ refugees or women, for example, but rather locks them away from the legal advice and health care they need.'[14]

On June 9, 2020, MSF released a report testifying that holding people in closed camps like Zervou only exacerbates the traumas they have already suffered as refugees, enhancing depression, breakdowns and suicidal tendencies among adults and children alike.[15] 'This system has inflicted misery on people, put their lives in danger and erodes the right to asylum,' the report declared, going on to quote Iorgos Karagiannis, Head of the MSF Mission in Greece: 'Despite claiming to change for the better, the EU and the Greek government are spending millions of euros to standardize and intensify policies that have already done so much harm.'

By 2022, Zervou was forbidding anyone who had not been issued an *Ausweis* to leave the detention center at all. It had become indistinguishable from a prison.[16]

The fear of being sent to Zervou only intensified Evans' agony over his asylum decision, for he knew a rejection would mean he would either be imprisoned there or deported back to Turkey, where he would face even worse mistreatment than in Greece. By May, four months after his interview, he could stand the wait no longer, so called his volunteer lawyer.

'I asked him to help me find out what my decision was but he said that he cannot help, that his organization is not permitted to check or tell me my decision. I told him, "But I'm disturbed, I'm depressed." He just kept on saying he is not allowed to do it. I got so angry, I hung up the phone on him. My head was filled with stuff! I was just walking around, trying to figure out what to do. I went back to my tent shedding tears, then it came to my mind – why don't you break the rules and just go to the asylum office yourself?

'So I went and asked the lady in charge. I said, please, I need to know if my decision is ready or not. I cannot sleep, I am crying, I need to know! So she said OK and asked for my case number. She went inside and checked. And she told me the decision is ready. But she did not say what it was! So, I asked, but is it positive or negative? That is when she told me it is positive! But I still have to wait for the official paper before I know it is really true.

'The next day, I went to the office and saw my name on the board. I had my open card! Now I could move to the mainland, leave this island. Oh God, I was so happy. I carried the card like an egg.'

Evans' persistence was unusually successful; most people never overcome the bureaucratic barriers in the camp, let alone the petty power plays of its minions.

On May 24, 2021, only a few days after Evans had received this good news, I arrived on Samos to meet him in person for the first time. We arranged to find each other on a Friday morning in the main square on the seafront, which everyone calls Lion Square because of the statue of a lion placed in the middle.

There are always surprises to meeting someone in person after only seeing them in the tiny rectangle of a phone. The first surprise was discovering how tall and long-legged Evans is. The second was how handsome. The third was that he was totally bald! 'I just shaved my head,' he told me with a shy smile. 'My hair, it was too much trouble and I did not like how it looked.'

For most of that afternoon, I accompanied him on what I thought would be a simple errand: opening the bank account and gathering the paperwork he would need to qualify for subsidized housing once he reached the mainland. Instead, our day turned into a nightmarish journey of long queues, bureaucratic hurdles, stubbornness and racism. One man wouldn't let Evans into his phone shop, mumbling about Covid, while he let in white people. Another man at a bank told him to leave and not come back for three months. A woman in a government office shouted at him to go away. Sometimes Evans did leave, but at other times he dealt with this antagonism by resorting to the same sort of begging he had used at the asylum office, which made me squirm, even as I saw that it worked. 'I have no choice,' he said about this more than once, an illustration of what happens to people when a government reduces them to total dependence.

As the next day was Saturday and banks and offices were closed, he suggested that I sneak into the camp with him to see the box he called his tent – the place that had been his home for the past year. Because journalists were still forbidden to enter the official camp, he suggested I disguise myself by carrying a plastic bag and exchanging my summer dress for long trousers and a shirt. 'This way you will look like a refugee, Ma,' he said with a smile, using the Nigerian term of respect for an older woman. I dressed as he suggested and we climbed the hill, taking a back way into the camp and slipping past the police guard booth as nonchalantly as we could.

The camp looked very different than it had on my previous visits because the tents were gone, replaced by box shelters like the ones Beth had shown me, draped in plastic sheeting and tarps, both within and without the camp fences. Like the tents, however, the boxes were so densely packed and numerous that they entirely obscured the white containers I describe earlier. The ground was still bare earth and rocks, intersected by rivulets of stinky green water, and the entire place was just as claustrophobic, buggy and clogged with garbage as ever. We wove down suffocatingly hot and narrow alleyways between these boxes, while I peered in the doorways of one after another, most of which were pitch black inside. A pair of shoes, a tattered piece of carpet, a plastic bag, a bottle of water, the bare feet of a sleeper. It's a wonder everybody hadn't died of Covid under such crowded circumstances. The camp did, in fact, have a fenced-off quarantine area for those who tested positive and their families. Evans pointed out that locking healthy family members in a compound with the infected seemed less than wise, and, indeed, infection rates were two-and-a half to three times higher for people living in island camps than for anyone else.[17] (The first vaccination clinic did not arrive until I was there on this same visit.)

Evans' box was squeezed in at the end of a row of similar boxes, each pressed tightly against its neighbor and sharing a sheet of plastic over its roof, the passageway between them so narrow that if someone opened a door, we could not pass. The boxes were perhaps two meters square and about the same height, most without windows. Evans' box, too, had no windows, no light, very little air, and was black as a tomb inside, even in the bright Greek sun of the day. The warren of boxes put me in mind of the cells of a vast wasps' nest.

The inside of Evans' box, however, was as clean and tidy as Beth's had been, if smaller, with a real wooden bed, its head-board painted the pale pink of a little girl's bedroom. In the back he had placed a small stack of shelves holding condiments and cleaning supplies, a bag for his clothes, a hanging cloth of shoe pockets for other items, his single burner cylinder stove and the small battery-powered lamp he used as his only light. He had no windows for fear of rats and thieves, but he did have the mirror in which he practiced his dancing.

We then slipped through a hole in the fence out of the official camp and into what was still called the Jungle, the unofficial spill of homemade shelters in the surrounding fields. There, he showed me his beloved gym, a jumble of objects spread out over a bare patch of dry earth: A set of barbells made of an iron rod with blocks of rough cement on each end, which had been molded in a bucket. Weights and a chinning bar made of scrap metal. A bench press that seemed to have been expanded out of an old wooden chair. A punching bag made of plastic stuffed with rags. 'We go around the town looking through the rubbish bins for these things,' Evans told me with a rueful smile.

He insisted on taking photographs for me because, he said, there were spies in the camp: people who are paid to inform. 'They won't care if I take pictures but you might get into trouble.' Eyad confirmed that what Evans said was true: there were informers in the camp. Later, Evans sent me seventy-two photographs.

He also showed me the way the camp was divided up between nationalities: the Afghan area here, the Arabs over there, the Iranians on this side, the Nigerians, Congolese and Cameroonians on the other, and so on, each with their own elected representatives. We passed homemade outhouses; the taps attached to rubber hoses where people fetched their water; a home-built mosque in the Afghan area; and a home-made church, which looked like a large rectangular wooden barn with spaces between the top of the walls and roof covered with chicken mesh to let in the air. We peeked inside to see a floor carpeted with rugs, rows of chairs, an altar and a cross, all colorful and cheerful. Evans told me he had much respect for the church's pastor, a fellow African refugee.

As we walked through the alleyways between shelters, small Afghan children played in the dirt by our feet, staring at our masked faces in fascinated alarm, while African men and women greeted us with smiles and introductions. Evans was polite and friendly in turn, but I could see the wariness in him and the determination to keep himself apart that he had described – not surprising, considering how often gay and lesbian refugees are attacked in the camp.

I saw more evidence of this danger when I accompanied him to Alpha Center for the first in-person meeting of the LGBTQI+ support group that had been held since Covid, and witnessed the security precautions Dan and his colleagues had to take. They only accepted members who had referral slips from their psychologists, doctors or social workers, and, once everyone was inside, Dan locked the doors. 'We have to be careful of infiltrators and people who might want to attack,' he explained.

As soon as we arrived, Evans busied himself sweeping the floor and helping to put out juice and cookies, yet even here, where he should have felt safe, he kept apart. For several hours, the twenty-three men and women who had come sat around on couches and in chairs, chatting and playing games to break the ice, the first time most of them had ever participated in such a group, LGBTQI+ support services being outlawed in most of their countries. But Evans stayed far in the back of the room by himself. The one time he spoke was to announce that he had received his positive decision and to thank everyone there for their support and courage.

Later, as he walked me back to my car, he said: 'There are days when I feel like committing suicide or doing something drastic to myself. Then I just stay alone in my tent, crying, crying, crying. Then I sleep. When I wake up, sometimes I feel better. But sometimes the stress continues.'

He broke off suddenly and kissed his ID card. 'Praise God! I'm just so happy about my decision. I just had this memory of crawling along on my hands and knees through the desert. So hungry. I was praying to God. "You didn't abandon Jesus in the desert, please don't abandon me now!"'

A few days later, just after I left Samos, Evans was evacuated to a camp called Serres, north of Thessaloniki, near the Macedonian border. We spoke over the phone a week after he moved. He said his new camp was better, with a concrete bungalow to live in instead of a tent or a box, although he still had to hide who he is day and night, even from his roommate. He also told me that he had found a live-in job on a farm near Athens, but that the bus ticket there cost forty-nine euros.

'Do you have the money?' I asked, knowing full well he did not but hoping he had managed somehow to borrow it.

'No,' he said, 'my money for this month is gone. I have to buy food because there is no food service at this camp.'

No job without the money; no money without the job.

I hesitated, in one of those dilemmas faced by everyone who knows refugees — whether and when to help, and how to do so with tact and respect. As I note earlier, I had long come to the conclusion that reporting on refugees requires a set of ethics that do not fall in line with the usual rules mandating that journalists should never give money or gifts to a source. So I asked Evans if I could send him the money for the bus ticket.

He paused barely a second. 'No thank you, Ma. It is too late for this job, anyway, I have lost it. But I will make it here somehow. With the grace of God, I will make it on my own.'

5

MURSAL

'I'm glad that I am a refugee. It's made me powerful.'

Langar
Khaney-Ye Kalan ■Kabul
Mazar-e-Sharif
Sheberghan *AFGHANISTAN*

Herat

Mashhad

I R A N

*Caspian
Sea*

Tehran

Maku

Tatvan

Kayseri

*Black
Sea* *TURKEY*

Istanbul
Bursa

*Aegean
Sea* *Mediterranean
Sea*
Thessaloniki
Malakasa
Athens
GREECE

Distance: 6,586 km

Mursal in Afghanistan

'I love to help my mom.'

Helen:

The first time Mursal and I saw each other was in Athens on a sunny afternoon in May 2021, not long after Greece had ended its coronavirus lockdown. A friend of Eyad's brother had brought us together, arranging to meet at an outdoor café in Monistraki, a teeming neighborhood in the middle of the city, where our table was nestled against a wall amidst the usual Athens cacophony: people shouting, laughing, smoking, singing, staring, clattering glasses and plates.

We were wearing Covid masks, so all I could see of Mursal's face was a wide forehead, so smooth it was almost shiny; deep brown eyes; and straight brown hair parted in the middle and hanging to her shoulders. Small and slight, dressed neatly in jeans, sneakers and a long-sleeved shirt, with a dashing red leather backpack, she looked both touchingly young – she was twenty-one – and yet ready for anything. Later, when I saw her whole face, I found her brimming with fierce intelligence and quick emotions, her cheeks smooth, mouth wide, expression warm. Above all, Mursal comes across as earnest, serious and deeply sure of herself. She wears no makeup and is not, she told me later in no uncertain terms, interested in boys.

'I hate boys. All my life I hear about boys raping and kidnapping. I stay away from them. My dad tells me do not judge, not all people are the same. But when I hear news of violence against girls, I just hate boys. So I am not interested, no.'

Mursal, her parents and two younger sisters had been in Greece for nineteen months by then, having arrived on October 27, 2019. The family was still awaiting their asylum interviews, scheduled at the time for more than a year from our meeting. They had been pushed out of Afghanistan by the Taliban; a foreshadowing of the persecution the fundamentalists were about to inflict on women and anyone else they didn't like when they seized power only three months after Mursal and I met.

In many ways, Mursal's life has traced both the defeat and rise of the Taliban. She was born on November 25, 1999, two years before the United States invaded Afghanistan in retaliation for the attacks of 9/11, and the Taliban, which had been in power since 1996, lost to the US-backed government in Kabul. While she was growing up, the Taliban continued to wage war against that government, steadily gaining ground. By 2019, when her family fled, the Taliban controlled more territory than it had at any time since 2001,[1] a fact seemingly ignored by the Trump administration when it entered supposed peace negotiations with them in 2020. By June 2021, only a few weeks after President Biden began withdrawing US troops from Afghanistan, the Taliban had gained even more power, and by August it had taken over completely. Now Afghanistan has once again become a country that denies women the right to go to school, work, engage in athletics or public life, or walk outside alone.

Mursal and her two younger sisters, Zuhal and Setayesh, grew up Dari speakers in the fourth-largest city in Afghanistan, Mazar e Sharif, in the northern province of Balkh. During

Mursal's girlhood, the Taliban had mostly stayed away from cities, consolidating their power in rural villages and towns, so Mazar was relatively liberal. These values are clearly reflected in her parents.

'My mom and dad, they are very open-minded,' Mursal told me in her high, gentle voice, her accent in English strong but easy to understand. 'They see boys and girls as equal, as having the same rights. My dad always told me, before you get married, you should stand on your own legs. And my mom said, you should have a job, you should achieve your dreams. After that, you can be married. Because when you marry, you will feel like your hands are tied.'

Mursal readily began her story in that noisy Monistraki café, continuing the next time we met in Athens, and then during our subsequent conversations over WhatsApp. She also sent me more than twenty pages she had written herself in English about her family's grueling journey from Afghanistan to Greece. With her permission, I have integrated some of those pages into her story here.

Mursal speaks English confidently, except for the occasional slip in pronunciation, such as 'nick' for 'neck'. She is mostly serious but has a smile that lights up her face and shows all her youthful optimism. She often looks anxious, though, and acutely aware of everyone around her, as if assessing danger. 'I am a shy girl,' she told me and I could see that, even though she was not shy about telling her story.

I asked her to begin, as I did with everyone in this book, with her childhood. She opened by talking about her parents, whom she clearly adores.

✳ ✳ ✳

I wanted to have a white coat of my own

My dad, he is a doctor. He worked for MSF [Médecins Sans Frontières] for more than two years, but after, because the Taliban did not allow MSF clinics, he opened his own clinic instead. My mom, she was just a home wife, but the duty she did was to support and teach us. This is such a great job, to help us go to school, continue our classes. I am proud of my mom. Even if she isn't a teacher, a lawyer, a doctor, I am proud of her.

My parents want me and my sisters to be educated. Even some of the families who are coming to Europe, they do not allow their daughters to go to school. But even when we were living in our own country, my parents allowed me to study and teach small classes in our home. I taught for free because I feel that if I have a little knowledge, I should share it. If I learn even one word, I want to teach this to my sisters.

The first memory I have is when my mom tried to send me to the school and the administration said, 'She is five years old, she is too young.' But at that age, I was very smart. I told them the numbers, some history, facts. They were surprised. But they still said no. After that, my mom continued teaching me, so as soon as I started school, they put me in second grade because my spelling and my mathematics, everything was too good for first grade! That is such a good memory.

When I was growing up in Afghanistan, my goal was to be a doctor like my dad. When I washed his coat, the white coat, I really wanted one day to have my own coat like that, to have my notes here, my pen there. I wanted to know how it feels to sit in a chair listening to a patient, helping them. But since I came to Greece, I have changed my mind. I see that some refugees are not able to go hospital, not able to see the doctors. Why? Because they don't have insurance. If I am a doctor, how can I support that? But if I am a lawyer, I can fight for them.

I wouldn't like to work in government, though. I don't know if Europe is the same, but in Afghanistan, the government, they never care about people. They never hear when we are shouting our problems. They never provide for our needs.

Even when I was a child, I loved to help my mom. I looked after my little sisters and cousins. And when I came back from school, even though I was too short to wash the dishes, I put a chair by the sink so I could clean everything. I washed the socks of my dad, brushed his shoes, washed our school uniforms. My cousins, my auntie, they told me, 'You won't grow taller if you work so hard.' I ignored them. From a young age, I knew how to cook, wash and clean the house. My mom taught me.

I also played with my cousins. Especially in the summer, we put water in the sun to make it hot because we didn't have a water heater. We washed ourselves, played with the water, washed our uniforms. But we didn't play games. My cousins were too young.

When I was a child, I read books for my courses. We took many courses at school: English, Dari, Arabic, Pashto, math, social studies, science, biology, history, geography, chemistry, religion, housework . . . I didn't have any other books. But I always loved to read my dad's books about anatomy. I would see the pictures and ask, what is this? My dad said, this is the uterus. I see another picture and I ask, what is this? And my dad said, this is the kidney, or this is the vagina. Because it was written in English and Persian – Farsi – it was very difficult for me to understand. So my dad explained. He learned Farsi in university because all the books are in that language.

Outside, we did not do much. Just on Fridays because in Afghanistan we only have one day for the weekend. Then, for two or three hours, I went to my auntie's house. I was so shy I wouldn't eat unless they told me. I just sat there, silent.

On some Fridays, my dad called a taxi and, together with my cousins, we went to a small river to go swimming and have a picnic. The whole day we would be there. Then we would go home and prepare for Saturday and school. After school, we had lunch, put on our hijab and the black dress, and went to the mosque. Not for praying but for learning how to read the Qur'an from the imam.

I loved our first house, where my dad was born and where I was born, too. But it didn't have any windows. I don't know why. We couldn't see the outside. My auntie, my uncle, all of us together in the one house. Just our rooms were separate. I had my own room with my sisters.

The house was my grandfather's and he divided it between his children. Then my dad, he bought the space from him. He built it to have two floors. We had a kitchen, a toilet, a basement, a guest room, our bedrooms and one extra room for storing oil and rice and sweets. My dad's patients would bring sweets and candies, so we had big bags of them in that room. My mom would give the sweets to my cousins, my aunties. She said we cannot eat all these and if we keep them here we will have a mouse!

The house was made of concrete and the outside was not painted, but the inside was. We had carpets, curtains in the doors and also in our kitchen. I was very happy there.

Patients were always knocking on our door at night. Some came for injections or medications. Boys came for circumcision. Even though during the day my dad was busy in the clinic and very tired when he came home, he always had more patients at night. But we had a good life in Mazar e Sharif, a good home. My dad even had a car.

I only accepted girls

When I was sixteen, we had to leave that house because it was too difficult to live there. The walls were always wet – they could never dry out because they were hidden from the sun. We tried to put in a window but the builders said it was impossible. So, my dad sold the house and bought a new one. It had only one floor and a basement.

At first, it was very difficult for me in the new house. It was too quiet. Nobody was living near us. It was in a new housing project and there were only four or five families in each row of houses. Everybody had their own house, some of them had walls, some had dogs to keep safe. We also had a dog because our house was far away from the people and if you went out for a picnic or shopping, anyone could undo the lock and enter.

It was in that house I began to be a teacher. A teacher's job is a such a holy job. I taught mathematics, English and sometimes Pashto. Because my mom was Pashto, she helped me if I didn't know the words. At least two girls came every day to our house to learn because in that area there weren't any good schools. Also, some families did not want to pay extra money for their daughters to learn a special subject. They allowed their sons to take computer or mathematics or English. But not the girls. So I only accepted girls, not boys. I didn't want to teach boys.

Most of the students were friends or classmates of my sister, some were my own classmates or neighbors. Or they knew me because I was always the top student of the school and I helped the teachers. And the parents, they knew we are a good family, so they allowed their girls to come. The girls were between fourteen and eighteen years old, and because I was seventeen I felt shy, like they were my teachers! But they were coming for learning, not to waste their time, so they kept the promise they gave to their parents and studied.

[When Mursal turned eighteen, her family was flung into trouble through no fault of their own, with disastrous results. She chose not to tell this part of her story in order to preserve their privacy and safety, but this trouble, a type of family feud, was so severe that it forced them to leave their home in the city and flee to the northern village of Langar Khaney-Ye Kalan. They did this partly to escape the feud, but also to save Mursal from being forcibly married to a relative. Unfortunately, they soon found out that they had walked into even more trouble.]

These are our children; we don't want them to die

We can never guess what life will give us, what is written in our luck, so we must be ready every moment.

After we had been in the village only a short time, we discovered it was under control of the Taliban. Nobody could go outside after eight o'clock. Anyone who was wearing a suit or jeans, they would be arrested, because the men could only wear *perahan tunban*, the knee-length shirt over baggy trousers. Men also had to wear a hat or turban and have a long beard. Small girls, too, had to wear long shirts over loose trousers, and the older girls and women, we had to wear burqas or *chadri*, which covered our faces as well as our whole bodies.

If we wore jeans and T-shirts, people in the village looked at us as if we had killed someone. So my mum decided that we had to change ourselves and dress the way the people wanted. It was really hard for me and my sisters.

There were two schools in the village and the Taliban only allowed girls to go to one, a very small school, and only if we wore a burqa. Some days we had teachers, some days we had none. They were afraid to come because twice the Taliban said they will bomb the school if the teachers do not close it and leave. But the chief of school would not accept this. He continued to keep the school open.

We didn't have many students, only four or five in each class, because the parents were too afraid to let their daughters come. Most of the families said, 'These are our children; we don't want them to die just for an education!' And it was already not a popular idea that girls should get an education anyway. They would say: 'When you get older, you will get married, so education for girls does not matter.' But my family, they are not like that.

I really wanted to continue my school, even though I was the only student who came to class every day. But I was afraid and so was my mom. She was our security. Every day, she took me and my sisters to school and picked us up again. She was afraid because sometimes the Taliban drove around the school in their car with guns sticking out.

But the school, it was not good. My teacher gave me a book that didn't have all the pages. It was really old. So I tried by myself to continue my education because my goal was still to be a doctor, even in the village.

I never walked alone in that village. I was always with my dogs or my mom. And it was very difficult because only my dad was able to bring us food from the city, vegetables and fruits. There was a shop but my mom and I were afraid to go because of the Taliban. Many days we had nothing for lunch. We only had what my dad brought.

One night my dad was so busy and tired, he forgot to bring us food. We tried to go to get some from the shop but because of the curfew at sunset, the shop closed early. My dad loves us a lot and it was difficult for him to see his children hungry, so he just tried to tell us stories, help us with our homework. I was going to tell my sisters not to complain because our parents are worried and have their own problems, but even before I said this, my sisters told me, 'Tell us if you're hungry, please don't say this to my mom, she will be sad.' I was surprised. I am older but they were telling this wisdom to me!

We had many bad moments in that village. We were still alive but we felt that this is not a life. Some nights the Taliban drove a car into our driveway and sat there shooting and shouting, telling us that they are coming to get us. They wanted to make us afraid of them all the time.

They attacked people a lot. This happened to my teacher. A Taliban fighter came to the school and seized her by the scarf and said, 'If you are here tomorrow, we will come and cut your throat.' We were all in the class and he looked at us and said, 'If I see her here tomorrow, I will do the same to you!' I told this to my mom and after that, I never went to the school again.

This was the second month we were in the village.

The Taliban also beat people who were teachers, lawyers – they would beat them in the street. They said: 'Why are you doing this? You should be in the mosque. You should not work for the government.' They made the name of Islam bad.

If you search about Afghanistan before, like twenty-five or thirty years ago, you'll see that the ladies were working, they wore skirts, and they were together with men in the same classes. Some were wearing the scarf, some of them no. They wore makeup, their legs were free. Maybe it was because of the government then, I don't know, but it wasn't terrible like this.

It was much better for us in Mazar. When we closed the door of our house, we did not lock it. But in the village our door was always locked and still we were afraid.

I will shoot you and your whole family

Because the Taliban knew that my dad was a doctor, every time one of their fighters was injured, they asked him to perform surgery for them or provide medication. Twice, when we were first in the village, he helped them because he did not know yet they were Taliban. Then, when he saw them coming back with more men who had been injured or shot by the police, he understood and told them: 'This is not for me. I cannot do this.'

They said, 'If you do not do this, we will shoot you and your whole family.'

My dad answered, 'I don't want to work with you.' So they beat him badly with a gun.

My grandmother, my mom's mother, she was also there. She spoke in Pashto with the Taliban, begging them to please stop. So they beat my grandmother, also – an old lady!

When my mother saw them beating her mother, she tried to stop them. So they beat my mom. They slapped me and my sister, too. But my grandmother, they beat a lot. She was so injured we took her to hospital. But she had heart problems and the beating was so bad she could not live. My mother lost her mother this way. Right in front of her eyes.

My mom was in shock after that. She didn't know what she was doing. And my dad was also injured because they beat him so much. For one week, he was not able to walk.

After they beat us all and they made my grandmother die, we knew they could do whatever they wanted. We knew we would always be afraid.

Three times we told the police about the Taliban and how they'd asked my dad to help them with their injuries. The police just said: 'You should prove it. You should have some videos and pictures.' But how can you take a picture of the Taliban? They will shoot you that second. It was a joke that the police said this.

We had been in the village for four months when my parents decided to leave. To stay alive, but also for the future of my sisters and me because the rules of our culture would not let us be who we wanted.

We left in the middle of the night. The date was August 29, 2019. First, we went to our auntie's house in Mazar e Sharif. After that, we said goodbye to Afghanistan, we will not be part of this type of violence anymore.

The day we left, my mom said: 'I feel like maybe Europe is not very far. God willing, we will get there on both feet.'

MURSAL IN FLIGHT:
AFGHANISTAN – IRAN –
TURKEY – THESSALONIKI

'I HAD TO BUY SHOES TWO SIZES
BIGGER THAN NORMAL.'

Helen:

The second time I saw Mursal in Athens, on Saturday, May 22, we met near her family's home in the residential neighborhood of Peristeri. We talked in a little park up a pretty hill of grass, flowers and trees, where a restaurant appropriately called The Treehouse Café sits overlooking the city view. Mursal did not seem comfortable in the café, however, which was full of Greeks, nor did she want so much as a glass of water. So we moved down the hill to a bench.

That day, Mursal was wearing blue jeans, a black-and-white checked cowboy-style shirt, red sneakers and her red backpack. Again, she wore no makeup or jewelry.

Several times as she talked, her eyes filled with tears, sometimes over terrible memories, as when the Taliban had attacked her grandmother, but more often when she was recalling the kindness of others. What clearly moved her the most, though, was her love of her family.

Mursal resumed her story, beginning with the day her family embarked upon the first leg of their two-month journey to Greece: the long and dangerous drive from Mazar e Sharif to the Iranian border.

* * *

Sitting there like sheep

When we left my aunt's house in the night, around four o'clock, we had no clothes packed or anything, just our backpacks from school. My dad had some identification documents, and we had my mom's medications and some milk and biscuits for Setayesh, who was only eight, but nothing else. In that moment we were just crying, we didn't care what we packed. The dress I wore, it was the long dress from the village. In the middle of the journey, I tore it shorter with my nails because we were walking in mountains and I couldn't walk in a long skirt. On our feet we had only sandals.

The nearest city to the Iranian border is in Herat province, yet going to Herat meant we had to travel through Taliban territory. This is why we older girls – Zuhal was thirteen then and I was nineteen – had to wear a hijab or *chadri*. If the Taliban spotted us without, they would flog us. So we covered our faces and hands.

We took a taxi for three hours until we arrived in Sheberghan. There, we bought water and biscuits, and searched for another taxi to continue our trip. My dad kept asking taxi drivers, '*Salaam*, brother, are you free? We want to go to Herat.' Most were too afraid to go, but finally, one driver accepted.

From Sheberghan, we entered the Dawlat Abad, which made us all afraid because the Taliban there often stops cars and buses. Fortunately, we passed through without any problems. After arriving, we rode a bus for nine hours and then a taxi for many more hours until we arrived in the city of Herat.

In Herat, we found a playground and sat there to wait for the smuggler my dad had hired to come or call. We did not know if he would come or when. We were so tired.

After an hour, the smuggler called and said he would come in ten minutes. We waited thirty minutes until, finally, we saw a van stop. A man got out, looked around nervously and said: 'Are you ready? Hurry up before someone sees us!' We got in the van and drove for about two hours to the border.

There, the man again stopped the van and said, 'I must wait till the checkpoint is cleared.' Someone called him and he drove at such a high speed we begged him to please drive slowly. But he didn't care! He continued speeding while my dad hugged little Setayesh and my mom hugged Zuhal. My eyes stayed fixed on the street until the van stopped. I was praying not to have an accident and to stay alive. By the time we arrived at the border of Iran, my hands were cold and I could not speak for fear.

There, we faced another hurdle: the police. The only time we could cross was during the night when it was dark and the police could not see clearly. If they saw us, they would deport and flog us.

We slept two nights on the ground, about fifteen minutes' walk away from the border. The border was on top of a mountain and so were the police. We were hidden at the bottom. Everyone was nervous. More than fifty or sixty families were just sitting there like sheep.

The second night there was a strong rain. We saw that all the police were inside their rooms, so we counted one, two, three, and a lot of people ran up the mountain and across the border. The police arrested some, but those who could walk fast or run managed to cross. We did not.

The police at the border will shoot anybody. They will shoot in the air. But sometimes, if they tell you to stop and you do not, they will shoot your arms or legs. They don't care.

We waited until the next night, when a person came and told us to get ready to move. When I heard this, my hands and legs shook so hard I felt I could not walk.

Everyone prepared to move and those who had children gave them sleeping syrup. When the smuggler said, 'Move!' some people ran and some, like us, walked fast. Some left their backpacks so they could walk faster. The single boys helped by carrying bags or children, and we managed to run across the border into Iran. But when we crossed that border and left Afghanistan, our home, I had a feeling like when you lose one of the most lovely members of your family. It was really the worst feeling.

The police will not allow even one fly to cross

After we crossed into Iran – this was August 31, 2019 – we walked up the mountains all night. Because of the dark, you don't know where you are. You don't have anything to eat. You don't know where you will sleep. And I was injured. I don't have experience walking in the mountains and I was in sandals, so I fell, got up and walked, fell again, hurting my knee on the stones. Little Setayesh took my hand and said, 'You will be fine, just try to continue, otherwise the police will come and stop us!' That moment I realized that having a family and a sister is a blessing.

I had to carry Setayesh some of the way because she was so tired and her stomach was in pain. Setayesh had a hernia operation two years before but some of the stitches had come undone, so her stomach hurt through our entire journey. Can you imagine how brave she is, my little sister? Eight years old and suffering pain but still walking and walking.

It was such a hard journey. My mom couldn't walk too fast or far because she has heart problems. She had also gained weight and was a little fat, so it was very difficult. My dad carried my mom and I tried to help my two sisters.

I prayed to God to make this day finished, this journey. I really wanted a room to sleep. When we continued, we again heard the sound of shooting. We were so tired.

We walked from morning till noon before we saw the place where the smugglers said they would meet us. Lots of cars passed but finally a truck approached slowly and stopped. We were afraid. Would he know we were refugees and call the police? But it was the smuggler, who was just waiting for the streets to empty enough so that it would be safe to come close. 'Hurry before someone sees you!' he said, so we climbed in with about thirty-five people. 'Now be silent, especially those with kids,' he told us.

We rode in the truck for four hours until we reached the city of Mashhad. There, the smuggler stopped at a park. Everyone climbed out and we all washed our faces and hands, and then sat in the park to wait for how long, we did not know. The sky was getting dark but I do not know what time it was because our phone batteries had run down.

After we waited a long time, two cars with new smugglers pulled up. The first smugglers chose only single boys, and the second one the families. We got in the cars and moved on again.

This time, we drove all night until next afternoon. The drive is almost ten hours if you don't have to stop. But most of the way, when the driver neared a checkpoint, he would change his direction and take another road. We spent the whole day like this till we arrived in Tehran, the capital of Iran.

In Tehran, a smuggler picked us up and drove us to a place in the north called Maku, close to the Turkish border. This was another drive that took all day – we were so tired and hungry and thirsty by then. We reached Maku on September 3, 2019. From there, we had no choice but to follow the smugglers on foot to the border.

The Maku mountains between Iran and Turkey are very hard to pass. At night it was completely dark and there were huge rocks in the way. We had no flashlights, no water, no food. We had to walk for four hours before we could find any water. If we wanted something to eat, we had to go to a village. All this time, the smugglers had food and water, but they never gave us anything.

Some people were lucky and crossed the border in only one night. Others, like us, were slower, so had to try again and again.

The first time we walked about twelve hours. Some of the children and women got sick. There were pregnant women with us, children even smaller than my sisters, families with babies. The smuggler brought some medication and told us: 'Give the children this so they will not talk or cry, only sleep. If they cry, the police will arrest us. Now, keep going and don't talk.'

The smuggler kept telling us to walk faster and faster. But we had no food, everyone was tired, we had no energy. When I said I was hungry to my mom, she just smiled and said, 'This will pass.' Her smile was such food for me. So, I shared that smile with my sisters and I, too, told them: 'This will pass. In just one or two hours, we will be in the city.' Because they were very young, they accepted our words, even though we were telling lies. It was difficult enough for me and I was an adult, so I thought how much more difficult it was for them.

All the time, I was afraid that the police would arrest and deport us. If they deported us, the Taliban would arrest my dad, I would be forced to marry and so would my mom.

After a few hours in the Maku mountains, my mom couldn't walk anymore. The path was teeny and steep and winding, right on the edge of the mountain. If we fell, we would die. We paid to borrow a horse for my mom but the horse jumped over a rock and she fell off. She was in pain, she couldn't breathe, couldn't move her arm. Some guys came and checked her legs and arms to see if they were broken. After she felt better, we just went slowly, sat for ten minutes or so to rest, then continued.

That night the Iranian police arrested us and told us to go back. They had a lamp and pointed it down the path and said: 'We do not have a problem with you. Why are you scared of us? We work with only single men and smugglers, not with families. Go back to where you came from. We will never let you cross the border.'

We walked all the way back until morning. The painful part is that every time you try to walk to the border and get caught, you become totally exhausted and lose your hope.

Again, we stayed in Maku, waiting for the smuggler, because you can't go alone or you would get lost.

For a whole week we tried many times to pass over the border with no success because the police of Turkey, they never allow even one fly to cross. We found some big tombs to hide behind, where the police couldn't see us. Some nights we heard the shout of a wolf. I was afraid. Sometimes I think we only survived because maybe before we did some good deed for somebody.

The only water we had to drink was from a small river between the two big mountains around us. It didn't seem clean but we had to drink it. If it made us sick, we never noticed because all we could think about was crossing the border. Coughing, fever, it was nothing to us. If my sisters were coughing, I told them it will pass. All we had to eat were the biscuits my mom brought from home. They got wet in the rain, so she put them out in the sun to dry. When I saw that, I cried over how my mom took care of us with the smallest things she had. Maybe it's not only my family, but a lot of families who experience these kinds of things.

Many fathers were worried about their daughters on that journey because there were men there who used that moment to rape. All night my dad stayed awake to watch over us. We didn't know who was sleeping near us – they touch your back, your legs, your bottom. You cannot do that! You should stop because all of us have the same problems and all of us just wish to pass the border.

[Numerous refugees have taken this treacherous walk over the Iranian mountains under even worse conditions. York, the young Sierra Leonean I mention in the Evans chapter, walked over those mountains for twenty-three days through the snow, dressed in nothing but sneakers and summer clothes. 'I didn't know how to dress for that weather,' he told me. 'In Sierra Leone, we just dress for the summer all year. I was cold and wet and, oh, my feet were frozen! Some people lost their fingers to frostbite. They had to cut their fingers away. There were babies there who died, women who were pregnant. If people got tired, we left them there. Everyone was on his own. If you got caught by the police, the smugglers would run away.' On that same trip, York, who was then Mursal's age, was robbed by smugglers of all his money and belongings, and orally raped by three of them. 'The smugglers raped men and women often. I saw it. The only way we could protect ourselves was to huddle tight together.' The fathers in Mursal's group had reason to worry.]

Maybe a wolf ate them

The second time we walked to the Turkish border, fifty or more people were also trying to cross, so the smuggler divided us into teams, the older adults in one and single persons in the other. The smugglers said the single boys should cross first, so if the police arrest them, we will have the chance to allow the next group to pass while the police are busy with the first group. Then he told us to hurry, saying this is a good time to cross because it is raining, there is lightning, the police will stay inside their cars and you will not come across any wolves.

We started to walk up the mountain again. My parents said: 'We cannot go faster, so you should go ahead with your sisters and follow everyone else. If you lose the people, you will not find the way.'

I said, 'How can I leave you?' But they told me, 'We are coming, do not worry, but we cannot walk as fast as you.'

I took the hands of my sisters and continued along the path. Then I felt that my mom was not behind me anymore. I looked back but could not see her or my dad! I could not decide whether to continue my way or to go back to find them. The other people were telling us, 'Come on, girls, hurry!' But I could only think, 'If I go back and cannot find my parents, where should we go, where should we stay?'

I asked the smuggler, where is my mom, my dad? He said: 'Maybe they crossed the border. Maybe a wolf ate them. This is not my responsibility.'

I didn't know what to do. I just cried. My sisters asked me, 'Where are our parents?' I didn't have an answer. Were they alive? Had they crossed? Or had the police shot them? There were lots of negative thoughts in my mind. Should I continue? If I do, I might die, or I might find my parents. Or maybe if I go on, I will be able to make a good life for my sisters. Only God knows.

Finally, I decided to continue because I would be completely lost in the mountains if I went back to look for my parents. We had to stay with the other people for safety, so we went on.

We were very close to the border when the police caught us again. I was scared because if they asked where my family was, I could not have answered. Luckily, they did not. They just sent us back the way we had come. At that moment I wondered how I would pass the night alone among all these people from different countries and cities. But I told my sisters: 'Do not worry. I am with you and we will find our parents.'

We spent four days without our parents and those four days were the darkest of my life. It was the first time that we were far away from them – I wish for no one to ever have to go through this!

We met another family who gave us hope by saying, 'You will pass the border and see your parents because, as you cannot find them, they must have crossed over already.'

I said to my sisters, 'We will be with our parents and this dark moment will come to an end.' But, after they fell asleep, I cried. I could not imagine what to do if we stayed without our parents forever. I knew I had to stay positive, however, because if you think positive thoughts, they will happen.

I am a man

While we were sleeping without my parents at the border, there were lots of men looking at my thirteen-year-old sister and me, trying misbehavior with us. I didn't care. I felt at that moment that I am a man, not a girl. When they called to me, 'Hey, come here,' I told them, 'No, I will never go with you.' When they shouted at me, I shouted back because I thought if something happened to me, if these men do rape me, it will be nothing for me because I lost my family.

In the middle of the way, some boys touched me, my hands, my leg. In that moment, I wanted to slap them in the face. But I realized if we start fighting, what will we gain? Nothing. So I told one of the boys: 'You don't have a sister? You don't have mothers? You don't have cousins?' I asked him if this kind of thing happened to your sister, what would you do? He said he would shoot the man doing this. I said, 'Then you should shoot yourself because you're doing this to me.'

There was a family there from Kabul and they said: 'Come with us. We know you because we spent one week with you. We see how you carry your sister, how strong you are. Don't feel weak, we are together.'

The third time we went to the border, we walked for six hours until it got dark. Again we had windy weather, rain, but we just walked and walked. I helped lots of ladies carry their bags. And some of the good men, they carried the bags of my sisters. One man said: 'Your sister looks like my own sister. I don't have any bad intentions, I promise. I'm a good man.' He showed me a picture of his wife. 'I am like your brother. Please give your bag to me. I know you are without food, without anything. I know that you don't have much energy to carry a lot. So let me help.'

So I made friends like that and received lots of love from them. That gave me hope.

After it was dark, we walked for fifteen more hours. We passed the Iranian border but not the Turkish border – we were in between. When we were close to Turkey, the Turkish police stopped and arrested us *again*, and told us, 'Go back.' So we had to walk all the way back to Maku.

By this time, I had worn through two pairs of sandals and a pair of shoes. I had blisters all over my feet and my knees were red and purple from falling and scraping them. My feet swelled so much from all the walking that I had to buy shoes two sizes bigger than normal.

Setayesh also was in pain. All the walking had opened the wound from her surgery even more. When you walk a lot, you sweat, and the sweat dripped into her wound and stung.

In Maku, the smuggler came and gave us some tomatoes and a loaf of bread, and then left for his home. We waited until the next day in a tent full of sheep because it was raining. So many people were in there with us that some had to sit or stand all night. But at least we were dry.

The next night, the smuggler brought us to the border again. But this time we walked for twenty-four hours! Everyone needed water but the smuggler only kept saying, 'Walk faster!' We did not have the energy to go faster but he didn't care. We knew the way he was taking us was dangerous, yet we had no choice but to keep going. It was raining and very dark, so we couldn't see the path and everyone began to lose hope. But after crossing over a tough, dangerous mountain, we finally made it across the border.

After four tries, I was in Turkey at last. But without my mom and dad.

I felt like I was flying

I do not know the date when we entered Turkey but all the families were running around, they were so happy. Everybody was going their own way but I didn't know what to do, where to go. Then I saw an old man. I didn't realize it was my dad. In only two weeks, the stress had turned his hair white.

When he saw me, he ran over, picked me up and cried. That was the first time I ever saw him cry. I had never seen any man cry, but especially not my dad because he is always laughing, he always has a smile on his face.

My mom was sleeping, but when she opened her eyes and saw my sisters and me, she cried out and ran and hugged us.

For four days, my mom and dad had searched for us in the woods while they stayed in a mountain hut with only dogs and sheep for company and nothing at all to eat. My mom said: 'Your dad had only thoughts for you. Whether you ate something or not. If anyone hurt or bothered you. Whether you felt cold. How did you sleep.'

At that moment, I felt that even if Europe didn't give me anything, it didn't matter because family is the most important. Without my parents I am nothing. Each refugee will learn something new in their journey. I learned how important family is. So I promised my mom: 'If you grow tired, if you say that you cannot continue our journey, I will stay with you. We should never leave a member of our family alone again.'

Now that I had my parents back, I felt like I was in paradise, that I was flying in the sky. I forgot my pain, my hunger, everything. And I couldn't control my crying. My dad said, 'Please stop, now we are together.' I said, 'My crying is from happiness.'

After that, slowly, slowly we continued walking. When my mom said she was too tired, we sat until she felt better. We would not continue alone. For me, family is a great gift that God has given to us. If now I am alive, if I never give up, this is because of my family, because of their support and love.

We walked for two hours until we saw the other families sitting on the ground, waiting for the smuggler again. When he came, he packed fifty of us into a small van, but everybody was happy because we had survived a very dangerous journey. Nobody complained, even though the windows were closed to hide us from the police. He said he would take us to Istanbul.

For more than eight hours we drove in that van. It was suffocating. When we got out, our legs were asleep. We couldn't walk. We couldn't stand. The smuggler shooed us out and said, 'Go find your way yourself.' But we were not in Istanbul.

We walked aimlessly for miles. We sat down a few times, then got up to walk again until we had no more energy to move. In front of us stretched only one long road. Sometimes we stopped cars and asked them for a ride but they only said, 'You are refugees. If we take you, the police will arrest us because they will think we are smugglers.'

We walked for fourteen hours.

Finally, we saw a small village. We thought maybe we could find food, water and shelter from the hot sun there. As we were searching, some villagers told us that we had reached Tatvan. [Tatvan is actually a city in eastern Turkey. I suspect Mursal's family had reached the outskirts and mistaken it for a village.] There, some people came over and asked us how we were doing. Here were people who love refugees, so we are grateful to the people of Tatvan. They gave us tomatoes, cucumbers, bread. After we finished our food, they said goodbye and again we walked until we met the next smuggler, who took us in a van to the city of Kayseri. [A drive of 759 kilometers.] The smugglers kept changing but they all knew our names. They worked together from Afghanistan, all the way to Turkey and then Greece.

In Kayseri, we slept by the side of the road until morning, when the police came and told us to go into the bus terminal. But the security guard would not allow us inside. We went back out and the police again said, 'I told you to go inside.' We went back and forth like this until some taxi drivers got permission to let us stay near the taxi stand. They brought us their own money, blankets, tomatoes, cheese and bread, and made us breakfast and tea.

We stayed outside until the afternoon. The taxi drivers tried to get bus tickets for us but the ticket seller would not let them have any because we were refugees. Finally, the smuggler came and put us into a truck with no window. The truck was worse than the van. It felt like stones were pressing into my bottom, into my back. We were squashed in there like sheep.

Nine hours later, we arrived in Istanbul. We knew no one, so we stayed in the street. But then we met a man who said, 'I have a hostel if you would like to stay with me.' This was in a neighborhood where there were a lot of Afghan people and shops. We ended up staying there for September and October because it took six trips to the coast before we succeeded in crossing the sea to Greece.

Burning our hope

The first time we tried to reach the sea, we had an accident. We were in a small van at night and it was raining. The van reached a police checkpoint, so the smuggler sped up and raced through it. Two police cars chased us. It was like a movie. We were rocking back and forth in the van, falling from side to side. We had no windows, everyone was calling to God, crying, 'We are too young to die!' The car swerved and slammed into a tree. The driver ran away. Some of us hit our heads and crashed into each other. Two people were badly injured.

Some men tried to kick the door open but couldn't. We were trapped! But then the police came and opened the door and took the injured to the hospital in an ambulance. They drove the rest of us to Istanbul and left us there. It was traffic police, so they didn't arrest us.

The second time, everyone was scared because of the accident. This time, the van reached the coast and we stayed in the forest there for four or maybe eight days – none of us can remember. Some nights we made a small fire to keep warm. It rained every evening and we had no blankets or jackets to cover ourselves. Our clothes were wet all night and morning, so we had to stand in the sun when it came out to dry them. As in the Iranian forest, we had no water or food. The children were crying and asking their mothers: 'When can we eat? Where are we? Why can't we go home?'

Their parents tried to comfort them by saying: 'This is a very famous park. Everyone has come here to see this park.' But their children didn't believe them. Can you imagine, all those days without food? How did we survive?

We faced all these problems but never lost sight of our goal. If we truly wanted to make it to Greece, we believed we would.

Then the Turkish police found and arrested us. We were so scared but the police said, 'We are not interested in you, only the smugglers.' The police brought us to a deportation camp, asked our names, gave us a piece of paper, and said, 'If you give us 100 Turkish lira for petrol, a driver will take you to Bursa.' If we did not pay them, they would have never let us go. So everyone paid. People who had no money borrowed it from others. We had to get out because the place they put us in was like a prison. The room had no windows and there were forty or fifty people in there. The children could not tolerate staying in a small room with so many people.

After giving our money to the police, they drove us for five hours to the Bursa bus terminal, but no one would sell us a ticket to Istanbul. They told us: 'You came here illegally. If the police see us selling you tickets, they will arrest us.'

We waited for two days outside the terminal. Finally, a smuggler came and, once again, we were put in a small van without a window and driven for hours. Inside, we tried to move our heads and focus so we would not be sick or faint. One of the Afghan guys had a key and he tried to make a hole in the ceiling with it so we could breathe. But at that moment our car stopped at a checkpoint. We were arrested again and turned back to the camp, where we had to pay the police again so we could go.

Four more times we went to the forest to try to reach the boat. Once, we had a second accident. The driver took us right near the sea and then lost control of his brakes. We jumped out right on the edge of the water. Some of us were cut and bleeding, so we tore up shirts and made bandages with them.

Another time it took nine hours to drive to the forest. After that, we walked for more than two hours before we reached the sea. We slept under the trees, thinking no one will come this way, even the police, because the paths were so dangerous with snakes and wild animals. The next day we woke up and waited for the smuggler. The weather turned cloudy and it rained. After a long time, the smuggler came and said: 'You cannot go because the sea is too rough. You must wait until tomorrow night.'

All of us were too wet and cold to sleep. Everyone got a fever, especially the children. We put our bags on the ground but only the children managed to sleep on top of them. The adults stood or sat all night.

The next day, the Turkish police caught us again and brought us back to the same camp we were in before. So we were back where we had been before we had taken that long walk!

Sometimes, the smuggler would call to say, 'Come, we have a boat for you.' But when we got there, the police had damaged it. Twice we were already in a boat when the police arrested us. Every time, they took us to that camp and made us pay them again to be able to leave. Every time, it cost up to 240 euros.

Also, each time we tried, we bought lifejackets for the boat. And each time the police made a fire and burned them in front of our eyes. You buy the lifejackets with hope, so it feels like they are burning our hope – like they are burning us.

You are alive

After we waited two more weeks in the Istanbul hostel, we again left for the forest. This time, we had so little money left we did not want to buy lifejackets yet again. And we were so tired. My mom said: 'We don't want to go. Again, the police will arrest us. Again, they will make a fire in front of our eyes.' So, the last time, we didn't buy anything. If we fall in the water, we decided, we will just die.

We stayed in the forest for six days. Some families began fighting each other because some boys annoyed the girls. People said: 'Please stop. We faced six days of cold weather, rain and also hunger together, so please calm down.' After five minutes, their fight finished.

When we finally saw the boat, we felt happy but also frightened. What if we drowned or were caught by the police again? The smuggler put us in and said, 'Choose someone to drive.' Then he left. But we never lost our hope. All the families just said, 'We will all pass through this.' And their smiles gave us energy.

There were twenty-one of us in the boat, including the children. The island we were trying to reach was just forty-five minutes away but it took four hours to get there. We felt fear because for some of us, this was the first time we had ever been on a boat. And what happened in the middle of the night? The petrol ran out! All we could do was pray. The batteries of all our phones were finished so we could not call anyone. We didn't know what time it was, where to go.

Then one of the refugee boys on the boat, he found he still had some charge in his phone after all. He said, 'I know the number of the police, 119' – something like that – 'Does anyone speak English?' I said I do, so he gave the phone to me. The number was for the Turkish police but when I called, it was picked up by the Greek police. We were very surprised.

The man who answered couldn't speak English. He just said, '*Parakalo*,' which means both 'please' and 'may I help you?' in Greek, but I didn't know the meaning of that then. I just knew it was not Turkish. Meanwhile, everybody was crying, especially the children. I think the policeman realized that we were in a boat because he asked if anybody there spoke English. Only I could, but at that moment, I forgot it! He said, 'Where are you?' I could only say: 'There is water. It is dark.' I forgot to say we are in the sea, in a boat. But he understood. He said, 'Turn on your lights so we can find you.' So I turned the phone light on my face to make a big light so he could see us.

After forty-five minutes, a ship came and took us on board. They dropped our boat in the sea and told the families with lifejackets to put them in the trash. Then they said: 'Sit here and don't worry. You are alive.'

Mursal in Greece

'In the middle of two governments, refugees are burning.'

Helen:

When I first began researching this book in 2018, Mursal was still a schoolgirl living happily in Afghanistan. By the time we met only a short three years later, she was supporting her family alone in Athens as an interpreter for her father's old workplace, MSF. Because her father cannot speak English or Greek, and because he had not yet received the necessary papers, he could not use his skills as a doctor or find work.

On June 15, 2021, only three weeks after Mursal and I met, the Greek Minister of Migration, Notis Mitarakis, made a shocking announcement: all new arrivals from Afghanistan, Syria, Somalia, Pakistan and India would be denied the chance to apply for asylum in Greece and sent to Turkey instead, which Mitarakis deemed a 'safe third country', parroting the same language that had been used in the 2016 EU-Turkey deal and that he had reiterated in 2019. If Turkey continued to refuse to accept these asylum seekers, as it had been doing since March 2020, the new arrivals would be held in detention centers until Turkey opened its doors, although when that might happen nobody could say.[2] In the kind of doublespeak immigration officials are using ever more often these days, Mitarakis insisted that this policy was not a violation of international law because the asylum seekers, 'are not in danger because of their religion, their nationality, their political opinions, or inclusion in a social group.'

Mitarakis's declaration was met with outrage by MSF and forty human rights organizations, who countered that by no stretch of the imagination was Turkey any more safe for asylum seekers than it had ever been, and that Greece was indeed violating international law, not only by denying people the right to request asylum, but by holding asylum seekers in prisons and by trying to send them to a country where they would be at risk of refoulement and exploitation.[3] Every one of these actions is explicitly forbidden by the Refugee Convention.

Meanwhile, the EU was busily planning to hand over 4.2 billion dollars more to Turkey to take back refugees from Greece.[4]

All this terrified Mursal. 'Turkey is no different for us than Afghanistan,' she told me. 'The Taliban can find us easily there. We can only be safe here.' And then she added the mantra that every refugee feels or speaks at some point: 'I just hope we can make the asylum office believe us.'

She then returned to the story of what happened to her family once they arrived in Greece.

❊   ❊   ❊

I felt like somebody was crushing my neck

After our boat arrived – this was October 27, 2019 – the police came and took us to a big room like a warehouse. We were in the north, near Thessaloniki, so we never landed on an island, only the mainland. The first morning, translators asked us about our language, names, ages and so on. 'You will stay here two nights and after that you must decide whether you want to go to Thessaloniki or Athens,' they said. They also did a checkup – our shoes, clothes, hair, everything.

My mom and sister were still suffering but there was no Dari translator there, only Farsi. I used Google Translate to explain that my mother has heart problems and my sister was in pain because of her hernia surgery. They told us we can go to hospital when we get to Athens. We didn't know how difficult that would be.

After that, they brought us to a camp named Fylakio, where we stayed for one day.[5] They said, 'If you go to Athens, every camp will accept you.' But we did not know how to get to Athens. People told us, 'Go to the train station and ask.' We tried to find a station but when we asked people directions, some of them walked away. Why?

We finally found the station with the help of one lady, but there was no train until the next day, so we waited there all night. We could not sleep because the station was outside and it was raining.

The next day, we took the train at noon. The ticket was fifty euros! We had to pay, we had no choice. After twenty-four hours of waiting in the station and then sitting on the train, we arrived in Athens. I asked the ticket checker if there was a camp or any place we could go. He said he has no English, just go. But he said that in English! You should be proud to help somebody, even a refugee. But he would not help.

We left the station. There were six families with us, all Afghan. One person called a relative in Athens, who told him we should all go to Victoria Park. But we did not know where that is. We were hoping that this relative might come and invite us to his home so we could have a shower, some food, change our clothes.

We kept asking people the way to the park. We saw some drunk Greeks laughing at us. They were drunk but they were cleaner than us.

From the train station to Victoria Park, it is just maybe ten or fifteen minutes, but we spent three hours finding it because we kept going in the wrong direction. I asked one person. They said go right. I asked another person. They said go left. Maybe they were telling me lies.

Finally we found the park. We saw a lot of Afghans there, so we thought, 'This place is like our own country.' But it was different, too. The relative came to speak with his family but he said his house was from an organization and he didn't have the right to bring us all there. Anyway, he only had two rooms. He said sorry and promised to bring us pillows and blankets and something to eat. We said, 'Do not feel bad, it's not your responsibility.'

While we were sitting in the park, some people put money in front of us. We were not there for money, we were there to find a place to stay. People gave us half-eaten food or empty bottles of water. Some spat at us. That made me feel like somebody was crushing my neck. I had such a bad feeling in my heart. I felt like the forest, the jungle, the mountains, they were better than that park.

That night it rained and we got so wet. It was early November by then, and cold. During the night, some drunk men came and stood right in front of us. We woke up and my sisters cried: 'Mom, please take us away from this place. It is not safe.'

Another Afghan family also told us, 'Don't sleep here because after midnight there will be fighting and drinking.' So we found a church and slept there on the steps until we were woken by the sound of voices. When we opened our eyes, we saw all these people looking at us. 'Why you are asleep here?' they said. 'Go away! Our morning has started!'

Every day, we searched for a camp with no luck. We had to sleep in the park for three days in cold weather without blankets. The next day, do you know what happened? A man came up to us and gave us food but he also wanted us to change our religion. Another day, we found people from Iran. They said we can support you, come with us. When we got to the place, it was a place of Jesus and they also said you should accept our religion. Everyone who spoke to us wanted us to change our religion! I find this unbelievable. You pass through a very difficult, dangerous trip, and they only want to help you if you will change your religion? The people doing this were not Greek. Some were Chinese, some Spanish. They even had their own translators.

After a few days, we found an Afghan shop and the man there said there is a camp but it is far and hard to find, you need internet or somebody who can show you the way. He told us about organizations that might help, too. We went to find them but no one helped us. Only one was left: KHORA.[6]

When I called KHORA, a very kind lady said, 'Hello?' and I felt lots of love with just that hello from her. She said you can come here, where are you now? I told her in Victoria. She said it is not far and told me how to use the GPS map.

After walking with the six other families for one hour, we found it. Two ladies there, Ruby and Ruth, welcomed us and explained how to make an appointment for an interview so we could collect the card for refugees that will allow us to get help. They told us about a place that will give us free lunch, another place that would give free coffee with biscuits in the morning and free wi-fi. They said they were sorry they could not give us accommodation, even though it was raining and cold outside.

But it was such a good feeling: we enter a building, they bring us a cup of tea, and even though we are refugees, they look at us in such a good way. This is everything for us.

Two days later, at the place that gives free lunch, a man said: 'You look Afghan. Why are you sitting here?' He did not know we were new. He said he knew a place we could go, the camp where he lives, Malakasa. [A camp forty kilometers north of Athens, surrounded by woods.] He paid for the train tickets there himself for all of us six families. He is such a kind person.

Sorry, we cannot help you

Together with all six families, we went to Malakasa, and as soon as we got off the train, a lady said hello in our language. 'How are you? Here are some books for you.' When I opened the book, it was about Jesus! Again, they did not want to help us, they just wanted us to do something for them.

When we entered the camp, some families told us to find an empty tent to stay in. We wanted to speak to the IOM staff but it was Friday afternoon and everyone was leaving for the weekend. We had to wait till Monday.

We found a tent, but when the weather turned cold that night, the tent did not protect us and soon a rainstorm soaked us all. Setayesh cried until the morning because she was in more pain than ever and sick, but we could do nothing to help her and could find no nurse until Monday. Some families brought blankets for my sister because she was shaking from fever, and for my mom, who was also sick.

The next day, Saturday, my dad heard there was an organization at the camp that cooks hot food, so he and I went to stand in the line. It is called FoodKind. The food was rice with salad. We ate but saved some of the food for that night in plastic containers. We did the same the next day. But some nights we had no food left.

The camp was made of lots of tents and also containers and some rooms. Only Arab and Afghan people were in the camp but every night there was fighting and men falling on top of our tent.

On Monday, we went to the IOM office, where they told us to go to the doctors' containers. But the doctors did not have the facilities to help us. They said: 'You need to go to a hospital but you cannot because you do not have ID or AMKA [health insurance] cards. So we can only send you to a clinic.'

We asked if we could register at the camp. They said, 'But we never requested that you come, who told you about our camp?' They said you can go to FoodKind for lunch but we cannot give you breakfast or dinner, shelter or any other help.

When my mom heard this, she fell down in a faint. Some nurses came to check her blood pressure and said it was very low. They also said her heart sounded weak and she needed rest. The staff of IOM helped carry her to the tent.

Early the next morning, my mom woke up saying she was very hungry and thirsty. I searched around. Everybody was asleep and I didn't want to awaken the other families to ask about water. The bathroom had no tap water that I could find. I told my mom the system of the bathroom, it is very modern, I cannot turn the water on. I didn't tell her there is no water. I didn't want to upset her.

After two hours, a nurse came to check on my mom. She brought bananas, water, two apples and a packet of biscuits. She put the food down outside our tent and said, please receive this. When I opened the tent, I saw it was the nurse from yesterday. She said: 'This is for your mom because I know she needs to eat something. Give this salty biscuit to her because her blood pressure is really low and this will help. Sorry I cannot do something more.' She also gave us painkillers to help my mom relax.

When my mom opened her eyes and saw everything in front of her, she was happy. 'How did you find this?' she asked me. I told her an angel brought it to us. Then I told her about the nurse.

The next day, the manager of the camp came, so we asked if he could give us a container and tell us how to find a doctor. He said: 'Everybody has the same problems as you. There are more than 3,000 people here. We cannot promise to help you. Just wait.'

We spent two weeks in the tent. Then my dad went to the camp mosque, where he met some men from our city in Afghanistan, who gave him food, blankets and jackets for us. They also told him there is a container that was in a fire, but if we wanted to clean it, we could use it – at least it has a bathroom.

Early the next morning, we went to the container and cleaned everything. One room was totally burned a dark black. It had a very bad smell. We closed the door of that room. The other room was half burned, as well, but it was better than a tent.

For one month, we slept in that container. The oven and heat did not work because they were burned, so we were very cold. Each month, the staff of IOM went around the camp counting how many families were left. They didn't know we lived in this burned container until they saw some clothes I had washed and hung outside to dry. They said: 'Why are you here? It's dangerous for your health!'

We answered that when we went to your office, you said you could not do anything for us, so this was our choice.

They had nothing more to tell us. They just said, 'As soon as possible you should leave this container, it's very dangerous. You're not allowed to stay here.'

But we stayed.

[FoodKind published a report in 2019 on Malakasa camp, which described exactly the predicament of Mursal and her family. Because they had arrived on the mainland instead of passing through an island reception camp, they were officially unregistered and so could be denied food, housing or any legal help. As a result, the report concluded, such people 'are now stuck in limbo in Greece with very few options'.[7]

In the meantime, Mursal's sister and mother were growing increasingly sick. Mursal told me more about this when we talked in Athens.]

A lady who loves refugees

This whole time, we kept trying to find a hospital for my mom and Setayesh, but they all turned us away because we did not have ID or AMKA cards. If someone is very ill, would you let him or her die because they do not have a card? It takes six or eight months to get these cards in Greece. Without them, you are left to just tolerate the pain.

Finally, I asked Ruby, the nice lady I met at KHORA, if she knew somewhere that could help my sister. Ruby became my new friend in Greece. She is very kind, a lady who loves refugees and wants to help us. She brought Setayesh to hospital and, after the checkup, the doctor said, 'She needs surgery.' But then again, 'We cannot help you without your card.' So Ruby pretended Setayesh was her sister and paid for the surgery. On February 9, 2020, my sister's surgery was finally completed.

Now, Setayesh does not cry anymore because her pain has stopped. She just wants to go outside and play with other children. She is only ten years old but she is very strong. She crossed borders even with the pain she suffered. She waited four months for her surgery. I'm sure if someone else had to go through this experience, they could not stand it.

My wish comes true

We lived in the burned container for two months, until IOM finally gave us a new, clean one. But my mom was still not feeling well. After visiting several clinics, she asked the doctors: 'Why is my belly so big and why do I feel like snakes are moving inside me? Am I pregnant or do I have cancer?' Before in our country, she would often go for two months before she saw her period, and she didn't have any classic symptoms of pregnancy, no vomiting, headache, nothing, so she didn't think anything of it. But now she wondered.

The doctor gave her a pregnancy test and it was negative. So he said, 'No, you have a uterine problem and stomach gas.' Although they have advanced medical machines, they were unable to detect what was wrong. I don't know why. Were they too shy to check up on refugees, or are we unclean for them? They clearly don't care about us.

For the next four months, my mother's belly grew bigger and bigger. She also had a lot of pain, so she went back to the camp doctor yet again.

This doctor, a woman, touched her and listened to her belly and said, 'I can hear the sound of a baby's heartbeat.' Without any machines, just by hearing and touching, she knew. 'Madam, you are pregnant.' For me, this is a good doctor.

My mom was so surprised! So was my dad. By then she'd had two negative tests, and also, we had gone to several clinics but nobody said anything about it.

We were all so happy! Finally, a good thing had happened to us. A newborn baby was waiting to come into our life!

Some weeks later, the doctor said because your mom has a heart problem, she has to go to another hospital called Alexandra. So she went there.

On March 5, 2020, a cute baby was born – my brother, Bilal. He endured a lot of problems inside of my mom's womb, crossing borders, climbing mountains. But now he is safe. My wish has always been to have a brother who loves me. Now I have him. And, although he is a baby now, one day he will support me and take care of his sisters.

After my mother gave birth, the doctors said it is not allowed for me to see her because they had just found out about the coronavirus. My mother said, 'I will not eat unless you let my daughter in!' So, the doctors let me in. I was not allowed to hug her, but it was such a good moment for me.

Baby Bilal, welcome to our life!

Always my dad was shiny

While we were living in the Malakasa camp, I found a school called Happy Caravan. This school was amazing and our teachers were so kind. They love refugees. I was so happy to find good people and a place to study. The school was not big but their love was everything for us. The first day, they gave us a notebook, a pencil, a folder. A student needs no more than this.

We had classes in English, mathematics, drawing. We watched movies to help our English – everyone wanted to learn new words. I found out that all those years I was learning English in Afghanistan, I was pronouncing it wrong! My teachers didn't know about silent letters, how to say the vowels, because none of them had ever lived in an English-speaking country. Now I am trying to speak better.

In December 2019, I began working with Happy Caravan as a Farsi interpreter. I learned Farsi not in school but from TV. And then, at the camp, everyone spoke only Farsi. When Happy Caravan asked my parents to allow me to work with them and said they would give me a salary, my dad said, 'We don't care about salary, we just want our daughter to be happy and busy.'

My dad, he was also happy in the camp. He went to the mosque to pray. He went for walks with his friends, he went jogging, he played football. He attended English classes. He helped with people who were injured.

Now, though, here in Athens, it's very difficult for him. He tries to wash plates and dishes like a woman because he doesn't want to do nothing. He's tired. He is totally changed. At home, when I opened my eyes, he was all dressed, prepared to go to his clinic. Six o'clock he left the house and when he came back, it was eleven at night. Some nights I didn't see him at all because we went to sleep early to be ready for school. When we opened our eyes in the morning, maybe he just kissed our faces as he left. And always my dad was really shiny. Just a smile and a laugh. He never thought about stress, he just made everybody happy. Most of the people who came to my dad's clinic, they said that they could not afford the pills, the injections, so he gave money to help them. Even though he had too many patients and he couldn't make enough money, he didn't care.

Now my dad just wants to make us happy. When I come home from work, he makes me a glass of lemon juice. He says, because it's sunny, you should drink more water. Do you need a massage, do you have a headache? I say no. He says why are you sad? I say, I'm not sad, this is just my mood. Always on the weekend, he says, let's go to the park, let's go for a walk. Always you're working, you will be getting stressed, don't pressure yourself.

A new life

Only after three months did they finally register us in the camp. That was when we got our *Ausweis* cards. But we had to live at Malakasa for nine months. When my brother was born, we were still there. We applied for accommodation but they said we must wait.

One day, I was in the container making lunch when the phone rang. I answered and the person asked for my parents. I told them my parents were not there, so they said they would call back. I didn't know who they were.

My dad came back from the mosque and, when they called, they said, 'We are Caritas.[8] [A Christian NGO that offers help to refugees and the homeless.] Your application was successful. Are you all together? Nobody in your family is in another country or camp?' My dad said, no, we are all together. They asked our ages, names. And then they said: 'Your apartment is in Peristeri in Athens, it is on the first floor, it has two rooms, one bathroom, one kitchen, a small balcony. If you accept, you can take it tomorrow. We will pick you up at 8:30 tomorrow morning.'

That night we packed and I went to say goodbye to my friends at Happy Caravan. Everybody was shocked. Some cried and said we will miss you. But they were happy for me and wished me success in starting a new life.

The next morning, July 29, 2020, the bus took us to the apartment. I was so happy to see it. We are not on the first floor but the third, it had been a mistake in translation. There was no lift, so we carried our things up the stairs. Now my sisters and I sleep with my brother in one room, my parents in the other. Only my mom has a bed. The rest of us have mattresses.

I am the only person in the family working. My parents are very proud of me. First, I worked for one month in a factory that made macaroons. But they would not allow me to work there wearing the headscarf. In Greek culture, they said, you should take it off. My dad said, 'You can take off your hijab if you want, it doesn't matter because your religion, it is in your heart.' When my dad told me this advice, I thought this is true.

But in the beginning, it was very difficult for me not to wear a hijab. I felt like I didn't have any clothes on, like everybody was looking at me. And I felt maybe I lost something. Then I got used to it. Also, I thought, without a scarf, maybe I would make more friends with the Greek people, get on better with them, be more in their culture. I was wrong. They still look at me as a refugee. I am proud of this name, but they still insult and hate us. People say rude things to me in the street. Because my skin is brown, they ask: 'Where are you from? Pakistan? India? Because you don't look as if you are from Afghanistan.' I ask them, 'Have you been there? Do you know how many languages we have, how many different kinds of people?' No, they do not. They just want to judge us.

In shops, in the train, I hear people being rude a lot. Asking us why we don't go home, why we are here. Once I entered a train with my mom and baby brother without tickets because we didn't have time to buy any before we got on. I offered the ticket taker the money. He threw my money on the ground, then told me to pick it up and give it to him. He wanted to humiliate me.

The job I have now is interpreting with MSF in Farsi and Dari and Urdu. I learned Urdu from watching Bollywood movies! Now my Urdu is better than my English and I am learning to write it. My mom also speaks Urdu and my dad understands a lot. At first at work, they did not believe I learned Urdu from the movies, so they tested me. But I proved it.

At MSF, they say if I want to wear a scarf to work, it is my decision. But if we decide on something, we should stand by our decision. Right? So I say no, I will not change. I am too busy thinking about my future.

✳   ✳   ✳

Helen:
While Mursal and I were speaking during May and early June 2021, her family was still enduring the two-year wait for their asylum interviews. Meanwhile, even though, by Greek and international law, both her younger sisters should have been in school, every time the family tried to enroll them, they met with an obstacle. The girls didn't have the right vaccinations. Or, if they did, the school was full. Or they needed another medical report. Or the school was still full, so they would have to wait until August 2021 to enroll for the next autumn. 'My sisters are fifteen and ten now and they have missed two years of school!' Mursal told me in distress.

Then, suddenly, on June 23, she received startling news. She texted me this message:

'Today the asylum-seekers' office, they called me and said your interview is on Wednesday! I am just shocked! I spoke with our social worker, she said best of luck. But how to do the interview I don't know, honestly! Since she called us about this my appetite is gone!'

This was the interview to determine whether Mursal and her family could be sent back to Turkey. 'If it was safe for us in Turkey, why would we sleep in the forest?' she asked me rhetorically. 'Why would we try six times to take a dangerous boat across the sea? All this is politics between governments. But in the middle of these governments, refugees burn.'

She then sent me this essay and gave me permission to include part of it here.

❊　　❊　　❊

Do you know about refugees' dreams?

If our country was at peace, we would never leave. No one wishes to live in a tent or a camp. Everyone loves their home.

Unfortunately, the Taliban came to our city and started fighting. Right before we left our country, we waited for the new year to come, but our new year opened with war and the sound of bombs, not with balloons. That night we had no dinner, only tears.

We come here to Europe because we hope to give our children a good life and a future. We want to wake up to the sound of clocks, not bombs. We want to sleep without fear. We want to hear only the sounds of our family's laughter.

We sold our home and everything we owned. Now we do not have anything. I hope one day we can find someone who loves and supports us, who will talk with us, not hate us.

My dream is every refugee's dream. I want to go to university and, after that, to work in the day and write in the night. I want to become a lawyer and solve refugee problems, and a writer to share the voice of refugees through my writing. Also, I want to establish a school for refugees, whether they have ID cards or not. I hope to open this school soon and invite those who helped me when I was in a bad situation to help with this, too. *Inshallah*, everything is possible.

It is not easy to talk about what I passed through. It is not easy to remember such painful times. But I want to tell everyone around the world: if you do not like us, it is OK. Not everyone is the same. If you want to insult us, we will not stoop to your level. But if you help and support us, we can show you our humanity and our character.

Refugees are not bad people. Please stop hating us. Just put yourself in our place. How would you feel if you were insulted every day on the bus? Would you be patient? If you look, you will see we are like you.

Some people see refugees as homeless, nameless, unclean, uneducated and criminal. Yes, we are homeless but not hopeless! We are nameless but not weak! If we are unclean, it is because we slept in the forest, streets and tents, but we have clean hearts. If our crime is speaking up for our rights and freedom, yes, we are criminals.

Please stop racism! Why do we have racism? If our skin, face, religion, language are not the same as yours, this is because God made us like this! So who are we to judge and make fun of others? Being different makes us beautiful. I will do my best to stop racism but I cannot control your mind. Only you can do that.

If you do not want to see any refugees or migrants, fine, but please do not insult us. Sometimes only one word or action from you can make us feel as if our whole life is a jail. My mom always tells me, 'Just calling someone a donkey does not make them a donkey.' Calling us bad and unclean does not make us bad and unclean.

Being a refugee means you are strong. You passed through a difficult, dangerous journey and, still, you are alive. You have hope. You have goals and dreams.

As my mom also says, 'When you find yourself in a bad situation, just remember this: after every dark night, a beautiful morning will come.'

6

CALVIN

'If you see me laughing, it is because I am just hoping the future will be better.'

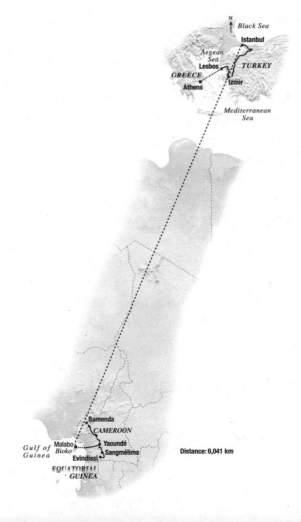

Calvin in Cameroon

'You have to learn to work hard.'

'When I was a little child and I awoke in the morning, everything around me was darkness and water. The dew is heavy in the equatorial forest where I lived, as is the night, the trees so tall they shut out the sky. And everywhere there are animals.

'I was afraid of the night and the animals. It would be dark by five o'clock and still dark when we woke up at seven. I would lie awake listening to all the noises, my eyes wide open in fear. Only when I could see light did I feel safe.

'I think it is a custom in my country, although I am not sure, but in my family we believe that when you are young, if you walk first along a path in front of everybody else and your clothes get wet from the dew, you will grow. So, every morning, after Father woke us up to make a prayer, my brothers forced me, the last born in the family, to be the first to walk along the path to fetch the water or take the animals from the traps, so the dew would make me grow. This is my strongest memory from childhood.'

❖   ❖   ❖

CALVIN IN CAMEROON

Helen:

Calvin told me this in April 2020, when he was sharing two rooms with some thirty other people in Athens, mattresses spread all over the floor and only one toilet for everyone. Even though we were in the initial wave of the coronavirus pandemic, miraculously nobody had fallen sick. 'Still, this is worse than anything I saw in Africa,' he told me over video phone, shaking his head.

A bass-voiced Cameroonian of thirty-six, with a long, thin face, high cheekbones and a bald head, Calvin comes across as cheerful and stoic, smiling frequently under his thin mustache, exposing a missing front tooth. It was knocked out by police officers during one of the many bouts of prison and torture he had endured, first in Cameroon for protesting the notoriously corrupt government of President Paul Biya, and then later in both Turkey and Greece.

Biya was first elected in 1982, and even though a Cameroonian president is only supposed to serve two seven-year terms, he has managed to hold onto power for forty years, thanks to a constitutional amendment he pushed through parliament in 2008. When his rivals protested, Biya had them imprisoned. 'It is as if President Trump imprisoned Joe Biden,' Calvin told me before the US election of 2020. He explained that anyone who challenges Biya, even ordinary protesters, is likely to be arrested, beaten and thrown into prison, often never to be seen again. Biya's current term will expire in 2025, by which time he will be ninety-two. He is, by all accounts, planning to stay in power.[1]

Calvin grew up far away from these political troubles, deep in the forest of south-central Cameroon. His school was taught in French, but at home he spoke a mix of the traditional language of Bulu and what he calls *Francam-Anglais*, a mélange of French, English and invented local words. 'I am of the Fang people, those who live in the forest,' he explained in a mixture of French and the English he had been learning in Greece. 'There are many languages among the Fang, but Bulu speakers can understand each other even if we are from different countries.' The Bulu people make up about a third of Cameroon's Fang population.

Cameroon, like all the countries of Africa, has a long history of colonization. The original inhabitants are thought to have been the Bakas, or pygmies, who, Calvin said, still live in the forest where he grew up. The Portuguese arrived in the 1500s, trading in human beings and goods off the northern coast, and bringing in malaria while they were at it, which, for a time, kept the rest of Europe at bay. During the late 1770s and early 1800s, the Fulani, one of the largest ethnic groups in West Africa, conquered most of Cameroon, displacing or subjugating the local people and installing Islam.

Once the malaria suppressant quinine was brought to Cameroon in the late 1870s, Christian missionaries soon followed, maintaining a presence to this day, probably the origins of why Calvin grew up Protestant. The northern slave trade was ended by the mid-1800s, and by 1884, most of Cameroon had been colonized by Germany, which called it Kamerun and eventually named Yaoundé the capital city, as it remains.

After World War One, the colony was divided up yet again, this time between Britain and France under the June 28, 1919 League of Nations mandate. France took the largest hunk of land, while Britain seized the heavily populated strip bordering Nigeria from the sea to Lake Chad. This set the stage for the civil war between the Francophone majority and Anglophone minority that has killed many hundreds of thousands of people and continues to rage today. Calvin was not much touched by this, although many Cameroonian refugees in Greece were, but his protests against Biya's corruption almost got him killed.

When I first met Calvin, he was suffering from nightmares and terrifying memories of his tortures and imprisonments, which often kept him from sleep. For help with this trauma, he traveled whenever he could from Ritsona, his refugee camp on the outskirts of Athens, into the city to see a psychologist at MSF – no Greek doctor would help him. It was while he was on one of these visits that the pandemic lockdown hit, trapping him in that overcrowded apartment.

Over the months, he and I talked whenever he could find free wi-fi, sometimes in an Athens park or that apartment, sometimes outside his container at Camp Ritsona, while children climbed all over his back, giggling. Once he had to interrupt our conversation to stop the children from teasing a dog. 'They are torturing that poor creature.' He said that telling his story was like therapy for him and that he enjoyed it, so, even though our connection was often barely audible, we persisted.

'My dream is to become a famous writer,' he told me once, enunciating his English carefully through his rolling Rs and French vowels. 'I love reading, especially novels. For now, I like to read in English because I am learning it. The way English people think isn't the same as the way French people think. We can have the same ideas but we don't express them the same.

'I am writing now. A collection of stories and a long movie. But I am writing it on my phone. I am not complaining but it is very slow to write on a phone. People ask me, why are you always on your phone, not making calls but typing, typing? They think I am crazy. But it helps me forget a lot of bad memories and angry stories.

'I do not want to write about my life, though. Maybe I am still embarrassed to talk about it. I need time to recover first. It is easier to tell you.'

❧   ❧   ❧

If you have bread, you are rich

My father was a catechist in a small Protestant church. He was paid no salary but he and my mother made a living with our farm. He was very strict and made us work hard harvesting cacao from our trees, but he cared about us and made sure we always had food on our table, no matter how difficult it was to provide. He also tried as much as possible to give us the best education he could with little money. He taught us the gospel and the ways of God.

After I fetched the water in the morning, we would have breakfast. My mother did not cook in the mornings, we ate leftovers from what she made the night before. The typical food was cassava leaf, pounded and mixed with cacao. This is a famous dish in my area: *le légume sans sel.* We mash the cassava leaves with a mortar and pestle, boil it with palm-nut sauce and eat it with cassava tuber. Cassava is essential for our nutrition. You can also kill animals and add the meat to the soup.

We did not have bread with breakfast, the way they do here in Greece. To me, if you have bread with breakfast, you are rich! Bread was reserved only for a special day like Christmas.

I miss my country now. You always miss where you grew up, no matter how bad the government might be. I do not know if I will ever see it again. Or if I will see my mother and father alive again, because they are old. And I miss my sister, Virginie, whom I love, and her children. I miss them all.

My family lived in the village of Evindissi, in the midst of enormous trees and plants. Because we were so deep in the forest, we had to build our houses close to the roots or around the tree trunks. To farm is very difficult in such terrain. You have to work hard to clear out even a little area – that is why we could not have cows. You have to cut trees, pull out the stumps, dig out roots, fertilize the ground with ashes, cinders. We grew cacao, cassava, agave, plantain, banana, macabo tubers, tomato, beans, pineapple.

Our farm was maybe six kilometers from home, a long walk through the forest. You cannot farm near the village because if your livestock escapes and destroys a neighbor's vegetables, he will complain to the chief and there will be trouble. Because of this, we had two houses, one in the village and one by the farm, where we could sleep for a few nights or a week when we were harvesting cacao. That was not really a house, just a shelter made of sticks, with a roof of woven raffia. It only had one room. And, because there were animals, we would make a big fire to burn all night to keep them away. We built the shelter in a clear area to avoid falling trees and branches. When there were strong winds and rains, we would rush into the shelter to stay safe. That killed a lot of people in my area, the dead trees and branches falling down from the sky.

We had many animals in the forest. Porcupines, bongo antelopes, palm rats, hares, giant forest hogs, black panthers. The panthers were the most dangerous. They would come into the village and attack sheep, wound people. We also had monkeys and gorillas. I saw the little monkeys a lot, but the gorillas stayed away from humans. People would cover themselves with leaves to hide their smell so they could get close to them.

The animals I was most afraid of, though, were the snakes. We had green snakes that were extremely poisonous and fast. We had black serpents. Vipers – those are slow and do not attack easily, but when they do, they are highly venomous. We also had a snake with two heads – that one liked to enter your house.

There was a little squirrel in the forest that made a noise whenever a snake was near. And *les hirondelles*, the swallows, they would always start their calls at six in the evening exactly. If you are working and you hear it, you know it is time to stop and go home. In one stream on the way to our farm, we always found parrots. Some guys in the village, they made traps to catch them. They used to sell them to a white man who was building roads in the nearby town of Sangmélima.

In the village, our home was made of wood and brown clay. The frame was constructed of wooden poles built in a crisscross pattern and filled in with mud mixed with mortar. Once you have money, you can plaster the walls and make the house look nice. Only in my region can you see this type of house. In French, we call it *maison à terre battues*.

Our villages are built alongside the road and each village has one chief. The village has a big house reserved for the men, which is plastered to look nice. And we build a kitchen house for the women. The kitchen has a living room, bedrooms, so the family and guests can sleep there, and an area to keep food. Near the big kitchen, we have a small kitchen for cooking with firewood – because of the smoke, we don't mix the buildings. We have a separate area for the toilets far away because of the odor.

My mum never allowed boys to go to the kitchen. She would say if you go into the kitchen, you will never get married. This is why I never learned to cook! But I am learning now. The other day I made spaghetti with potatoes and sardines. It is hard to find fresh ingredients here by the camp, and expensive, but when I do, I can make a good meal.

My mum did most of the farm work but we children helped. We were seven; four brothers, three sisters. But now we are six because one of my brothers was killed by people in the family. I cannot talk about that story . . . it is still too painful for me. But he died in 1988, when I was four.

Father worked on the farm from time to time, but not always. Women work harder than men on the farms, especially in my area. The men just sit around drinking palm wine. Father was also often busy with the activities in the parish, which was nine kilometers from our village. Sometimes he used to stay there for weeks.

As a boy, I was shy and quiet. If I was given something to do, though, I would do it efficiently. I tried not to complain. You cannot complain or your parents will punish you.

Father did not allow us to have friends, so I was by myself a lot, but I had friends sometimes. I found ways. I would pretend to fetch water or wood, for example, so I could go play football. Father would not allow us to play in case we hurt ourselves and could not work – he would beat us if he found out. We played barefoot because our parents didn't have money to buy us football shoes – we mostly only wore normal shoes on Sunday to go to church and we did not want to ruin them. But it meant that if I hurt my foot during the match, I could never tell Father because he would ask me how it happened. I also played football at school. It was the only sport we had. I liked school. I wanted to learn.

My mum was very kind to me, very patient. I had a good time with her when I was young, she was never violent to me. The side of me that never gives up, that keeps trying, that is my mum.

Her name is Paulina. She was very pretty. I cannot see her clearly very young but I have seen pictures. She had really long hair, no makeup, everything was natural. My sister used to treat her hair with black palm kernel oil and braid it with black string until she looked like an African queen. They do not do that style anymore, I think.

My mother was black, darker than me. When you don't use artificial oil, your color is a true black color. But my father's mother was like an albino with white hair, even when she was young, so my father has a light color, especially in his feet. He was tall, my mother was average. I am 1.75 meters, so I am average, too.

It has been a really, really long since I saw my mother. When I was in Sangmélima, we talked on the phone. But when I started to have problems with the government, I stopped speaking to her because she would always ask so many questions and I did not want to stress her. Now, we never talk because she lives in the village where there is no telephone. She must walk a long way through the forest to another village to use a phone. And she is really old now, seventy-eight.

My father is still alive also, but he cannot move. He is very sick. The last time I spoke to him, he was in hospital and I was in Turkey.

The only time I saw my family happy

My best memory of childhood is Christmas.

We had no electricity – we used a storm lamp on ordinary days and a bigger oil lamp on Christmas Day and New Year's. So, when Father told us to go clean the big lamp, we knew it was a special day.

Every Christmas when I was young, Father would make us happy by killing a pig, and everybody in the family would come to feast with us. We raised the pigs ourselves, but there were also wild boar in the forest. People would hunt them with bows and arrows.

Before Father could kill the pig, we children had to catch it. Pigs are very stubborn and catching them was not easy! You hook a piece of cassava on wire as bait, then tie the wire to a long stick. When the pig tries to eat it, you trap the leg – *pas facile*! Father would say, 'If you cannot catch it, we will have nothing to give to people to eat.'

Once we caught the pig, we would call my uncle to come and kill it. He was a butcher and knew exactly how to cut it up. He would always reserve one part for him, then give us the back part with the tail. We cooked the whole pig and ate it over five days because there was nothing like refrigerators to keep it fresh. But for Christmas we also cooked chicken, fish, antelope or any bushmeat we had. And we would wear new or clean clothes.

When I was around four or five years old, a lot of people would gather for the Christmas meal. It seemed like a big party to me, a festival. That was the only time I saw my family happy.

[Calvin smiled here, his thin face lighting up. He had shaved his head recently, which made the black mustache curving above his lips more prominent.]

But after, there were too many problems for that to happen. My father's mother had twelve children – well, she lost three or four but twelve were alive. And they would all come for Christmas. But after she died, they quarreled and it stopped.

I was only with my parents when I was young and when we celebrated Christmas together. After we children grew a little, we all went to different homes. You do that a lot in Africa. When you are poor, you cannot support all your children, so you send them to other people who can take care of them.

Father wanted me to have a good education and to learn to repair cars so I could always make a living. And I wanted to study. I started in primary school but, because we were many in my family, he could not afford to keep paying for my studies. So when I was eleven or twelve, he sent me to his older brother, who lived in Sangmélima. I was born on April 15, 1984, so this was in the 1990s. He wanted my uncle to give me a better chance because he had more money than we did. I never lived with my parents again.

You cannot complain

My uncle and aunty treated me very badly. They made me work like an adult all the time. Every day I had to clean the house and the kitchen, run errands, wash their clothes. My aunty made me go to the market before I went to school. I was supposed to go with other children, but she made me go alone after the chores, so I was always late, which got me into trouble. And often my uncle and aunty, they would not give me food, saying I had not cleaned well enough. They never treated their own children like that, only me. When it was time to eat, I would have to eat last and my aunty always gave me less food than she gave to her children. If the food wasn't enough, she would leave me to starve. One day my uncle accused me of stealing his money when it was his son who stole it. My uncle beat me that day. And he was not teaching me anything.

I told my father that I did not want to stay with my uncle anymore. When you are young, you expect people to see you as a child, but my uncle treated me as if I was not human. But my father only said, 'You have to do it, it is good for you. You have to learn to work hard. Do not compare yourself with his children because you are not them.' He could not see how bad it was. When he visited me they acted as if they were giving me so much love. But as soon as he left they would get hard again. And if Father brought me something to eat when he came, my uncle took it away as soon as he left. Anything I was given they would take away.

Because my uncle was cruel, I ran away when I was fifteen. I left his house by myself and took a bus for three hours to Yaoundé to look for a job.

They will not allow children to dream

In Africa, no matter how much a member of your family does wrong, you cannot do anything about it. So I told no one my plans. My uncle and aunt looked for me, they sent a message to my village asking for me, but I waited for months before I told anyone where I was. It was only when I made some money a long time later that I wrote to Mum and Daddy telling them why I ran from my uncle's house and that I was in Yaoundé. I did not inform them before because they would just say again that I shouldn't expect my uncle and aunt to treat me like their children. That always made me feel very bad.

Yaoundé is a big city compared to Sangmélima, so when I arrived on the bus, I decided to stay in the bus station, where there are people. I tried to make money by carrying bags for passengers, helping the drivers pack bags in a car. Families would come with a lot of food, plantains, sacks of goods, so I helped pack those. I also washed cars.

My first week, I slept in the station. It was always busy because the bus station had shops selling alcohol all night. I knew it was dangerous there but I was focused on making my future in the big city, not on the danger. I talked to people in the bus station, told them I was homeless but willing to work. It was rough but I was thinking, 'Better this than my uncle's house.' I knew I never wanted to be treated like that again.

I think now that maybe my uncle helped me grow up early, to become a man very young. But the bad side is I could not go to school, so I missed the good education I was supposed to have. When you are young you learn every day, you absorb so much. I wanted to have that, to grow up normally. I wanted to become a teacher of languages and stories. If I had a good education, I would like to teach writing, poetry and storytelling. But it did not happen.

I was scared to tell people about my dreams, though, because in my country people will not allow children to dream because conditions are so difficult. They will say, 'My friend, you are dreaming, you will not make it, you do not even have education.' So I kept my dreams secret.

The bus station was a very, very tough environment. When a passenger arrived, you had to race the other guys to carry the bags. It was very aggressive. Some people would fight over their customers. I always tried to keep myself apart from that but when I was a newcomer many times older guys slapped me away. Because I was the youngest, sometimes passengers chose me to carry their luggage and that would make the others jealous and angry. They would try to frighten me, saying they do not want to see me around, it is their area. Some men forced me to give them money or buy them food so that they would give me the freedom to work.

People were also smoking marijuana and there were always drunks in the station. There were some sexual predators, too. If you get hooked on marijuana or something, they would force you to have sex with them. And some people want to pay for you, buy you. When I was new at the bus station some men tried to do that with me, but other people defended me. Also, to keep myself safe, I avoided going to the areas where those guys were smoking or drinking and taking drugs. And I always looked for an older person to protect me. I am always friendly to people and that makes them want to help me.

I made very little money, although some passengers would give me money or food. It was difficult but God told me to do my best.

After about a week, I made friends with some other boys and we got a room together. We crowded in . . . it was like a ghetto, very bad. Any time, people can come to rob you. You just go there to sleep, and early in the morning you go to work. I would work from early till nine or ten in the evening. Sometimes I worked at night and slept during the day because there was more space when the other guys were working. Later, I changed flats a couple of time, looking for a cheap room to rent where it was not so easy to be robbed.

In the station, I made friends with several drivers. Some people working with drivers try to steal their money but I never did that, so they loved me. The one who helped me the most was called . . . it will come to me . . . ah, Monnaie. In English it means money. I met him four to six months after I arrived at the bus station, and when he saw how willing I was to work, he protected me. He was like my godfather. Once people knew I worked with him, they left me alone.

When I worked with Monnaie, my schedule depended on him. When you find a driver like that, you stick with him. You wash his car, guard it, help with the passengers' luggage. Eventually, he will give you a jacket to mark you as working for him. Monnaie told me he would teach me how to drive if I worked well with him. At that time in Cameroon, if you were a driver, you were a big man. You could take pride in your life. Getting a car in Cameroon is harder than getting a job.

Monnaie would give me his keys and that is how I learned to drive – without a license. I was seventeen or so by then. If a driver was not feeling well, he might hire me to drive for two hours and then let me keep a portion of the money I made. If I did that well, he would recommend me to other owners of cars. I also continued to carry bags for passengers.

I worked for Monnaie for many years without a license. With a bribe, I could always get the police to leave me alone. They told me, 'You are a very good driver but you need a license.' I was twenty-three or twenty-four when I finally got it.

Once I made some money driving, I found a little room only for me. It was not too bad – I could close my door. It was not in a family home, just a building of rooms.

After that, I got a job driving for a company, taking the boss places, carrying his bags. Then I began doing the same work for the government party in Cameroon. I would arrange rooms for them to stay in, drive people from this place to that. I was in the party then, hoping that would help me get a better job because the leader can do that. But they just used me, paid me nothing, exploited me. Sometimes I did not even have the money to put fuel in my car. But if you complain, you get into trouble.

Still, I had a normal life by then. I was renting a small flat, one living room, one bedroom, toilet, kitchen. I had a girlfriend who lived with me from time to time. We were planning to settle down together, but in the end, she was too demanding. I had a small income and I needed to take care of my mummy, send her money. I could not manage both.

I was living like that till I was around twenty-eight.

Why are you in the opposition?

In 2008, when President Biya got his parliament to change the law so he could be re-elected in 2011, everybody was hoping he would not run again, even if we were not free to say so. Biya was no good for young people and he was corrupt. So, when he changed that law, people protested. The army killed many peaceful protesters that year, mostly young people. That made me deeply shocked and angry.

In 2013, a member of the party, Professor Maurice Kamto, resigned from the government in protest and created an opposition party, the MRC: Movement for the Renaissance of Cameroon.[2] That is when I asked myself why I was still in the government party. So I left and joined the MRC instead.

I began then to drive for some of its leaders. I would take them to meetings; I was always available. They really appreciated me. The MRC was not élite like the government. The leaders would talk to me, tell me I was doing a great job, pay me. Even Professor Kamto himself was kind. I talked to him from time to time during the campaign because he was very close to poor people and simple.

When, in the election of October 2018, President Biya claimed he had won 78 percent of the vote, Professor Kamto contested the results. We all knew Biya had cheated. The MRC asked us to gather in Carrefour Nlongkak, the biggest square in Yaoundé, to hear Professor Kamto give his opposition speech.

The government sent the police to beat us. They were extremely violent and they hurt people badly. They also arrested many of the opposition leaders, including Professor Kamto himself. He was the most important law professor in all of Cameroon, he had taught at many universities around the world. But, in spite of that, he spent eight months in the Central Prison of Ngondengui. They let him free eventually but some of the other leaders are still in prison today.

At the protest, I put some of the injured people in my car to take them to hospital. But the police started smashing cars and setting them on fire. They got to my car, burned and destroyed it.

I tried to run away but the police caught and beat me. Later that day, they came to where I was staying, arrested me and put me in a cell. They never gave me a trial, just locked me up. They said: 'You are from the South like the president. You were a member of the ruling party. Why are you now in the opposition?'

In the prison, they beat me up again. Then they took me to the basement, made me and some other protesters they had arrested clean the cell, and then locked us inside with maybe forty people. The cell was small and narrow, like a corridor, and so dark we could not see each other. We would bump into people whenever we tried to move.

They kept me in that cell for an entire month. When they opened the door, I would hide my face because the light hurt my eyes. I could not tell if it was night or day. It was terrible. There was no toilet in there; we had to request one. They would give us a bucket. Many people were using it, so the odor – that part was not easy to live with. And there was no shower, no bed. You sleep on the concrete, no bedsheets, nothing. All they gave us to eat was corn, sometimes mixed with beans. Because it was November and December it was cold at night. And all the time, I was in pain from the beatings.

After I had been there more than a week, they called me and some other people to see a lawyer. That was the only time they let us out of the cell. But all the lawyer said was that we broke the law by protesting. After that they locked us back in. I asked if I can have a lawyer for myself but to have a lawyer in Cameroon is difficult. They said I will not get a lawyer until they finish the investigation. The MRC tried to find a lawyer to defend us but they were not allowed to.

At the end of that month, the prison guards asked me to sign a letter resigning from the MRC. The police officer said, 'If you sign, I can help you to get out.' I was so scared and desperate that I signed the letter. They did release me then, but first the police said: 'We will watch you as long as you are in Yaoundé. We will watch everything you do.'

I knew I could not stay in Yaoundé after that. So, I went to live with my sister, Virginie, in the English part of Cameroon, in a place everybody calls Ghost Town.

You are a terrorist!

I am closer to my sister than to anybody else in my family. She is always kind and available to me. From time to time I speak with her still. She lives in Yaoundé now and has seven children, like my mum, including twins. I miss them all.

When I went to stay with her, though, she was living in Bamenda, a town in the northwest. She had a business selling food, although she did not make much money.

Because I had lost my car and my way of earning a living, I was broke. So, when there was a peaceful protest about the marginalization of Anglophones in Cameroon, and the MRC party offered me a little money to go, I took it.

Every week in Bamenda, all the shops closed down for one day because everyone went to these protests. That is why we called it Ghost Town. At first, the protests were peaceful and I marched twice without trouble. But at the third protest, the police came and arrested us. They beat me up a little but not too much. But then, because this was the second time I was arrested, when they looked me up in the system and saw I had a case in Yaoundé, they said, 'You are a terrorist!'

That is when I learned that I could be arrested anywhere in Cameroon. I thought my case was over, that I would be safe. But no.

Three policemen took me to an empty room after that and beat me severely. They tortured me, too, burning me all over with cigarettes, every part of my body. I have a lot of scars.

[Calvin lifted his shirt here and used his phone camera to show me the circular scars all over his torso.]

They whipped me with a baton, punched and kicked me. They knocked out my tooth. They did all this in a secret room, so the others were not aware. They tried to make me confess that I was a terrorist.

For three days they kept me there while they beat me. Because it was so painful, I was begging them, 'Do not kill me, I am not a bad person!' I ended up saying anything they wanted me to say. They only stopped when I was bleeding so much that I lost consciousness.

When I awoke, I was lying on a bed but I did not know where. It turned out the police had taken me to a small private health center. The police told the doctor that I was an Amba Boy – the name of a gang who fought the forces of order in the Anglophone zone – so, for the doctor, it was normal to see a person like me. I was in very bad condition but I suppose he was used to taking in people who had been tortured. Either way, he asked me no questions. He just gave me some pain tablets, that is all.

Then the police took me back and put me in a prison cell. They kept me there for two weeks – this was the winter of 2019. At least in this prison I could have visitors. You had a toilet, although you had to knock to ask to go. But it was better than the first prison.

I had to pay money to be released. My sister and her husband helped me pay. Every place in Cameroon, there is bribing and corruption like this. But, before I left, the police told me: 'If we catch you again, you will see what we will do to you. We don't want to see you around.'

That is when I knew that if I wanted to stay alive, I had to leave Cameroon.

CALVIN IN FLIGHT: CAMEROON – EQUATORIAL GUINEA – TURKEY – LESBOS

'WHEN YOU FACE THE WATER, YOUR LIFE HAS NO WORTH.'

Helen:

While Calvin and I were talking, through the spring and summer of 2020, he was dealing with the usual labyrinth of problems that Greece inflicts upon refugees. He had not yet received asylum and so was at least allowed to stay in Ritsona camp and receive his monthly allowance, but, because the coronavirus had closed all the asylum offices, the paperwork he needed to take a legal job – already delayed by Greek's clogged and inefficient system – was now frozen in limbo.

Finding work as a refugee in Greece is nigh on impossible in normal times, but this grew much worse during the pandemic. Nonetheless, after months of searching, Calvin did finally find a job as a cleaner. In July 2020, he was telling me about this with excitement and relief when he received a phone call. A few minutes later, he rang me back, his cheerful mood replaced by gloom.

'The company wants to give me the job, but I need to provide documents that are very difficult to get with Corona.' He rubbed his face hard with one hand. 'They are asking for my AMKA number. I was supposed to get the number with my blue card but the number was missing and now they say they cannot give it to me. My blue card expired during Corona and all the offices are closed, so I can't renew it.'

This is the kind of Kafkaesque tangle to which refugees are constantly subjected. A typo on an ID card, a mis-spelled name, a missing detail – little mistakes like this can spin a person into months of misery and dead ends. After a few more moments of distress – here he was with an employer who wanted to hire him but couldn't – Calvin recovered himself and continued his reminiscences.

✶   ✶   ✶

I thought I would die

After I decided to leave Cameroon, my sister advised me to go stay with a friend in Equatorial Guinea, but I was not there very long before I found out that if you are known to be with the opposition in Cameroon, you can be arrested in Equatorial Guinea, too. When I realized that, I became scared of everything. I could not sleep, could not breathe well. I would wake up at night shouting, 'Please don't kill me!' with all the images from my beatings and arrests crowding my mind. I became afraid if I even saw a policeman.

Because of this, a friend suggested I go to Turkey. He used to help people travel, so he arranged to get me a passport, a visa, a plane ticket. I gave him a little money I had made driving a taxi part-time and he hired a smuggler to help me in Turkey. I thought the papers were legal but they were not.

[As soon as Calvin landed at Ataturk Airport in Istanbul, he was arrested, undergoing many of the same ordeals as Evans had in Iran: the language barrier, the arbitrary and terrifying imprisonments, the mistreatment of him as an African.]

They put me in a prison called Maltepe.[3] It is an enormous, concrete prison in Istanbul full of real criminals. The police took all my things and sent me into a big room with a mix of nationalities. It was extremely rough in there. People were fighting to get food. They took my pillow, my blanket. I became very afraid. I thought if I had to stay many days in that place I would be killed.

I passed three days in that room and the entire time I thought I would have to stay there for years. But then I was taken to the health center and asked some questions, after which I was conducted to a cell reserved for Africans. There were Nigerians, Somalis, Kenyans, Gambians, Guineans, the majority there for trafficking in drugs, scamming and stealing on the internet. When I told the other prisoners that I was only there because of an issue with my documents, they called me a liar because people with my problems were usually sent to a deportation camp, not Maltepe. Some people there were locked up for twenty years and some were violent because of too much isolation and long imprisonment. Not everyone told you what they had done because they were ashamed. I was terrified that I would be in there for years, too.

In the African cell, it was better organized, mostly by the Nigerians. But we also had crazy people in there with mental problems. They were not supposed to be with us and the guards said they would remove them, but they never did. One man kept beating himself and saying he wanted to die. Other men were so violent, you did not want to sleep near them.

The guards would not allow you to call anybody on your phone, so nobody knew where I was. I had no idea how long I would be there without being able to inform my family or a friend.

My public lawyer told me maybe if I am lucky, I will get two years. I said: 'Two years just to investigate my nationality and documents? Why?' I could never get an answer. In Turkey they do not know how to communicate. The lack of information and communication can make you go really crazy.

In the prison, you had to follow a timetable and a list of chores, such as cleaning the toilet. We were around thirty people per section, all men. We had beds, a fridge, TV. Each cell held four people and had a wall of bars in the front. Several times every day, we had to stand against a wall so the guards could count us.

There was a tiny courtyard surrounded by tall concrete walls, where we could go for one hour a day for air. The walls were so high and the courtyard so small that almost no daylight could reach it. That was the only time we saw the sky.

They do not explain in Turkey

After I was in Maltepe for a month, the guards came one morning and said, 'You are free.' They told me to collect my belongings and go. I thought I was really free, so I walked out with great relief. But then the police stopped me, put me in a small room where there was no camera and one of them punched me two times and said, 'Do not ever come back.'

After that, they brought me to another police station and locked me in a jail cell inside. It was in the basement, like the one in Cameroon. 'Why are you doing this?' I asked them. 'You told me I was free.' No answer. I was with people from Afghanistan, Pakistan, Syria . . . I was the only African. Nobody spoke French or English.

In that jail, they gave us food only once a day. The toilet was outside but you were only allowed to ask to use it at one in the afternoon. Everyone goes, then they lock you in again. They would not let you go in the morning. And it was bitterly cold. It was winter but they left the window in the cell open all the time. We begged them to close it, but no. We had no bed. No blankets. No heater. We slept on the cement floor. I never felt cold like that in my life.

One morning, after I had been in that jail for a week, they brought us out, took our fingerprints, snapped our pictures and asked us to sign something. Everything was in Turkish and there was no translator, so you cannot know what you are signing. I wanted to say I would not sign but I was the only Black. When you are Black in that position, you cannot object . . . so I signed.

After that the police put me in a car with five other guys and drove for three or four hours out of Istanbul and onto a small road. For all those hours I was thinking: 'My God, I am finished. They are going to take us out, shoot us and bury us somewhere.' The others were scared, also. But we could not ask where they were bringing us, again because of the language.

It turned out they were taking us to a deportation camp. When we arrived, the police took our phones, every-thing, and put us in a big room with a mix of many people.

A lot of Algerians were there and they were always fighting. There was no law in that room. People fight, you call the police, they do not come. Or they come only to beat people up. There was no way to escape the violence.

The deportation camp was in a small village in the mountains. I was there for three weeks. At the end of that, the police called me into an office and asked me again to sign a paper in Turkish. People had told me if I sign anything, it would be an agreement for them to deport me, so this time I refused. I even put my hands behind my back so they would not grab my fingers and force me to press them on a document.

Then they asked me to buy a ticket so they could deport me – they wanted me to pay for my own deportation! They had someone there who could speak English, so I told him I need protection, I cannot go back or I will be executed as a terrorist. He said they are not asking; they are telling you that you have to go back. I said you can kill me if you want, but I cannot go back.

Three times they called me in to sign that paper. I kept saying no. The last time they called me, they said you are free.

Why they suddenly let me go, I do not know. Maybe because I did not commit any crime in Turkey, it was only that my papers were not in order. They do not explain in Turkey. They called one guy in the prison to explain to them what I was saying, but even then, my English was better than his.

There is nothing like freedom

When they let me out of that deportation camp, I had no idea where I was going or where I would sleep, but I did not care. I was only excited because there is nothing like freedom. My phone was dead, I could not call anybody, but, still, I was happy. When you have never been in prison, you cannot know how valuable freedom is. Even if I had to sleep outside, the most important thing was that I was free.

The police put me in a car with an older Syrian who could not speak English and drove us towards Istanbul. They asked us, where can we drop you? I did not know the city but I remembered hearing about an area called Aksaray that has many Blacks. So I asked them to leave us there.

Aksaray was on the outskirts of the city, far away from the center. They left us in the street at night. It was very cold. I had a little money but not enough for a hotel. It was a bad neighborhood. My phone was off – no credit, no internet. I had no idea where I was but I did not care because I was still so happy to be free.

I walked up and down until I heard a man speaking English. I asked him, can you tell me where I can sleep on the street? He gave me the name of an area I could go and let me use his phone. I tried to call my family – I had not been able to reach them for more than two months – but had no luck. I asked the man if I could sleep in his building. He said no, he had family problems.

I walked some more until I saw my first Black, but he also said he could not help me. Then I saw two more Blacks, a man and a lady with a child. I talked to them. One was from Gambia, one from Cameroon. They said they would help me for the night. Later the Gambian man said he knew of a room I could rent.

I went there and showed the landlord a paper the police gave me when they released me. He translated it for me. It said that I had the right to stay in Turkey for three months. So he let me stay in a room.

The guy from Gambia helped me a lot. He found me a job in Istanbul ironing clothes, the kind of job you can get easily because they do not ask about papers, and he invited me to stay with him. He told me he could get me to Greece, where it would be better for me. So I worked for a small amount of money for more than a month and, each week, I would give him some. Once it added up to 500 dollars, he bought me a bus ticket to Izmir, gave me the number of a guy there, and I left.

Now I'm laughing

When I arrived in Izmir, I contacted the Gambian and he directed me to the neighborhood of Basmane. Most people who want to go to Greece stay there – it is as if Turkey just gave up that area for refugees. But everything is bad in Basmane. They rob, they rape girls. Alcohol. Drugs. You cannot believe it. And there are no jobs. You have nothing to eat, no food, nobody to help. You see families sleeping on the ground with small children. Many girls turn to prostitution because they lack the money to pay for hotels. Some guys become gay to make a little money. Some people wait a whole year or more trying to cross and they get very desperate. When I was there, I did not know who to trust.

I found a small hotel in Basmane where people stayed to wait. Many hotels there are like this. You must pay each day for a room or they will throw you out on the streets. I am calling it a hotel but you need to see it with your own eyes. Even in Africa I had never seen such a nasty place.

The smugglers said I should wait there and be ready for them to contact me at any time. They don't talk about what they are going to do because it is illegal. I waited for two weeks.

The first time they called me was in an afternoon – this was in May 2019. They told us to wait until night, when they would send several small lorries to pick us up – we were a group of maybe thirty.

In my lorry, they stuffed me in with perhaps sixteen people and locked the doors to hide us because they knew if the police saw so many Blacks inside, they would arrest us. We were so squeezed that pressure from our bodies was trying to burst open the door. There were pregnant women and children in there. It was hard enough for me, but at least I am a strong man. How did they do it?

The lorry drove us to the beach and, when it finally stopped, we had to carry some people out because they had fainted. The smugglers did not care. They were from Syria. Some even had guns.

One of my friends told me that his smugglers drove him and the others to the forest, separated the women and took them away to rape. Some of those smugglers have no human feeling. They can do these things because they bring you to the forest or isolated houses, where you are helpless.

We stayed at the beach for about thirty minutes. Then the police came. We tried to run but they shot in the air to stop us. After everything we had gone through, they caught us all! Now I am laughing, but then I was crying.

They brought us to a police station, where we slept for one night. We were more than sixty. In the morning, they sent a long bus to carry us to a small deportation camp, where they kept us for an hour. They put the Africans on one side, Arabs on the other. They think if we are Black, we all speak the same language.

At the police station, they took our fingerprints, pictures, names, ages, where we were from. Then a European lady came who could speak English. She told us that we did not commit any crime but what we are doing is illegal. We said we want to seek asylum. She negotiated and they released us after four days or so. I do not know who she was working for but she really cared about us.

We were also lucky because this was during Ramadan, when Muslims have to do good deeds. So the police released us. But they said if they saw us again, we would be in big trouble.

After they let us out of the camp, they told us to pay for the bus back to Izmir. There I had to find a place in a hotel again. You paid for a bed among many beds in a room or you slept in a corridor. I stayed there almost two weeks. You cannot walk very far from the hotel and you must keep your phone on always because the smugglers might call you at any time and, when they do, you have to pay for the taxi to wherever they are. When a taxi driver sees you are Black, he will charge fifty euros when it should be ten. If you argue, he will threaten to call the police because he knows you are illegal.

When you face the water, your life has no worth

The second call came at night. This was June 6 or 7, 2019. At midnight, they drove us to the beach in one of those tiny lorries and made us inflate the boat ourselves. There were around fifty-three or so of us in the boat, women and children, too, although it was only made to hold at most twenty. But even if you want to turn back, the smuggler will not allow you.

When you are facing the sea like that, everything is in the hands of God. I don't know how to say what I mean in English. *Quand tu es devant l'eau, tu sais que ta vie vraiment n'a pas de valeur. Tu peux mourir.* [When you face the water, you know that your life truly is worth nothing. You could die.]

The first time I tried to cross, I bought a lifejacket. I can swim in a small river but not in that sea! This time I did not have a jacket. Most people had none because the smugglers say do not bring a lifejacket because if the police see it they will arrest you.

At one in the morning we moved out into the water but the boat turned back and hit some rocks in the dark. The smugglers showed our driver how to steer again and we tried once more. We sailed for maybe twenty-five minutes and then the engine stopped. It was very old and could not process the petrol. We managed to fix it. The whole way, we had to stop every twenty-five minutes to pump the engine. We sailed all night like this, stopping and starting. Everybody was scared.

At seven in the morning we came across the Greek coastguard. They asked us if there were children. They transferred the children first, then the women, then the men onto their boat, tied our empty boat to the back and took us to an island. We were so happy. We had arrived in Freedomland!

CALVIN IN GREECE

'I THOUGHT MY SUFFERING WAS OVER.'

Helen:

Like Asmahan, Calvin had arrived on Lesbos, only by then it was a year later and the number of asylum seekers in Camp Moria had more than doubled to 16,800.[4] Moreover, thousands more were arriving every month, most from Afghanistan, Syria and the Democratic Republic of Congo, more than half of them women and children.[5]

Conditions in Moria were so appalling by then that the EU, UNHCR, Red Cross and the Greek courts all demanded with outrage that Greece do something to fix them.[6] Human Rights Watch also issued a damning report on the camp at the time, quoting an unnamed high-level Greek official both admitting to and yet blaming Greece's violations of refugee rights on lack of support from the EU. 'Greece cannot be the gatekeeper of Europe, as it is being asked to be by the EU, and also be expected to respect human rights fully.'[7] Yet none of this outrage made any difference. By 2020 Moria held one of the most dense and underserved populations of any refugee camp in the world: 203,800 people per square kilometer.[8]

Bad as this was, the situation only worsened when, that same year, the new government stepped up its anti-refugee efforts, denying refugees access to public-health services except in emergencies, imprisoning asylum seekers for ever more arbitrary reasons and narrowing the criteria for asylum. All this was to affect Calvin severely.

❖   ❖   ❖

A nicer place

When our boat arrived in Lesbos, *j'ai pensé que ma souffrance était terminée.* [I thought my suffering was over.] The Coast Guard took us to a police station at the port, where they made us wait, wait, wait while they called us into a small container one by one and asked us questions. We were rescued at about eight that morning but we did not leave the police station until eleven.

I was excited to be in Europe but also worried because nobody explained what would come next and because, when you give the police information about yourself like that, you cannot be sure how they will use it. The police separated us then by nationality. There were only three from Cameroon – myself and two other men.

After that they sent a long police bus to carry us up the hill to the Moria camp. It was like a war zone. So dirty and stinking! Rubbish bags heaped like mountains. Filth and crowds everywhere. I was shocked. I asked myself, 'How can people live like this?'

The police did not let us mix with other people, they only took us to a special area and questioned us. We stayed there until three or four in the afternoon. Then they sent us to the doctor for a checkup. But the doctor only asked if we had any diseases, filled in a paper and said, 'Go.' I was still suffering from the torture and beatings and my broken tooth but he did not examine us. Still, I thought it was over now and I could go free. Then a strange thing happened. The police released everybody except for me, the other Cameroonian men and the Ghanaians. Us, they put in handcuffs and shoved us into a small police car. Even then I did not realize what was happening. I thought maybe we were lucky and they were taking us to a nicer place.

The police drove us to what looked like a camp inside the camp. It was a group of gray buildings, shabby and old, surrounded by chain-link fences and barbed wire. When we arrived, they told me to leave my bags and sent me inside, where they asked if I had money, jewels or anything with me. That is when I realized, my God, I am in prison again! I was shocked and angry that we were the only ones arrested. But you do not ask questions in circumstances like that.

At about six they took us into the prison and locked the gate. The people behind the bars were calling out, 'New arrivals, where are you from?' I asked them why they were locked up but, before they could answer, the police opened a cell and put us inside with nine other guys. Then they said, 'You will stay here for three months.'

I had just arrived in Greece and here I was being treated like a criminal again. I was thinking, why did I ever run away? I came to Greece because I wanted to be free. Now I was again going through everything I faced in my country and Turkey. We were locked in. We could not go outside except for one hour in the morning and one hour in the afternoon. The building had a small open area in the middle, a courtyard, so you could walk back and forth there just to breathe a little air for those two hours. We were only allowed access to our phones Saturday and Sunday.

They never gave us a reason for why they locked us up like that. Some people were in the prison because their asylum had been rejected and they were going to be deported, or they got caught selling drugs or committing other crimes. But me? And I still do not know why they kept certain nationalities and not others. People from Congo and Somalia were free. Other countries were free. But people from Cameroon, Ghana, the Ivory Coast, Nigeria, Guinea, they locked up. The only reason they gave was that there were not many people seeking asylum from our countries. It was very unfair.

On Lesbos they try to tell you that the place they put me is not a prison but only a 'pre-removal' center. But it is a prison. The buildings are containers made of a composite board covered with something you cannot break. There are tall, chain-link fences all around with barbed wire on top. A guard booth with police who have guns. Everything is old and worn and gray. It brought back all my bad memories.

While I was in that Moria prison, the backache and pain from the injury in my mouth returned very badly. Ever since I was beaten up, wounds will appear on my tongue and lips when I am stressed. Also, because of my memories, it was difficult to sleep. I kept having nightmares about the other prisons and what I went through in Cameroon. I asked many times to see a psychologist or a doctor who could help me and give me sleeping tablets, but the police said no sleeping tablets in prison. All they gave me was paracetamol. And it was impossible to see a doctor. Anytime you asked, you were told there is no doctor, or that you are pretending, you are not sick. This was very difficult not just for me, but for many people.

The Red Cross visited us and made a lot of promises that they would do this and that and send us a doctor. They said we could speak freely. So we spoke our minds – that many of us are sick, we never see a doctor, some of us have contagious diseases. We told them all that. After the Red Cross left, the guards reduced our food to punish us. And nothing changed.

The guards were often very hard with us. When we asked for water, one of them refused to give it to us. One said: 'Why you come here? We don't have money! When we have a problem, we don't go to Africa.' He was very angry. We tried to tell him we did not come to Greece for pleasure, we are running for our life.

I stayed in that prison for June, July and August without seeing the outside once. That was the seventh time I had been arrested. I hope never again. But it has left me afraid of being arrested all the time. Now, when I see people getting arrested here in Athens, I grow frightened. Even when I have my documents, I feel afraid of the police, especially the ones who are shouting, giving orders, acting rough. I always try to avoid them.

The Moria prison did not release me or the other Cameroonians until early September. They never explained why I was locked up or why I was released. They only spoke Greek anyway.'

[They locked Calvin up because Greece had a policy of imprisoning anyone for three months who came from a country with a less than 25 percent acceptance rate for asylum, as was the case for Cameroon at the time. Since then, such imprisonments have become so routine that Greece is incarcerating seven out of ten asylum seekers, no matter where they came from.[9] This is not only a violation of the right not to be penalized for seeking asylum, but of the right to an impartial and individualized examination of one's case, as it is much harder to find or consult with a lawyer from inside a prison, or to get a fair hearing when dragged to court in handcuffs, looking like a criminal. Furthermore, the justifications for these imprisonments are so vague and convoluted that it is almost impossible for lawyers to challenge them.[10]]

✻   ✻   ✻

I took all these risks to come here and look!

When I finally left the prison, I walked outside and, ah, it was so overcrowded! People were sleeping everywhere! On the street, in the fields. When you see people living like that, you ask yourself if we are even human anymore. It made me think Moria was even worse than my country. Never in my life had I thought there was something like that in Europe. It made me desperate. I took all these risks to come here and look at these conditions!

By the time they released me, my health was much worse, in my mind and my body. I was having difficulty being around people, I couldn't sleep. My mouth was hurting. It was so stressful to wait in the queue to get food while people were fighting that sometimes I had to walk away, even with nothing to eat. My friends said you are dying, you need to go for food and water. But you had to wait two hours just for a bottle of water and sometimes you get there only to find it is finished. The same with a meal. I lost a lot of weight because of the stress and not eating. Even now when I am anxious, I cannot eat.

For the first two weeks I was out of the prison, I slept in a big tent for new arrivals. That place was the worst in Moria for me. If you put anything down even for a minute, people will steal it – your phone, everything. And because they mixed all sorts of nationalities, there was a lot of fighting, even with knives. There were no beds, you just had to find a spot on the floor. It was extremely dangerous in there.

So I made some friends and we tried to sleep outside. An NGO called EuroRelief gave us sleeping bags, toothpaste, toothbrushes, shampoo. If you had nowhere to stay, they tried to help.[11] [This was the same organization that Asmahan had liked so much.]

The camp was divided into two areas. The first was made up of rows of white containers inside walls and chain-link fences, like a giant cage. The second was tents spread all over the fields, under fig and olive trees on the side of the mountain. That area was initially illegal – refugees built it themselves. The owners of the olives were not happy.

Some tents were big, like the first one I slept in, some were for about ten people, and then the tiny ones where you cannot stand, you must just crawl. Because the administration was so bad, an NGO called Movement on the Ground took control of this area.[12] It brought in small tents because even children and babies and pregnant women were sleeping on the street. And more people were coming every day.

In the end I got a little bit lucky because Movement on the Ground gave me and some friends a tent of our own. We shared it with around eighteen people. The NGOs are doing a lot but, to be honest, no matter what they do it cannot be enough.

At one point when I was there, a big fire broke out. It was close to the administration building. The fires started in two areas at the same time. That was very scary. I was lucky that my tent was not nearby.

[Fires have remained a problem in Moria for years, rendering conditions in the camp steadily worse. In September 2020, fires left close to 13,000 asylum seekers with no shelter at all.[13]]

The camp and the tents were at least ten kilometers from the town of Mytilene, so you normally did not see many Greeks, aside from the ones who worked in the camp. In Mytilene, they had a very bad image of the camp and were scared of it. The local Greeks did not even go to the camp side of the village. So, I was never really in touch with Greeks, except in the prison.

After I left that prison, the camp officials told me that I had ten days to collect all the papers for my pre-interview – doctor reports, police papers, anything I had to show who I was. If you miss that deadline, they said, you could be rejected. But anything you wanted to do in that camp, 2,000 other people wanted to do it too. People fighting, jumping place in queues. And there were not many police to keep order.

My pre-interview took place in September 2019. This is the interview when they give you an open or closed card. I got a closed one, the red stamp, so I could not leave the island. Lesbos became an open prison for me. Each time I had to renew my card, four or five times, they gave me the red. They never said why. I spent most of the time in Moria trying to get my open card. It is like trying to win a lottery because, once you have it, you can request accommodation on the mainland and you can get off the island of hell.

In the camp, my daily life was all waiting in lines. For a toilet, for food. It was not well organized. Sometimes you wake up at 6:30 and don't get food until nine. I do not like to do nothing but wait like that, so when I heard you could go to an NGO in Mytilene called the Mosaik Center and take classes, I took a class in Greek.[14] I completed the first level. They issued me the certificate. I also began a volunteer job for One Happy Family, teaching children.[15] After all, I had been hoping that in Europe I could get more education, take some training, learn something, find a job. In Moria, all that hope fell down, but at least I could take these classes. I was thinking it would be easy for me to get a class in Athens, too, but when I got here, there were no available seats. Instead, I started to improve my English.

On Lesbos, I always tried to stay busy because that camp is hell. It is not fit for humans. At least they allowed us to have books. The other guys were not interested in books but I was reading all the time. This I still do, but it is hard to find books now.

I also began studying the Bible with Jehovah's Witnesses. They used to come to Moria all the time, ask if you speak English or French, and then tell you about the Bible. I attended their meetings every week. On Wednesdays they would meet me in Moria, take me to study the Bible in their café downtown, and then bring me back. They gave me clothes, shoes, help like that.

I did learn new things studying the Bible with them but I could not totally agree with them. For example, they refuse to recognize the Holy Trinity: the Father, the Son and the Holy Spirit. They say there is only God, Jesus is not on the same level. Their target was to convert us to become a Witness, but it was not for me.

I was terribly shocked

In November 2019, after I had spent almost five months on Lesbos, I finally got my blue card. When you do, the asylum service puts your name in the system. Still, you might have to wait for two, three months for space in a mainland camp or hotel. So I decided not to wait but instead go to Athens on my own and find a job.

Many times I called a friend who had left for Athens to ask if it is truly possible to find a place to live and have a normal life there and a job. He kept telling me yes. So I left with my own ticket on a ferry. The ticket costs fifty euros and you have to buy food on the boat. I was only getting ninety euros a month, so this was a lot of money.

We traveled the whole night to Athens, arriving at eight or nine in the morning. One of my friends said he would pick me up at the seaport, but instead he sent someone else. That guy took me to a building and, when I saw it, I was terribly shocked. There were maybe thirty people sleeping everywhere on the floor. No room to move. My friend had told me it would be fine, but he lied. [This was where Calvin was living when we first met.]

I thought, I did not leave Moria to live like this. I hoped to get a normal life!

I looked for an NGO that could find me somewhere better to live. It was not easy because NGOs are so overwhelmed. I looked for two months and meanwhile I had to sleep on the floor with all those people. You could wait three hours to take a shower or use the one toilet, just like Moria! But in Moria at least you could sleep outside. In Athens, we were on the second floor and the landlord didn't want to see you outside. It was winter and there was no heat, nothing. I had to pay fifty euros a month to live like that?

Also, the police checked the area all the time because a lot of Blacks were selling drugs there. It is called Plateia Amerikis. Many Africans and refugees live there. Two or three times, the police stopped me and searched my backpack. It is better, I think, not to carry one.

After two months like this, I heard that the government had opened a new camp called Ritsona, so I went there and begged for a place. I moved there in January 2020. Ritsona is about an hour away from Athens by train because the government does not like to have camps in the city. They put them far away in villages where nobody can see us. The nearest city to Ritsona is Chalkida, nearly twenty kilometers away.

Here, we live in containers. Each has two rooms, with a mix of bunks and single beds. We are nine people living in my container, sometimes ten. We have only one small closet to keep our clothes. There is no space. It is very untidy and difficult to clean. But we have a toilet, a kitchen, heat and A/C. And beds.

That was the first time I slept in a real bed since I came to Greece!

※　　※　　※

Helen:

At about this time, the Greek government announced that it was banning many NGOs from camps, a move it justified with the baffling contention that the volunteers were both enticing refugees to Greece and making money off them.

'There is a galaxy of dodgy NGOs operating alongside a network of doctors, lawyers and other people making a mint out of the human misery of these people,' declared Greece's deputy migration minister at the time, George Koumoutsakos, in October 2020. 'They are leeches and these practices must end. All of this contributes to illegal migration.'[16]

With this claim, the government decreed that only those organizations that had re-registered with the government and filed a complicated set of paperwork by June 14, 2020 – a process that included budget scrutiny, criminal background checks of all staff and clearance for the NGO's missions – would be allowed to work in the camps. As a result, the government managed to force all but eighteen NGOs to close, leaving camp dwellers bereft of most of the classes and services that had helped to make life tolerable.[17]

Calvin talked about the effect this had on Camp Ritsona.

✻   ✻   ✻

Fighting with my past

The volunteers from Europe, America, Canada, all had to leave. I had a teacher from Canada who spoke English and French. I was learning English really well with him. But he left. They had activities for children, classes in English, German . . . Now, nothing. So we are organizing ourselves and teaching each other. I am teaching French and taking English lessons. I need something to do. Otherwise all I do is sit and remember the past. When you are busy, your mind is quiet and you are better.

I still go to Athens every month to see my psychologist at MSF. He gave me a paper report to show I am diagnosed with PTSD. If your case is not serious, they cannot give you that paper. He also gives me tablets for sleeping and for anxiety.

I also go to Athens to buy food because Ritsona has no food service. It is cheaper to buy food in Athens and keep it in the refrigerator than to buy food near the camp. There is nothing here but a small village, abandoned buildings, fields, farms. I tried to find a job on a farm but without luck. People built a small shop here of Arab food but it is too expensive. In Chalkida, the food is expensive also.

I am happy to have a bed here, a kitchen. But there is no security, no order. It is becoming normal for people to steal. I put under my bed the things that are important, like oil or onions or tomatoes, because if you leave them in the kitchen everyone will take them.

Most of the time I am very lonely because my roommates are all from the Congo and we do not speak the same language. The authorities here put all Africans together because they think we are the same. So often I am just alone with my phone. I do have one Cameroonian friend. We met in Turkey and crossed the water together. Now we are both here in the camp. Three times a week we go outside in the morning, take walks for exercise. We call it in French *une randonnée*. The camp is surrounded by farms and *les vignes* – vineyards.

Also, I still cannot sleep because of bad memories. I am still fighting with my past.

I do not know what will happen next. I am just waiting for my asylum interview. It was supposed to be this past April but, because the virus closed the offices, it has been postponed. Now I have to wait five months to even find out the date of my interview. It is a long, long wait. [He was finally given a date more than a year in the future – May 2021.] I just want to get my residence and my ID so I can work and travel.

I would like to have children one day, to try to correct my mistakes and lack of opportunity and give them what I did not have. My dream country is Canada because I like English. I think I could go to school, learn more there.

If you see me laughing, it is because I am just hoping the future will be better.

✻   ✻   ✻

Helen:

In July 2020, Calvin sent me a series of texts:

July 16: Hello Helen, I feel bad sharing all my problems with you but if you don't mind this is what happened to me: I went to Athens as usual but unfortunately somebody stole my bag at the bus station and that bag had all my Asylum papers, my police papers, all my doctors papers since I am in Greece and also my HCR Bank card. Only my Asylum international protection card is left. So I'm very stressed and desperate. I don't know where to start and who I can ask for help even to go back. I am feeling so bad I don't know how I am going to survive this month. I have been going up and down trying to figure things out but nothing.

July 17: Hello Helen. Sorry to not have reacted to your messages.

I have been through very difficult times these days. I wanted to take time and step back to think about everything that is happening in my life. I spent two nights in a park. Fortunately a friend of mine paid transport for me so that I returned today to the camp. I will try as much as possible to rest. I have lodged a complaint with the Omonia Police Station and I will see if they can help.

July 31: I cannot concentrate to write or do something better for myself.

Aug 1

[7:11am]: It's difficult here. I don't have anything to eat but I don't like talking about my problems. I have always struggled on my own since Cameroon.

[7:13am] About our work, I just want to be in the best state of mind to be able to give you my best you know.

[7:13am] Hope you understand me.

❖   ❖   ❖

I never heard from Calvin again.

EPILOGUE:
WHAT CAN BE DONE

BY HELEN BENEDICT AND
EYAD AWWADAWNAN

Much time has passed since we began our conversations with the people in this book. So now, as we write in 2022, this, briefly, is what has happened to each person since.

Hasan stayed with friends for two months until he eventually found a job as a parking attendant, and a basement apartment in the house of a friendly Greek family in Thessaloniki. He lived happily like this, cooking for himself, feeding a stray cat, earning a small income – until finally, in October 2021, three years after his trial for human trafficking, it was time for his appeal to be heard in the Samos court. He traveled back to the island with his legal expert friend, Nick, only to find that, because of a strike, the hearing had been indefinitely postponed. This left Hasan deeply disappointed but as determined as ever to forge ahead.

Asmahan began asylum procedures in Germany in April 2021. After moving from one refugee camp to another, she settled in a camp in Berlin, where she and little Aziz live in a small container on a monthly stipend. She spends her time between the immigration office and taking him to a psychiatrist because, she says, he suffers from cognitive deficiency as a result of isolation in their tiny apartment in Greece. As for her hopes to reunite with her sons, Muhammad and Shehab, so far there is no sun on the horizon.

Evans found a temporary, low-paid job as a dishwasher, working fifteen hours a day for about two dollars an hour. Meanwhile, his mother wrote asking him to forgive her. After long deliberation, he did. 'I have to, she is my mother.' Evans received his passport in October 2021, which gave him the freedom to travel but also left him one month before he would lose all support and have to leave the camp. After failing to find a Greek landlord who would rent to him, he began moving around the country working at various jobs such as picking olives or oranges on farms. When I asked him if he was going to try to return to school, he replied, 'That would make me the happiest man on earth.' But then he added: 'I have a problem. I cannot trust anybody.'

Mursal was overcome with worry for her aunts, uncles and cousins in Afghanistan once the Taliban took over in August 2021. 'They cannot leave the house, it is too dangerous. My uncle is targeted because he worked for the government, and his daughter, my cousin, is just the age when she could be forced to marry a Taliban fighter.' Soon after, the family bought fake passports and tried to leave Greece so that Mursal's sisters could go to school at last. Her mother and sisters made it through, but Mursal, her father and baby brother were stopped at the airport and turned back, resulting in the very situation she most dreads: the separation of her family. Then came more news: Mursal's second interview was held in November 2021 and, on December 10, she was granted asylum, only to be told that within a few weeks she had to move out of the apartment she shares with her baby brother and father and live on her own, as the authorities plan to move another family in. Mursal is now trying to find a home for herself, Bilal and her father, while he still awaits his second interview, trapping them in Greece.

Calvin has never resurfaced. When Eyad went to work as an interpreter at Ritsona Camp in late 2021, he was only able to find out that Calvin was no longer there and had still not received asylum.

As for the other people whose stories we were, to our regret, unable to include in this book – York from Sierra Leone, Abbas from Iraq, Hamidou from Mali, Sari and Yasmine from Syria, Fatima from Morocco, and Brice and Liliane from Cameroon – some received asylum, some did not. Almost everyone tried to flee Greece several times, only to be caught and turned away. One made it to Germany at great risk and expense, requested asylum, but was sent back to Athens. One landed in France, where he is living illegally. One walked most of the way to Bosnia, losing everything but his phone on the journey. Some are living on the street, some have returned to Turkey, some have disappeared.

Meanwhile, the abuse of refugees by the EU and Greece is growing dramatically worse. The EU is testing 'sound cannons' to blast at asylum seekers trying to cross into Greece from Turkey by land, devices that can emit as much noise as a jet engine.[1] The coast guards of both Greece and the EU are pushing refugees – children included – back out to sea, causing many to drown.[2] Greece is still denying new arrivals the right to request asylum, unless those arrivals are Ukrainian, even Afghans fleeing the 2021 Taliban takeover. And Greece is imprisoning seven out of ten asylum seekers for administrative reasons, including unaccompanied children, pregnant women and people with medical emergencies or trauma, while arresting the activists and volunteers who try to help them.[3]

Many other countries are no better. As if inspired by the past Trump administration's extreme anti-immigration policies in the United States, Italy, Belarus, Poland, Croatia, Spain and Hungary are imprisoning and sometimes beating refugees who arrive at their borders, or using them as political pawns.[4] Denmark is committing refoulement by sending Syrians back to Syria, even after they have lived in Denmark for years.[5] The Biden administration in the US has yet to dismantle the Trump-era policy of forcing asylum seekers to wait in lethally dangerous Mexican camps for months or even years while their applications are being reviewed. Australia is incarcerating asylum seekers in terrible conditions on isolated islands. And, since Brexit and the election of Boris Johnson as prime minister, Britain has locked thousands of refugees in detention centers, despite outbreaks of Covid-19; has continued deportation flights even during the pandemic travel bans; and has passed laws denying basic rights like health care and housing.[6]

All this exacerbates the tragedy of being a refugee, only 2 percent of whom end up finding stable homes and lives around the world. The rest typically live in marginal, even desperate conditions for some seventeen years, while those who fled war stay in this cruel limbo for an average of twenty-five.[7]

Nobody who has fled war, violence or persecution should be treated like this. All the young refugees we spoke to long to work and build careers, just as all yearn to continue their educations. Yet every one of them has been held in place, as if encased in plastic, unable to move forward for year after year.

What could we be doing better? Here is a list of suggestions we culled from human rights organizations, activists and policy makers, our own research, political philosophers and refugee writers. In particular, we would like to acknowledge Serena Perekh, author of *No Refuge: Ethics and The Global Refugee Crisis*;[8] David Miliband, president of the International Rescue Committee; and Dina Nayeri, author of *The Ungrateful Refugee*.[9]

How the European Union can help

Rather than funneling billions of euros into Turkey to keep refugees in miserable conditions, and billions more into Greece to build prisons for asylum seekers, the European Union and its governing arm, the European Commission, should implement the following reforms:

1. Help refugees to travel without endangering their lives or relying on smugglers

Over 47,000 refugees and migrants have died or gone missing during their journeys since 2014, most of them drowned.[10] Amnesty International and UNHCR suggest three main ways to avoid these heartbreaking deaths:

- Bring more people into the **UN Refugee Resettlement** program, which enables the most vulnerable, such as torture survivors and the severely ill, to travel, usually by plane, to a safer country and settle there.

- Issue more **Humanitarian Visas.** These allow refugees who are unable to procure passports at home to travel safely and legally, and to apply for asylum when they arrive.
- Help more refugees join relatives in EU countries through the **Family Reunification** program. As Amnesty says, 'Why force someone to endure a long, dangerous journey if they already have a family that can support them in Europe?'[11] Although the right to reunite with family is enshrined in European Union law, definitions of who family is and how to apply vary from country to country, resulting in confusing, arbitrary and often cruel barriers to reunification. This, coupled with the lack of clarity or help available to refugees, leaves too many eligible people, even children, unable to join their families at all. UNHCR has long called on Europe to apply a broader and more consistent definition of what family means, and to lift the unnecessarily burdensome restraints that prevent families from being together.[12]

2. Instead of paying to trap refugees in Greece, the EU should help them settle evenly across the Union

Greece is still suffering from its decade of austerity and bankruptcy, a major reason why it is so hard for refugees to find work there and why so many try to leave illegally. Rather than trapping them in poverty, the EU should fund Greece to help them move quickly and easily to other countries that offer better opportunities, and incentivize those countries to share the settlement of refugees more equitably.

In general, refugees should be welcomed more evenly across the globe. Aside from Ukrainians, only one out of every 300 people in the world is a refugee, as most forcibly displaced people stay inside their own countries.[13] Yet politicians and journalists constantly talk about an overwhelming number of refugees 'flooding' the West. In fact, 86 percent of today's refugees are clustered into a handful of the world's poorest, developing nations, while the wealthiest countries take in the fewest. Europe holds only 11 percent of today's refugees; the United States a mere 1 percent.[14]

3. Reverse new laws that block people from gaining asylum, and push asylum services to review applications quickly, consistently and fairly
At present, asylum procedures vary wildly between and even within countries. The EU should standardize these procedures and open them to anyone who requests them. It should also give people time to find the documents, legal assistance and translation services they need to avoid being rejected on technical, bureaucratic or other arbitrary grounds.[15]

4. Use EU funds not to imprison or paralyze asylum seekers and refugees but rather to help them regain independence
Too many countries force asylum seekers into dependence and depression by either imprisoning them or preventing them from working. Instead, these countries should provide cash assistance, put people in homes and schools rather than camps, allow them to use hospitals, invite them to get involved in local politics and communities, and offer employers tax and trade incentives to train and hire asylum seekers and refugees.

Some might object that giving refugees money only encourages dependence and is too expensive for a government to maintain, but no evidence supports this. On the contrary, cash aid not only restores a person's wellbeing by saving them from desperation, it also benefits the local economy.[16] When such assistance is coupled with enabling refugees to find jobs, this is the best path toward helping people regain their independence and dignity.

5. Rather than portraying refugees as a burden, encourage Western countries to welcome them as potentially productive immigrants

Given the chance, refugees, like other immigrants, increase a country's median income and gross domestic product by starting new businesses and replacing aging populations[17] – something of note in Europe, where eighteen countries are losing people.[18] How much refugees can help depends on their skills and the country they are in, but even the International Monetary Fund found that, although the influx of refugees and migrants can be initially expensive, over the years they 'raise economic growth . . . by contributing young, energetic workers to the European workforce.' Germany and Sweden, the EU countries that took in the most refugees in 2015, are already showing economic and employment expansion as a result.[19]

6. Stop painting refugees as criminals and terrorists

The fact is, refugees and immigrants are strikingly less likely to commit crimes or terrorist acts than are native populations.[20] In Europe, almost all the terrorist attacks of this past decade were committed not by refugees but by radicalized natives, including those in Paris and London.[21] In the US, not a single refugee has been involved in a terrorist attack since 1980, and even before then the numbers were fractional compared to domestic terrorism.[22] The EU must denounce governments that use lies and disinformation to whip up hatred of refugees.

7. Reject and discourage the view of refugees as inferior or different from 'us'

This was the same rhetoric used during World War Two to turn away Jews. As Mursal and everyone else in this book has made clear, xenophobia like this only allows governments and ordinary people alike to mistreat refugees.[23] Certainly, some might come from cultures foreign to Westerners, but this is something to be addressed by encouraging understanding, not by perpetuating misinformation and prejudice.

8. Stop making the false claim that Turkey is a safe country for refugees

Turkey not only denies full refugee status to non-Europeans, leaving them with no protection from exploitation and no legal way to make a living, but returns many to the very countries they fled, putting them at risk of torture, imprisonment and death.[24]

9. Stop referring to refugees as 'migrants'

'Migrant' has become the word of the day among politicians, pundits and journalists, yet using that word for people fleeing for their lives denies them recognition of both their plight and their right to protection.

Some policy makers insist that the distinction between refugees and economic migrants should be sharply defined.[25] Yet how to make such a distinction? Take Abbas, an Iraqi we met on Samos. He was a child during the worst of the US bombing of Baghdad. His family survived, but the chaos and corruption that resulted from that war made living in Iraq so impossible that he fled. So is he a war refugee or an economic migrant? Or take an Afghan who has fled the starvation afflicting her country since the Taliban took over in 2021. Is she a civil-war refugee or a migrant? Many people have been forcibly displaced because of the chaos caused by European and American powers: dividing up countries, erecting false borders, invasions, occupations, racist and homophobic laws, etc. Without acknowledging this, the West is placing the blame on the victims and shunning its own responsibility.

10. Stop the practice of pushing refugees back out to sea and otherwise endangering their lives

During the pandemic, Greece and Frontex – the Border and Coast Guard of the EU – have pushed some 40,000 refugees back out to sea, causing the drowning of at least 2,000,[26] while Italy, Hungary, Malta, Croatia, Spain and Belarus, all of which signed the Refugee Convention, have also been inflicting unspeakable violence on the asylum seekers at their borders.[27] The European Commission should enforce the laws governing refugee protections and prosecute those who break them. It should also investigate and better oversee Frontex, which is riddled with scandal and violations of human rights.[28]

11. Stop criminalizing asylum seekers

As we have said, seeking asylum is a human right, not a crime. Yet Greece and many other countries are arresting and imprisoning asylum seekers under an array of unjust accusations. One of the most egregious cases is Greece's 2021 child-endangerment charge against an Afghan whose small son drowned when their rubber dinghy broke in two on its way to Samos. The bereaved father, who is only twenty-five, faces up to ten years in prison.[29]

12. Stop Greece from imprisoning asylum seekers for steering their own boats
Smugglers almost always abandon boats off the shore of Turkey, as the people in this book attest, forcing refugees to choose between steering for themselves and their fellow passengers or drowning together at sea. For passengers then to be charged with smuggling, as was Hasan, is a nightmare of injustice. Yet in Greece this is an everyday event. In 2019 alone, 1,905 refugees were imprisoned for human smuggling, each of whom will serve up to twenty years.[30] The EU must insist that Greece ceases this inhumane practice.

13. Stop criminalizing NGO volunteers who work with refugees
The Greek government has also been arresting NGO volunteers under the charge of human trafficking, most notoriously twenty-four activists who were saving people from drowning at sea.[31] Italy, too, has done this, while both countries try to paint such volunteers publicly as criminals. This not only punishes the very people who help refugees the most, it leaves people to drown.[32] The EU should pressure the Greek and Italian governments to eliminate restrictions on NGOs, stop arresting volunteers, and make their work easier instead.

14. Transfer people out of the closed detention center on Samos and stop building new ones
Holding asylum seekers in Zervou and the other new, expensive island prisons is not only unconscionably cruel, but also a violation of international law and a waste of money.[33] These prisons must be closed immediately, and vulnerable people, such as survivors of sexual violence and torture, unaccompanied children, single women and those

who identify as LGBTQI+, must be moved quickly to safe and humane accommodation on the mainland.

15. Reinstate support for refugees

Since the Greek government's withdrawal of support, thousands of refugees are now without homes or income, leaving young people to fall prey to pimps, sex traffickers and drug dealers at a cost not only to themselves, but to Greek citizens, too.[34] Similar policies are inflicted on refugees in the UK, forcing many into homelessness and despair.[35]

16. Arrange guardianships for unaccompanied children and keep them out of prison

For years, the Greek government has been illegally imprisoning unaccompanied children under the name of 'protective custody.' After an international outcry, the Greek government announced in 2020 that it would cease this practice and move children to shelters and homes instead, but the implementation of this plan has been slow and erratic.[36] The EU and UNHCR must press Greece to do better.

17. Increase oversight of Greek use of EU funding

In spite of widespread condemnation of Greece's inhumane refugee camps, so far there has been little transparency and virtually no accountability for how the country is using the EU money that funds them.[37]

How the rest of us can help

Any one of us can help a refugee. We can vote for politicians who do not villainize or weaponize human beings, and who promote policies that aid rather than punish asylum seekers and refugees. We can donate, volunteer, demonstrate and protest against hateful rhetoric. We can befriend refugees, invite them into our homes, share tea and meals and walks. We can take courage from the fact that many a survey has found that most people in the world believe in the moral obligation to help those who are fleeing war and catastrophe, and in the right of human beings to live in safety, freedom and dignity.[38] And we can apply this generosity not only to European refugees such as Ukrainians, but to all those who flee for their lives, regardless of their race, religion or origin.

As Mursal says: 'We were not born refugees. We had homes and jobs. But because of the problems in our country, we had to leave. I am sure if you were us, you would do what we did.'

Here are some ways to help:

Donate or volunteer to work with refugees

Doctors Without Borders/MSF – doctorswithoutborders.org
HIAS – hias.org/where/greece
Indigo Volunteers – indigovolunteers.org
International Refugee Assistance Project – refugeerights.org
International Rescue Committee – rescue.org
MADRE: Global Women's Rights – madre.org
Samos Volunteers – samosvolunteers.org
Still I Rise (education for refugee children) – stillirisengo.
    org/en/

Help refugees find a home, or invite them to dinner

In Europe or the UK:
Refugees at Home – refugeesathome.org
United Invitations – unitedinvitations.org
Refugee Action – refugee-action.org.uk

Refugees Welcome – https://www.refugees-welcome.net/#
  countries
In the United States:
Welcoming America – welcomingamerica.org
Borgen Project – borgenproject.org/3-ways-to-host-refugees-in-
  your-own-home/
Welcome.US – welcome.us

Keep up with what is happening to refugees

Aegean Boat Report – aegeanboatreport.com
Amnesty International – amnesty.org/en/
AYS (Are You Syrious) Newsletter – medium.com/are-you-
  syrious/ays-newsletter-ays-special-from-bosnia-the-
  game-bdcadd6b9c3
Doctors Without Borders/MSF – doctorswithoutborders.org
Human Rights Watch – hrw.org
International Rescue Committee – rescue.org
Reliefweb – reliefweb.int

Further reading on how to help

Serena Perekh, *No Refuge: Ethics and the Global Refugee
  Crisis*, Oxford University Press, UK, 2020
David Miliband, *Rescue: Refugees and the Political Crisis
  of Our Time*, Simon & Schuster, NY, 2017
Dina Nayeri, *The Ungrateful Refugee*, Canongate Books,
  UK, 2019
Jessica Goudeau, *After the Last Border: Two Families and The
  Story of Refuge in America*, Penguin Random House,
  NY, 2020

ACKNOWLEDGMENTS

Helen

I thank:

Hasan, Mursal, Evans, Calvin, Abbas, Hamidou, York –
it is only because of your trust, honesty and kindness that this
book exists.

Eyad, for opening your world to me, for believing in
our work, and for the treasure of your friendship.

Giulia Ciccoli, Nick van der Steenhooven, Dan Chapman,
Eliza and Alice Cornwell, Agus Oliveri, Freya Hodges, and
the others I met at Samos Volunteers. Without your courage
and dedication, many lives would be so much worse.

Tommy Olsen, creator of the Aegean Boat Report, for
your unflagging work and care.

Ali, for your precious friendship; Moira Lavelle, Nicholas
Boggs and Robert(a) Marshall for your time and help; Gabriel
Profumo for your work on this book.

The PEN Jean Stein Grant for Literary Oral History of
2021, and the War & Peace Initiative at Columbia University
for recognizing this work with grants. Likewise, Yaddo, Blue
Mountain Center, VCCA and I-Park for time and peace in
which to work.

My generous and patient friends for listening to me talk
for so many years about this book.

Steve, Emma, Simon and Iggy for being my anchors and my loves.

Eyad

Asmahan, Sari and Yasmine – thank you for your generosity and vulnerability in telling your stories, in spite of endless hardship and suffering. To the people who work tirelessly to make our world a kinder place, either with their actions, and if not with their actions, then with their words, and if not with their words, with their respect for human dignity – thank you for all that you do.

Helen, thank you for believing in me and for honoring me, not only with your partnership and co-authorship, but with your invaluable friendship. You have impacted my life in more ways than you know and I'll be forever grateful.

Thank you to my family, who are my reason to keep moving forward; and to Little My and her family, who have cheered me on since the very beginning.

BIBLIOGRAPHY

Leila Abouzeid, *Last Chapter (Modern Arabic Writing)*, The American University in Cairo Press, Egypt, 2000

Rania Abouzeid, *No Turning Back: Life, Loss, and Hope in Wartime Syria*, WW Norton & Co, New York, US, 2018

Afghan Women's Writing Project, *The Sky is a Nest of Swallows: A Collection of Poems and Essays by Afghan Women Writers*, Afghan Women's Writing Project, Afghanistan, 2012

Maram Al-Masri, *Liberty Walks Naked* (poems), Southword Editions, Cork, Ireland, 2017

Melissa Fleming, *A Hope More Powerful Than the Sea: One Refugee's Incredible Story of Love, Loss, and Survival*, Little, Brown and Company, Massachusetts, US, 2017

Malu Halasa et al, *Syria Speaks: Art and Culture from the Frontline*, Saqi Books, UK, 2014

Zeyn Joukhadar, *The Map of Salt and Stars*, Orion Publishing Group, UK, 2018

Khaled Khalifa, *No Knives in the Kitchens of This City*, Oxford University Press, UK, 2016

Khaled Khalifa, *Death is Hard Work*, Farrar, Straus and Giroux, New York, US, 2019

Tima Kurdi, *The Boy on the Beach: My Family's Escape from Syria*, Simon & Schuster, New York, US, 2018

Alia Malek, *The Home That Was Our Country: A Memoir of Syria*, PublicAffairs, New York, US, 2017

Alane Mason et al, *Literature from the 'Axis of Evil,'* A Words Without Borders Anthology, The New Press, New York, US, 2007

Dina Nayeri, *Refuge*, Penguin Publishing Group, New York, US, 2017

NH Senzai, *Escape from Aleppo*, Simon & Schuster, New York, US, 2018

Kao Kalia Yang, *Somewhere in the Unknown World: A Collective Refugee Memoir*, Metropolitan Books, New York, US, 2020

Samar Yazbek, *A Woman in the Crossfire: Diaries of the Syrian Revolution*, Haus Publishing, UK, 2012

Samar Yazbek, *The Crossing: My journey to the shattered heart of Syria*, Rider, UK, 2015

Haifa Zangana, *Women on a Journey: Between Baghdad and London*, University of Texas Press, US, 2007

Haifa Zangana, *City of Widows: An Iraqi Woman's Account of War and Resistance*, Seven Stories Press, New York, US, 2009

Notes

PREFACE

1. Ehab, who goes by the last name Onan, made a series of short videos in English and Arabic about life as a refugee on Samos and his rejection called *Diary of a Refugee*: youtube.com/channel/UCjcMAyO46 ng4FrVQeslzzQA/videos?view=0&sort=dd&shelf_id=1

INTRODUCTION

1. unhcr.org/refugee-statistics/
2. nytimes.com/2020/09/08/magazine/displaced-war-on-terror.html?refe rringSource=articleShare
3. reliefweb.int/report/greece/issue-brief-blocked-every-pass-how-greece-s-policy-exclusion-harms-asylum-seekers-and
4. bbc.com/news/world-europe-34832512; france24.com/en/france/202 10908-paris-november-2015-attacks-a-timeline-of-the-night-that-shook-the-city
5. reliefweb.int/sites/reliefweb.int/files/resources/EUR2556642017 ENGLISH.PDF
6. 'As of the 30 June 2020, there were 122,000 forced migrants in Greece, with 86,500 of them on the mainland and 35,500 on the islands.' migrants-refugees.va/country-profile/greece/
7. unhcr.org/en-us/1951-refugee-convention.html
8. For a list of which countries signed, see: unhcr.org/protect/ PROTECTION/3b73b0d63.pdf
9. capital.gr/english/3385967/mitsotakis-most-arrivals-in-greece-now-are-economic-migrants-not-refugees
10. 'At the end of 2019, Greece hosted over 186,000 refugees and asylum-seekers. This included over 5,000 unaccompanied children. Most persons of concern were coming from Afghanistan, the

Syrian Arab Republic, the Democratic Republic of the Congo and Iran.' unhcr.org/en-us/greece.html?query=Greece; rsaegean.org/en/majority-of-asylum-seekers-in-need-of-international-protection-according-to-eurostat-first-instance-asylum-statistics/#footnote-2

HASAN

1. globalr2p.org/countries/syria/
2. amnesty.org.uk/licence-discriminate-trumps-muslim-refugee-ban
3. mail.google.com/mail/u/0/#inbox/FMfcgzGmtXBJSmZfWBlpz TdkgRThJQCV; UN Refugees news story tinyurl.com/2s3vzwrj
4. unhcr.org/3bcfdf164.pdf; unhcr.org/4ca34be29.pdf; ohchr.org/Documents/Issues/Migration/GA74thSession/Greece_annex.pdf
5. abcnews.go.com/International/wireStory/critics-greece-criminalizes-migration-prosecutes-helpers-81174380; borderline-europe.de/eigene-publikationen/stigmatisiert-inhaftiert-kriminalisiert-der-kampf-gegen-vermeintliche-schleuser?l=en

ASMAHAN

1. infomigrants.net/en/post/9047/tension-still-high-in-lesbos-after-racist-attacks; theintercept.com/2018/07/25/lesbos-moria-kurdish-refugees-isis/
2. solidaritynow.org/en/
3. EuroRelief was one of the first NGOs to help on Lesbos: eurorelief.net/about/
4. greece.iom.int/helios-national-campaign

WOMEN ON SAMOS

1. theguardian.com/global-development/2019/feb/22/greece-races-to-move-refugees-from-island-branded-new-lesbos-samos
2. In the first four months of 2019, 9,233 asylum seekers had landed in Greece, 1,444 on Samos, and many more were expected as the weather warmed.
3. data2.unhcr.org/en/situations/mediterranean/location/5179
4. facebook.com/stilliriseNGO/posts/today-our-small-volunteer-organization-filed-a-lawsuit-against-the-management-of/42580 7718012792/; fxb.harvard.edu/the-migrant-diaries2019pt2/

NOTES

5. bbc.com/news/world-europe-50260597; https://www.theguardian.
   com/global-development/2019/feb/22/greece-races-to-move-
   refugees-from-island-branded-new-lesbos-samos
6. medequali.team/en/news/
7. foreignpolicy.com/2019/01/19/al-shabab-wants-you-to-know-its-
   alive-and-well-kenya-somalia-terrorism/
8. fxb.harvard.edu/the-migrant-diaries2019pt2/
9. samosvolunteers.org/situation-on-samos; hrw.org/news/2019/10/29/
   greece-asylum-overhaul-threatens-rights
10. glocalroots.ch/en/samos-safe-space/

EVANS

1. cnn.com/2019/04/17/opinions/nigeria-opinion-lgbt-attack/index.html
2. theinitiativeforequalrights.org/wp-content/uploads/2017/05/Social-
   Perception-Survey-On-LGB-Rights-Report-in-Nigeria3.pdf
3. legislation.gov.uk/ukpga/Vict/24-25/100/section/61/enacted
4. humandignitytrust.org/lgbt-the-law/map-of-criminalisation/
5. statista.com/statistics/1082077/deaths-of-migrants-in-the-medite
   rranean-sea/; newsbook.com.mt/en/med-is-the-largest-cemetery-in-
   europe-pope-francis/
6. Serena Perekh, *No Refuge: Ethics and the Global Refugee Crisis*,
   Oxford University Press, p 32.
7. theguardian.com/world/2021/sep/19/why-greeces-expensive-new-
   migrant-camps-are-outraging-ngos
8. infomigrants.net/en/post/27510/after-moria-eu-to-try-closed-
   asylum-camps-on-greek-islands; theworld.org/stories/2021-04-06/
   island-prison-migrants-say-plan-refugee-camp-lesbos-too-isolating
9. Algorithm Watch, 27 April 2021, tinyurl.com/5apncwh6
10. theguardian.com/global-development/2021/mar/29/
    eu-announces-funding-for-five-new-refugee-camps-on-greek-islands
11. theguardian.com/world/2021/sep/19/why-greeces-expensive-new-
    migrant-camps-are-outraging-ngos
12. Algorithm Watch, 27 April 2021, tinyurl.com/5apncwh6
13. Der Spiegel, 3 Nov 2021, https://tinyurl.com/2p93p934
14. From a blog by Dr Ignacia Ossul-Vermehren, an Associate Staff at
    the Development Planning Unit, University College London, tinyurl.
    com/4ea3zy2c

15. msf.org/constructing-crisis-europe-border-migration-report
16. Samos Volunteers, tinyurl.com/mr39yehs; amnesty.org/en/latest/news/2021/12/greece-asylum-seekers-being-illegally-detained-in-new-eu-funded-camp/
17. pubmed.ncbi.nlm.nih.gov/34258570/

MURSAL

1. bbc.com/news/world-asia-49263537; cfr.org/global-conflict-tracker/conflict/war-afghanistan
2. trtworld.com/magazine/how-greece-s-new-asylum-policy-endangers-refugees-and-violates-eu-laws-47357
3. middle-east-online.com/en/rights-groups-tell-greece-turkey-not-safe-refugees
4. 'Top European Union leaders agreed in principle June 24 on a new financial package for Turkey for hosting refugees and taking back migrants from Greece while also warning against "instrumentalization of migrants for political purposes." The 3.5 billion euros (nearly $4.2 billion) for Turkey would be part of a larger aid package that aims to continue to stop migrants from reaching the EU.' al-monitor.com/originals/2021/06/eu-leaders-back-funding-warn-erdogan-against-instrumentalizing-syrian-migrants#ixzz6zNt2IG7q
5. borderlandscapes.law.ox.ac.uk/location/fylakio-pre-removal-centre
6. khora-athens.org
7. foodkind.org/our-work
8. caritasathens.gr/en/

CALVIN

1. For more of Biya's history, see theguardian.com/world/2020/nov/02/for-the-sake-of-cameroon-life-president-paul-biya-must-be-forced-out; theconversation.com/cameroons-biya-is-africas-oldest-president-assessing-his-38-years-in-power-156221
2. mrcparty.org
3. hurriyetdailynews.com/inmates-in-turkeys-maltepe-prison-producing-slippers-for-luxury-brands-hotels-142158
4. hrw.org/news/2019/12/04/greece-camp-conditions-endanger-women-girls

NOTES

5. reliefweb.int/report/greece/greece-sea-arrivals-dashboard-july-2019
6. hrw.org/news/2019/12/04/greece-camp-conditions-endanger-women-girls
7. Ibid.
8. rescue.org/press-release/new-irc-analysis-reveals-risk-coronavirus-transmission-rates-moria-al-hol-and-coxs; reliefweb.int/report/greece/residents-moria-camp-must-be-moved-now-red-cross-head
9. hrw.org/world-report/2021/country-chapters/greece#; reliefweb.int/report/greece/detention-default-how-greece-support-eu-generalizing-administrative-detention-migrants
10. For a detailed account of the Moria prison that held Calvin and the Greek laws behind the locking up of asylum seekers, see: dm-aegean.bordermonitoring.eu/2018/09/23/the-prison-within-the-prison-within-the-prison-the-detention-complex-of-moria-camp/
11. eurorelief.net/about/
12. movementontheground.com/about-us
13. bbc.com/news/world-europe-54082201
14. lesvossolidarity.org/en/what-we-do/mosaik-support-center
15. ohf-lesvos.org/en/welcome/
16. dw.com/en/greece-ngos-accused-of-stoking-unrest-in-refugee-camp/a-52320720
17. keeptalkinggreece.com/2020/06/17/greece-refugees-migrants-centers-ngos-minister/

EPILOGUE

1. aljazeera.com/news/2021/5/31/migrants-refugees-will-face-digital-fortress-in-post-pandemic-eu
2. unfilteredvoices.org/2021/07/02/frontex-the-controversial-european-union-agency-on-the-brink-of-closure/; aegeanboatreport.com/blog-posts/
3. oxfam.org/en/press-releases/detention-default-how-greece-and-eu-are-generalising-administrative-detention
    For a damning report of how Greece is treating asylum seekers and refugees, see: Human Rights Watch end of 2021 report hrw.org/world-report/2021/country-chapters/greece; and a 2021 report by Oxfam tinyurl.com/2p9bt2re

319

For more on cases against volunteers, see: dw.com/en/greece-ngo-workers-could-face-prison-for-helping-migrants/a-59857314

4. nytimes.com/2021/12/14/world/europe/european-union-schengen-migrants-borders.html; theconversation.com/the-eu-is-the-real-villain -in-the-poland-belarus-migrant-crisis-172132

5. aljazeera.com/podcasts/2021/12/10/denmark-is-still-trying-to-send-syrians-back

6. nytimes.com/2021/04/01/opinion/uk-immigration-boris-johnson. html?referringSource=articleShare

7. Serena Parekh, op cit, pp 5-6.

8. Ibid.

9. Dina Nayeri, *The Ungrateful Refugee: What Immigrants Never Tell You*, Canongate, 2019.

10. missingmigrants.iom.int

11. amnesty.org/en/latest/campaigns/2015/09/what-can-europe-do-to-welcome-refugees/; unhcr.org/uk/5f5743f84.pdf

12. refugeerights.org/issue-areas/family-reunification; unhcr.org/en-us/ news/briefing/2021/10/616935614/unhcr-calls-states-expedite-family-reunification-procedures-afghan-refugees.html;amnesty.org/ en/i-welcome-community-2/welcoming-refugees-solutions/; unhcr. org/refugee-statistics/

13. unhcr.org/refugee-statistics/; gapminder.org/upgrader/q16/; this point was inspired by *The Ungrateful Refugee* by Dina Nayeri, op cit.

14. David Miliband, *Rescue: Refugees and the Political Crisis of Our Time*, Simon & Schuster, 2017, pp 22-23.

15. reliefweb, tinyurl.com/28773pej

16. Parekh, op cit, p 184

17. icmc.net/2020/07/14/refugees-good-or-bad-for-economy/; migrationobservatory.ox.ac.uk/resources/briefings/the-labour-market-effects-of-immigration

18. worldpopulationreview.com/country-rankings/countries-with-declining-population

19. Parekh, op cit, p xviii

20. Ibid.

21. cnn.com/2015/12/08/europe/2015-paris-terror-attacks-fast-facts/ index.html

NOTES

22. In the Introduction to her book, Parekh breaks down the statistics of refugee crime in several countries, op cit, p xv, pp xi-xiii.

23. Parekh, p 194.

24. amnesty.org/en/latest/news/2017/03/the-eu-turkey-deal-europes-year-of-shame/; middle-east-online.com/en/rights-groups-tell-greece-turkey-not-safe-refugees

25. politico.eu/article/solve-migration-crisis-europe-schengen/

26. theguardian.com/global-development/2021/may/05/revealed-2000-refugee-deaths-linked-to-eu-pushbacks; dailysabah.com/politics/eu-affairs/greece-pushed-889-migrant-boats-into-turkish-waters-in-2021; aegeanboatreport.com

27. theguardian.com/global-development/2021/may/05/revealed-2000-refugee-deaths-linked-to-eu-pushbacks

28. medium.com/are-you-syrious/frontex-and-human-rights-2021-a-reading-list-7c2d5cf132a9

29. aljazeera.com/news/2021/3/19/refugee-father-charged-with-sons-death-on-journey-to-greece

30. Borderline Europe: tinyurl.com/yckjzkcx; https://tinyurl.com/5yedtxuu

31. hrw.org/news/2021/07/22/greek-authorities-target-ngos-reporting-abuses-against-migrants#; dw.com/en/greece-ngo-workers-could-face-prison-for-helping-migrants/a-59857314

32. reliefweb.int/report/world/criminalization-search-and-rescue-operations-mediterranean-has-been-accompanied-rising

33. aljazeera.com/news/2021/10/22/prisons-in-paradise

34. Reliefweb briefing, tinyurl.com/3pphwj5z

35. nytimes.com/2021/04/01/opinion/uk-immigration-boris-johnson.html?referringSource=articleShare

36. hrw.org/news/2021/12/22/submission-committee-rights-child-concerning-greece#

37. reliefweb, tinyurl.com/28773pej

38. pewresearch.org/fact-tank/2019/08/09/people-around-the-world-express-more-support-for-taking-in-refugees-than-immigrants/; rescue.org/press-release/irc-report-nearly-60-percent-americans-believe-us-has-moral-obligation-help-refugees

About the Authors

Helen Benedict, a professor at Columbia University, is the author of eight novels, including the forthcoming *The Good Deed*, about refugees in Greece, and five books of nonfiction. A recipient of the 2021 PEN Jean Stein Grant for Literary Oral History and the Ida B. Wells Award for Bravery in Journalism, Benedict also wrote the award-winning book, *The Lonely Soldier: The Private War of Women at War Serving in Iraq*, and the play, *The Lonely Soldier Monologues*. Her writings inspired a class action suit against the Pentagon on behalf of people sexually assaulted in the military and the 2012 Oscar-nominated documentary, *The Invisible War*. For more information, visit helenbenedict.com.

Eyad Awwadawnan, formerly a law student from Damascus, Syria, is a writer and aspiring poet currently living as an asylum-seeker in Reykjavik, Iceland. During his four years in Greece, he worked as a cultural mediator, translator and interpreter for various NGOs, as well as publishing a featured article in *Slate Magazine* detailing his escape from Syria.

INDEX

323

INDEX

INDEX